CHANGING FACES OF TOURISM

By

Sudesh Bansal

2008

CYBER TECH PUBLICATIONS
4264/3, Ansari Road, Daryaganj, New Delhi-110002 (India)
Ph.: 011-23244078. Fax: 011-23280028
E-Mail: cyberpublicationsdelhi@yahoo.com

CHANGING FACES OF TOURISM

Sudesh Bansal

First Edition 2008

Published by :

G.S. Rawat for **Cyber Tech Publications**
4264/3, Ansari Road, Daryaganj, New Delhi-110002 (India)
Ph.: 011-23244078. Fax: 011-23280028
E-Mail: cyberpublicationsdelhi@yahoo.com

Printed at : **Amit Enterprises**, Maujpur, Delhi, (9810878184)

Preface

Tourism is one of the fastest growing sector of the global economy, which account for about 11 percent of the gross Global Domestic Product (GDP) and employ about 200 million people worldwide. There are about 700 million international travellers per year. Tourism and travel related sectors have become dynamic sources of income and a major strategic sector for development in many countries.

Tourism businesses operate globally and many have opted for a competitive advantage of internationalisation. Technology, information and reduction of boundaries have created new forms of service companies, not only the large multinational corporations, but also small niche specialists. The growing importance of strategic alliances in creating networks of business relationships has become a trend also in tourism.

The book examines the current trends in international tourism markets along with emerging opportunities and challenges in the field. It provides a set of tools for monitoring tourism management, policy implementation, promoting sites in a changing global environment. It also reviews roles of government organisations, international organisations and private sector. The book will be highly useful for tour operators, policy makers, administrators and general readers interested in tourism.

—*Author*

Contents

1

INTERNATIONAL TOURISM

HISTORICAL PERSPECTIVE

Wealthy people have always travelled to distant parts of the world to see great buildings or other works of art; to learn new languages; or to taste new cuisine. As long ago as the time of the Roman Republic places such as Baiae were popular coastal resorts for the rich. The terms tourist and tourism were first used as official terms in 1937 by the League of Nations. Tourism was defined as people travelling abroad for periods of over 24 hours.

Health Tourism and Leisure Travel

It was not until the 19th century that cultural tourism developed into leisure and health tourism. Some English travellers, after visiting the warm lands of the south of Europe, decided to stay there either for the cold season or for the rest of their lives. Others began to visit places with supposedly health-giving mineral waters, in hopes of relieving a whole variety of diseases from gout to liver disorders and bronchitis.

Leisure travel was a British invention due to sociological factors. Britain was the first European country to industrialize, and the industrial society was the first society to offer time for leisure to a growing number of people. Initially, this did not apply to the working masses, but rather to the owners of the machinery of production, the economic oligarchy, the factory owners, and the traders. These comprised the new middle class.

The British origin of this new industry is reflected in many place names. At Nice, one of the first and best-established holiday resorts on the French Riviera, the long esplanade along the seafront is known to this day as the Promenade des Anglais; in many other historic resorts in continental Europe, old well-established palace hotels have names like the Hotel Bristol, the Hotel Carlton or the Hotel Majestic-reflecting the dominance of English customers.

Winter Tourism

Winter sports were largely invented by the British leisured classes initially at the Swiss village of Zermatt (Valais), and St Moritz in 1864. The first packaged winter sports holidays (vacations) followed in 1903, to Adelboden, also in Switzerland.

Organized sport was well established in Britain before it reached other countries. The vocabulary of sport bears witness to this: rugby, football, and boxing all originated in Britain, and even Tennis, originally a French sport, was formalized and codified by the British, who hosted the first national championship in the nineteenth century, at Wimbledon. Winter sports were a natural answer for a leisured class looking for amusement during the coldest season.

Mass Travel

Mass travel could not really begin to develop until two things occurred.

- improvements in technology allowed the transport of large numbers of people in a short space of time to places of leisure interest, and
- greater numbers of people began to enjoy the benefits of leisure time.

A major development was the invention of the railways, which brought many of Britain's seaside towns within easy distance of Britain's urban centres. The father of modern mass tourism was Thomas Cook who, on 5 July 1841, organized the first package tour in history, by chartering a train to take a group of temperance campaigners from Leicester to a rally in

Loughborough, some twenty miles away. Cook immediately saw the potential for business development in the sector, and became the world's first tour operator.

He was soon followed by others, with the result that the tourist industry developed rapidly in early Victorian Britain. Initially it was supported by the growing middle classes, who had time off from their work, and who could afford the luxury of travel and possibly even staying for periods of time in boarding houses. However, the Bank Holiday Act 1871 introduced a statutory right for workers to take holidays, even if they were not paid at the time. The combination of short holiday periods, travel facilities and distances meant that the first holiday resorts to develop in Britain were towns on the seaside, situated as close as possible to the growing industrial conurbations.

For those in the industrial north, there were Blackpool in Lancashire, and Scarborough in Yorkshire. For those in the Midlands, there were Weston-super-Mare in Somerset and Skegness in Lincolnshire, for those in London there were Southend-on-Sea, Broadstairs, Brighton, Eastbourne and many others. In travelling to the coast, the population was following in the steps of Royalty. King George III is widely acknowledged as popularising the seaside holiday, due to his regular visits to Weymouth when in poor health.

For a century, domestic tourism was the norm, with foreign travel being reserved for the rich or the culturally curious. A minority of resorts, such as Bath, Harrogate and Matlock, emerged inland. After World War II holiday villages such as Butlins and Pontins emerged, but their popularity waned with the rise of package tours and the increasing comforts to which visitors became accustomed at home. Towards the end of the 20th century the market was revived by the upmarket inland resorts of Dutch company Centre Parcs. Other phenomena that helped develop the travel industry were paid holidays:

- 1.5 million manual workers in Britain had paid holidays by 1925
- 11 million by 1939 (30% of the population in families with paid holidays)

Similar processes occurred in other countries, though at a slower rate, given that nineteenth century Britain was far ahead of any other nation in the world in the process of industrialisation.

In the USA, the first great seaside resort, in the European style, was Atlantic City, New Jersey.

In Continental Europe, early resorts included Ostend (for the people of Brussels), and Boulogne-sur-Mer (Pas-de-Calais) and Deauville (Calvados) (for Parisians).

International Mass Tourism

Increasing speed on railways meant that the tourist industry could develop internationally. By 1901, the number of people crossing the English Channel from England to France or Belgium had passed 0.5 million per year. However it was with cheap air travel in combination with the package tour that international mass tourism developed after 1963. For the worker living in greater London, Brindisi today is almost as accessible as Brighton was 100 years ago.

World Tourism Rankings

The World Tourism Organization compiles the World Tourism Rankings.

Income from foreign tourists in 2002, 2003 and 2004

Rank (2004)	Nation	Billions of USD (2002)	Billions of USD (2003)	Change (2003/2002)	Billions of USD (2004)	Change (2004/ 2003)
1	United States	66.7	64.5	-3.3%	74.5	15.5%
2	Spain	33.8	41.8	23.6%	45.2	8.1%
3	France	32.7	37.0	13.1%	40.8	10.3%
4	Italy	26.9	31.2	16.2%	35.7	14.4%
5	Germany	19.0	23.0	21.2%	27.7	20.4%
6	United Kingdom	20.5	22.8	10.7%	27.3	19.7%
7	China	20.4	17.4	-14.6%	25.7	47.7%
8	Turkey	11.9	13.2	10.9%	15.9	20.5%
9	Austria	11.2	14.1	25,2%	15.4	9.2%
10	Australia	10.3	12	11.7%	13.0	16.1%

Number of foreign tourists in 1990, 1995, 2000 and from 2002 to 2005

Rank (2004)	Nation	1990	1995	2000	2002	2003	2004 (provisional)	2005	Change 2001-02	2002-03	2003-04 (provisional)	2004-05
1st	France	52.497	60.0	77.2	77.0	75.0	75.1	76.0	+2.4%	-2.6%	+0.1%	+1.2%
2nd	Spain	34.085	34.9	47.9	52.3	52.5	52.4	55.6	+4.5%	+0.3%	+3.1%	+6.0%
3rd	United States	39.363	43.5	51.2	41.9	40.4	46.1	49.4	-6.7%	-3.6%	+11.8%	+7.2%
4th	China	10.484	20.0	31.2	36.8	33.0	41.8	46.8	+11%	-10.3%	+26.7%	+12.1%
5th	Italy	26.679	31.1	41.2	39.8	39.6	37.1	36.5	+0.6%	-0.5%	-6.4%	-1.5%
6th	United Kingdom	18.013	23.5	25.2	24.2	24.8	27.8	30.0	+5.9%	+2.6%	+12.3%	+8.0%
7th	Mexico	17.172	20.2	13.1	20.6	18.7	20.6	21.9	+4.6%	-4.9%	+10.5%	+6.3%
8th	Germany	17.045	14.8	19.0	18.0	18.4	20.1	21.5	+0.6%	+0.4%	+9.5%	+6.8%
9th	Austria	19.011	17.2	18.0	18.6	19.1	19.4	20.0	+2.4%	+2.6%	+1.5%	+3.0%
10th	Canada				20.1	17.5	19.2	18.6	+1.9%	-12.6%	+9.2%	-2,2%

• Note: Russia and Hong Kong (China) have not been included due to contradictory UNWTO data (compare the figures for 2003 here and here).

• Sources: 1990, 1995 & 2000, 2002 & 2003, 2004, 2005 (provisional).

Regional Statistics (2002)

Europe

	International Tourist Arrivals		International Tourism Receipts	
Major destination	**Number in thousands**	**Percentage share**	**Number in US$ million**	**Percentage share**
Europe	399,759	100	240,490	100
Austria	9,611	4.7	11,237	4.7
Belgium	6,724	1.7	6,892	2.9
Croatia	6,944	1.7	3,811	1.6
France	77,012	19.3	32,329	13.4
Germany	17,969	4.5	19,158	8.0
Greece	14,180	3.5	9,741	4.1
Hungary	15,870	4.0	3,273	1.4

Contd...

	International Tourist Arrivals		International Tourism Receipts	
Major destination	**Number in thousands**	**Percentage share**	**Number in US$ million**	**Percentage share**
Ireland	6,476	1.6	3,089	1.3
Italy	39,799	10.0	26,915	11.2
Netherlands	9,595	2.4	7,706	3.2
Poland	13,980	3.5	4,500	1.9
Portugal	11,666	2.9	5,919	2.5
Russian Federation	7,943	2.0	4,188	1.7
Spain	51,748	12.9	33,609	14.0
Switzerland	10,000	2.5	7,628	3.2
Turkey	12,782	3.2	9,010	3.7
Ukraine	6,326	1.6	2,992	1.2
United Kingdom	24,180	6.0	17,591	7.3

WORLD TOURISM DAY

Since 1980, September 27 is celebrated by the World Tourism Organization as World Tourism Day. It was established at the Third Session of the UNWTO General Assembly in Torremolinos, Spain, in September of 1979. The purpose of this day is to display awareness that tourism is vital to the international community and to show how it affects the social, cultural, political and economic values worldwide. September 27 is important since on that day in 1970, the Statutes of the WTO were adopted. The adoption of the statutes is considered to be a milestone in global tourism.

At its Twelfth Session in Istanbul, Turkey, in October of 1997, the UNWTO General Assembly decided to designate a host country each year as the Organization's partner for celebrating World Tourism Day. At its Fifteenth Session in Beijing, China, in October of 2003, the Assembly decided the following geographic order to be followed for the World Tourism Day celebrations: 2006 in Europe; 2007 in South Asia; 2008 in the Americas, and 2009 in Africa.

2

Tourism by Country

TOURISM IN AUSTRALIA

Tourism in Australia is a large sector of the economy. In 2003/04, the tourism industry represented 3.9% of Australia's GDP at a value of approximately A$32 billion to the national economy. It should be noted that tourism's share of GDP has been slightly decreasing over recent years.

In 2004-05, international visitors consumed AUD$18.3 billion worth of goods and services produced by the Australian economy. This represented 11.1% of total exports of goods and services.

Australia was also the received the 10th biggest revenue from being a tourist destination in 2002, 2003 and 2004.

Trends

At least until September 2001, tourism and particularly international tourism had grown rapidly for the past two decades.

During 2001-2002 and 2002-2003, external events such as the September 11, 2001 attacks and the Severe Acute Respiratory Syndrome (SARS) scare caused changes to the level of international visitors to Australia.

Visas

All visitors to Australia, apart from New Zealanders, require advance permission to enter the country. For most countries, a full visa is required, but holders of certain passports from some OECD and some East Asian countries are able to apply for the simpler Electronic Travel Authority which enables one to apply and be granted a visa.

Marketing

Australia's international tourism campaigns have largely centred around the image of Australia as a wild, expansive, almost uninhabited continent, with all manner of exotic scenery and wildlife, endless beaches, large coastal cities and friendly, relaxed locals. A famous advertising campaign of the 1980s featuring Paul Hogan offering American tourists the chance to "throw another shrimp on the barbie" serves as an example of this marketing approach. (Ironically, this statement is a misquote; Hogan's actual line was "I'll slip an extra shrimp on the barbie for you.")

The marketing focus has changed over the years, for example with specific advertisements created for individual countries. A 2006 Tourism campaign using Australian colloquialisms was typified with the slogan: "So where the bloody hell are you?"

Popular Destinations

International Tourists

Tourism Australia lists the following as the most visited regions in Australia:

- Sydney, includes sights such as Sydney Opera House, Sydney Harbour Bridge and Bondi Beach.
- Melbourne
- Brisbane
- Far North Queensland including Cairns, known as the gateway to the Great Barrier Reef and Daintree Rainforest
- Gold Coast, famous for its beaches and theme parks
- Perth, Western Australia
- Adelaide

- Sunshine Coast, Queensland
- Uluru (Ayers Rock) and surroundings such as Kata Tjuta
- Whitsundays, Queensland

Top Ten Visited Regions in Australia

Domestic Tourists

This list varies for domestic tourists and focuses on destinations relatively near capital cities. A notable omission is Far North Queensland mainly due to its distance from capital cities.

- Sydney
- Melbourne
- Brisbane
- Gold Coast
- northern coastal New South Wales including Coffs Harbour and Byron Bay
- Perth
- Sunshine Coast, Queensland
- South Coast, New South Wales including Nowra and Batemans Bay
- South Western Western Australia including Bunbury and Busselton.
- Hunter region, New South Wales including Newcastle, Port Stephens

Top 10 Domestic Regions

Popular Activities

Tourism Australia reported the following as the most popular activities for overseas tourists:

- Dining or eating out at a cafe
- Shopping
- Beach

- Markets
- National parks
- Pubs, Clubs and Discos
- Zoos, Wildlife parks and Aquariums
- Botanical Gardens and Public Parks
- Charter boats, ferries, cruises
- Historical sites, Heritage

Top 10 Activities

This list varies for domestic tourists:

- Dining
- Visiting friends or relatives
- Shopping
- General sightseeing
- Pubs, Clubs and Discos
- Beach
- Picnics and Barbecues
- Bushwalking
- National parks
- Fishing

Top Activities for Domestic Tourists

Types of Tourists

International Tourists: The top 10 countries for short term visits to Australia:

- New Zealand
- United Kingdom
- China
- Singapore
- Hong Kong
- Japan
- United States
- South Korea
- Malaysia
- Germany

Source: ABS Overseas Arrivals and Departures August 2006

Whilst the above list may include personal and business visits, a considerable proportion of these visitors would engage in tourist activities. 52% of visitors to Australia in 2005/06 visited for a holiday.

Tourists from countries such as United States and Japan benefited from the weakness of the Australian dollar against their own currencies over much of the 1980s and 1990s, making Australian holidays quite cheap. Japanese tourists make up a distinctive part of the Australian tourism market, usually taking short package tours which concentrate heavily on the iconic sights (typically Sydney, Uluru, Gold Coast and Cairns), and viewing Australian native animals (particularly the koala).

UK Tourists

Due to the close cultural connections and the working holiday visa scheme between the United Kingdom and Australia, British visitors are commonplace. A particularly noticeable part of this market coincides with visits of British sporting teams, such as the English cricket or rugby union team. The Barmy Army, numbering into the thousands, provides fanatical support to English cricket tours. At the final of the 2003 Rugby World Cup, played in Sydney's Telstra Stadium between Australia and England, about half of the 83,500 crowd supported the visitors.

Backpackers

Another major source of tourists to Australia include backpackers, mostly young people from Western European countries (particularly the United Kingdom) and Canada. Spending more time in Australia, these travellers tend to explore considerably more of the country.

Many backpackers participate in working holidays enabling them to stay longer in the country. Working holiday visas for Australia are available for those aged 18 to 30 for most Western European citizens, and also citizens of Canada and some developed East Asian nations such as Japan and South Korea.

Domestic Tourism

Australians are big domestic travellers as well, with a profusion of seaside resort towns in every state (many located on or near good surfing beaches), mountain retreats, plentiful national parks, rivers, fishing locations, wine growing regions, as well as domestic visitation of the major tourist spots.

Major Events

Major events attracts large number of tourists.

Sporting

The 2003 Rugby World Cup attracted 65,000 international visitors to Australia. The 2000 Sydney Olympics resulted in significant inbound and domestic tourism to Sydney. During the games, Sydney hosted 362,000 domestic and 110,000 international visitors. In addition, up to 4 billion people watched the games worldwide.

So where the bloody hell are you?

So where the bloody hell are you? is a AU$180 million advertising campaign launched in 2006 by Tourism Australia created by the Sydney office of the London headquartered advertising agency M&C Saatchi.

The advertisements feature images of Australians preparing for visitors to their country. It begins in an Outback pub with the barkeeper saying, "We've poured you a beer." Further imagery to a similar effect is then shown, including a young boy on the beach saying, "We've got the sharks out of the pool," and partygoers watching Sydney harbour fireworks saying, "We've turned on the lights". The commercial ends with bikini-clad model Lara Bingle stepping out of the ocean and asking, "So where the bloody hell are you?"

The campaign has received massive press coverage, and British prime minister Tony Blair even asked "Where the bloody hell am I?" when speaking to the Australian Parliament and suffering from jet lag. However, despite the press coverage, the campaign appears to be failing to attract tourists to Australia, with figures released in December 2006 showing a fall in tourists visiting Australia in markets where the campaign was run.

Controversy

The advertising campaign caused controversy in March 2006 when it was banned by the Broadcast Advertising Clearance Centre in the United Kingdom, which would not allow the word "bloody" to be used in television versions of the commercial. Following lobbying by Tourism Australia, including a visit to the UK by Australia's tourism minister Fran Bailey and Lara Bingle, the ban was subsequently lifted, although a 9 p.m "watershed" was imposed on television commercials in May. In March 2007, however, the Advertising Standards Authority in the UK ordered the removal of roadside billboards bearing the slogan. The ASA stated that they had received 32 complaints about the advertising, and warned Tourism Australia to refrain from using swear words in future billboards. Tourism minister Fran Bailey responded:

"What an absolutely, incredibly ludicrous stance and a greater example of double standards you'd never find. Everyone is shaking their heads, especially as it's in a country where they allow the FCUK billboards... I mean what is it about our campaign that they find offensive? I just don't understand it."

The advertisement has also been banned by regulators in Canada, owing to the implication of "unbranded alcohol consumption" by the opening line, "We've bought you a beer". There was also some concern in Canada at the word 'hell' being used as an expletive. It has been allowed to run with no adverse regulator action in several other countries such as the United States and New Zealand (although New Zealand operates upon complaints rather than banning advertisements before airing).

In Singapore, the advertisement campaign is presented as "So Where Are You?", with the words "bloody hell" removed.

Parodies and Influences

Australian comedy writer Dan Ilic produced and released a parody of the ad towards the end of March 2006. The parody uses the structure of the Tourism Australia ad to make satirical reference to various current political controversies that might be of concern to potential tourists (eg. "We got you some free accommodation" over shots of the Villawood Immigration Detention Centre). The parody was the subject of controversy in its own right when Ilic removed the ad from his company's web-site because Tourism Australia's lawyers had threatened legal action claiming the music "was infringing their copyright." According to Ilic, however, Downwind Media "commissioned [their] own song that is different in tune and tempo." As of 28 March 2006 four "new special edition versions" of the parody were made available for download.

The Chaser's War on Everything released a similar version with the slogan "So get your fucking arse over here!" to parody a perceived Australian propensity for common vulgarity, and later took to the streets to see what tourists thought of similar campaigns which made extensive use of swearing.

The Coromandel region of New Zealand also released a parody with the words, "We're bloody well in the Coromandel."

Australian Financial Review columnist Peter Ruehl speculated how effective an advertising campaign promoting the United States would be if Australians were cajolled to get their 'cracker butts' over stateside.

At the 2006 Melbourne Comedy Gala, American comedian Arj Barker replied to the ad, saying, "Whoa! Take it easy Australia! I never even said I was going there man... Australia, have you been drinking? It's eleven in the morning!"

Ashes Version

An advertisement was produced to promote the Nine Network's television coverage of the 2006-07 Ashes series, in the style of this ad but on a cricketing theme (eg 'We've rolled the ground, we've put in the stumps'). The next sentence parodied the beer quote from the original ad but this time referencing the supposed English predilection for warm beer ("we've warmed up the beer"), then "we've hidden the sunscreen, and we've brought you some soap", and finally the Australian captain descending the steps of a cricket ground stating "And we've been waiting all year" (ie to get the Ashes back).

This ad also culminates in a bikini-clad Bingle asking "So where the bloody hell are you?"-this time addressed to the English team and supporters, with Lara on the centre cricket pitch at the Sydney Cricket Ground, holding a cricket bat and wearing nothing but a green and gold bikini (based on the design of the one day International uniforms of the Australian cricket team), white shoes, and leg pads. A coda is then provided by Richie Benaud saying "Marvellous".

After success by the England team early in the second test that year, one Australian paper ran the front-page headline "Australia-where the bloody hell are you?", in reference to this advert.

Effectiveness of the Campaign

On December 6, 2006, News Limited newspapers around Australia drew attention to the campaign's shortcomings. The $A180 million campaign had hoped to attract visitors to Australian from Japan, Germany and the United Kingdom, but tourist figures show that during October 2006 the number of Japanese tourists visiting Australia fell by 5.7% in comparison with the same period in 2005.

German tourists were down 4.7% and UK visitors dropped 2.3%, although there was a slight increase in tourists from the United States and the People's Republic of China. Critics argue that the expensive campaign has failed to deliver the promised increase in tourist numbers, with opposition tourism spokesperson Martin Ferguson saying "We've been told it was a huge success and generated all these hits on a website but the latest tourism figures show the numbers are down."

In March 2007, however, The Age newspaper credited the ad with a $1.8 billion increase in tourism spending, and Tourism Australia stated that the primary goal of the campaign was to attract higher-spending, longer-staying visitors, not just to increase tourist numbers.

Immigration to Australia

Immigration to Australia began at least 40,000 years ago, when the ancestors of Australian Aborigines arrived on the continent via the islands of the Malay Archipelago and New Guinea. Europeans began landing in the 1600s and 1700s, and the continent was colonised by Great Britain in 1788.

The overall level of immigration has grown substantially during the last decade. Net overseas migration increased from 30,000 in 1993 to 118,000 in 2003-04. The largest components of immigration are the skilled migration and family re-union programs. In recent years the mandatory detention of unauthorised arrivals by boat has generated great levels of controversy. In 2005, total 123,424 people immigrated to Australia. Of them, 17,736 were from Africa, 54,804 from Asia, 21,131 from Oceania, 18,220 from United Kingdom, 1,506 from South America, and 2,369 from Eastern Europe.

History

Human migration to the Australian continent was first achieved during the closing stages of the Pleistocene epoch, when sea levels were typically much lower than they are today. It is theorised that these ancestral peoples arrived via the nearest islands of the Malay Archipelago, crossing over the intervening straits (which were then narrower) to reach the single landmass which then existed. Known as Sahul, this landmass connected Australia with New Guinea via a land bridge which emerged when prevailing glacial conditions lowered sea levels by some 100-150 m.

Australia's coastline also extended much further out into the Timor Sea than at present, affording another possible route by which these first peoples reached the continent. Estimates of the timing of these migrations vary considerably: the most widely-accepted conservative evidential view places this somewhere between 40,000 to 45,000 years ago, with earlier cited (but not universally accepted) dates of up to 60,000 years or more also proposed; the debate continues within the academic community.

On January 26, 1788, a date now celebrated as Australia Day, a landing was made by the British at Sydney Cove for the purposes of establishing a colony. The new colony was formally proclaimed as the Colony of New South Wales on February 7.

The Gold rush era, beginning in 1851, led to an enormous expansion in population, including large numbers of British and Irish settlers, followed by smaller numbers of Germans and other Europeans, and Chinese. This latter group were subject to increasing restrictions and discrimination, making it impossible for many to remain in the country. With the Federation of the Australian colonies into a single nation, one of the first acts of the new Commonwealth Government was the Immigration Restriction Act 1901, otherwise known as the White Australia policy, which was a strengthening and unification of disparate colonial policies designed to restrict non-White settlement.

After World War II, Australia launched a massive immigration programme, believing that having narrowly avoided a Japanese invasion, Australia must "populate or perish." Hundreds of thousands of displaced Europeans migrated to Australia and over 1,000,000 British Citizens immigrated under the Assisted Migration Scheme, colloquially becoming known as Ten Pound Poms.

During the 2001 election campaign, immigration and border protection became the hot issue, as a result of incidents such as the September 11, 2001 attacks, the Tampa affair, Children overboard affair, and the sinking of the SIEV-X. This incident marked the beginning of the controversial Pacific Solution.

Australian Immigration Law and Policy

The Commonwealth Migration Act 1958 is the primary legislation regulating immigration law in Australia and is administered by the Department of Immigration and Citizenship (DIAC). The Migration Act replaced earlier legislation which had been in place since 1901. The Migration Regulations 1994 is the subordinate legislation which deals with the operational aspects of the Act. Amongst other things the regulations set down the qualifying criteria for the 200 or so classes and subclasses of visa.

There are currently two immigration programs that allow permanent migration to Australia, the migration program and the humanitarian program. Foreigners currently living in Australia under one of a number of temporary visas may apply for permanent residence. New Zealanders are a special case and can migrate to Australia under the Trans-Tasman Travel Arrangement. Illegal migrants are typically unauthorised entrants and those who have either violated conditions of, or overstayed their visa.

Migration Program

To be accepted into Australia under the migration program a person must be a skilled migrant or sponsored by a family member who is "an Australian citizen, permanent resident, or eligible New Zealand citizen aged 18 years or over who lives in Australia".

A third class covers special eligibility migrants which includes Australians returning to Australia who had to give up citizenship to live overseas. DIAC states that the migration program for 2004-05 has 120,000 places available for migrants, with a strong focus on attracting skilled people and people who agree to live in regional areas of Australia. 42,000 places were allocated to the family stream.

On April 13, 2005, Australia announced that it will take an extra 20,000 skilled migrants in 2005-06 to help meet labour force needs. Immigration Minister Amanda Vanstone said that between 130,000 and 140,000 non-humanitarian migrants would be taken, with a skilled migrant component of 97,500.

Some in Australia have expressed concern that skilled migration is being used as a solution to the current shortage of skilled labour in Australia, as opposed to training Australian workers. During the 2006 budget "right of reply" on 12 May, 2006, Opposition Australian Labour Party leader Kim Beazley stated that under a Labor government, foreign apprentices would be banned from seeking work in Australia.

New Zealanders

New Zealand citizens are entitled to live and work in Australia under the Trans-Tasman Travel Arrangement. New rules in 2001 divided New Zealanders living in Australia into two categories: those who were resident in Australia before 2001, and those who arrived in Australia after 2001. Those who were resident before 2001 may claim unemployment benefits after two years' residence, as is the norm for permanent residents of other nationalities. New Zealanders who arrive in Australia after 2001 are not entitled to any unemployment benefits at all, as is the norm for people living in Australia indefinitely only on work permits.

Humanitarian Program

The humanitarian program is designed for refugees and others with humanitarian needs, and comprises "offshore" and "onshore" components. The offshore resettlement program assists people in humanitarian need overseas for whom resettlement in another country is the only option, while the onshore program assists people already in Australia who arrived on temporary visas or in an unauthorised manner, and who claim Australia's protection. The offshore program comprises two categories of permanent visa ("refugee" and "special humanitarian program") and two categories of temporary visa ("secondary movement relocation" and "secondary movement offshore entry").

For the humanitarian program period 2005 to 2006, a total of 14,144 visas in all classes were granted (of which 1,805 were brought forward from the period 2006 to 2007). This period saw the highest number of visas granted in ten years, and for the third time in seven years there were no unused places to carry over to the next period. Of the 14,144 issued visas, 12,758 were granted to people overseas and 1,386 were granted to people in Australia.

The United Nations High Commission for Refugees estimates that Australia accepted 16,000 people through its humanitarian program in 2004. This consisted of both UNHCR assisted refugees and those taken through bilateral arrangements. This is the second largest program in the world after that of the United States and Australia takes 19% of those refugees being assisted by the UNHCR.

Types of visas issued under the humanitarian program include the protection visa, temporary protection visa, temporary humanitarian visa and return pending visa.

Illegal Immigration

Illegal immigrants to Australia are those who:

- enter Australia without authority; or
- overstay visas, work without appropriate approval or have their visas cancelled.

The Migration Act 1958 requires that all non-Australian citizens who are unlawfully in Australia must be detained and, if they are not given permission to remain in Australia, must be deported as soon as practical. In 1992 mandatory detention for illegal immigrants was introduced, and has been maintained by successive governments. In 2001 the Australian migration zone was reduced by excising many offshore islands which had been used by unauthorised arrivals to seek entry to Australia, particularly those guided by people smugglers.

DIAC statistics show that the most common nationalities of people detained as illegal immigrants since 2000 are: Afghan, Iraqi, Iranian, Chinese, Indonesian, Sri Lankan, Palestinian, Korean, Indian, Vietnamese, and Bangladeshi. However, the single largest group of illegals in Australia are British nationals who have overstayed their visas. As of 31 December 2005, DIMA (as it then was known) estimated the total number of visa overstayers in Australia at just under 46,400, a figure which has been reduced by around 10,000 each year since December 2003.

Environmental, Economic and Social Impacts

There are a wide range of views in the Australian community on the composition and level of immigration, and on the possible effects of varying the level of immigration and population growth, some of which are based on empirical data, others more speculative in nature. In 2002, a CSIRO population study entitled "Future Dilemmas", commissioned by DIMA, outlined six potential dilemmas associated with immigration-driven population growth. These dilemmas included the absolute numbers of aged continuing to rise despite high immigration off-setting ageing and declining birth-rates in a proportional sense, a worsening of Australia's trade balance due to more imports and higher consumption of domestic production, increased green house gas emissions, overuse of agricultural soils, marine fisheries and domestic supplies of oil and gas, and a decline in urban air quality, river quality and biodiversity.

Replacement

The fertility rate in Australia has dropped over the last generation below replacement levels, meaning that without immigration, Australia's population would both age and decline, raising the question of long-term social and cultural sustainability.

In 2006, Treasurer Peter Costello warned Australians to increase their birth rate to replacement levels or run the risk of Australia's population composition being fundamentally transformed by immigration. Raising the spectre of social fragmentation and violence under a low birth rate, high immigration scenario, Costello cautioned that immigrants might not be absorbed successfully if the Australian-born population dwindled. He stated: "Increasing immigration to cover natural population decline will change the composition of our population and raise concerns about social dislocation."

Environment

Some members of the Australian environmental movement, notably the organisation Sustainable Population Australia, believe that as the driest inhabited continent, Australia cannot continue to sustain its current rate of population growth without becoming overpopulated. SPA also argues that climate change will lead to a deterioration of natural ecosystems through increased temperatures, extreme weather events and less rainfall in the southern part of the continent, thus reducing its capacity to sustain a large population even further. The UK-based Optimum Population Trust supports the view that Australia is overpopulated, and believes that to maintain the current standard of living in Australia, the optimum population is 10 million (rather than the present 20.86 million), or 21 million with a reduced standard of living. Other members of the environment movement point out that Australians are, per capita, the highest users of water on the planet and the worst emitters of greenhouse gases, so any consideration of changes to standard of living needs to consider a broader context regarding appropriate use of resources independently of population.

Housing

Some claim that Australia's recent level of immigration has (along with natural population growth and other economic factors) contributed to a widespread shortage of affordable housing, particularly in the major cities. A number of economists, such as Macquarie Bank analyst Rory Robertson, assert that high immigration and the propensity of new arrivals to cluster in the capital cities is exacerbating the nation's housing affordability problem. According to Robertson, Federal Government policies that fuel demand for housing, such as the currently high levels of immigration but also capital gains tax discounts, have had a greater impact on housing affordability than land release on urban fringes. However, the Productivity Commission does not accept "population pressures" as a major driver of strong increases in house prices, stating that "increased demand for better quality and better located dwellings, rather than for more dwellings, has been the primary driver".. Furthermore, demographer Wendell Cox has argued that Australian cities are among the least affordable in the world due to government policies of urban consolidation.

Employment

According to one researcher, there are thousands of low-cost IT workers entering Australia who are undermining the job prospects of new computer science graduates and reducing salaries in the IT industry. However, other research sponsored by DIAC has found that Australia's structured labour market along with the larger number of immigrants with higher education levels has tended to raise employment levels for Australians who are relatively unskilled.

Australian trade unions have sometimes exposed attempts by employers to introduce foreign workers into the country in order to avoid paying local workers higher wages. The government's policy of mandatory detention, especially regarding the impact upon children, has come under criticism from a range of religious, community and political groups including the National Council of Churches, Amnesty International, Australian Democrats, Australian Greens and Rural Australians for Refugees.

Economy

The Federal Treasurer, Peter Costello considers that Australia is underpopulated due to a low birth rate, and claims that negative population growth will have adverse long-term effects on the economy as the population ages and the labour market becomes less competitive. To avoid this outcome the government has increased immigration to fill gaps in labour markets and introduced a subsidy to encourage families to have more children. However, opponents of population growth such as Sustainable Population Australia do not accept that population growth will decline and reverse, based on current immigration and fertility projections. In terms of using immigration to offset an aging workforce, a 1999 parliamentary research paper entitled "Population Futures for Australia: the Policy Alternatives" concluded: "It is demographic nonsense to believe that immigration can help to keep our population young."

Ross Gittens claims that the Liberal Party's focus on skilled migration has reduced the average age of migrants. "More than half are aged 15 to 34, compared with 28 per cent of our population. Only 2 per cent of permanent immigrants are 65 or older, compared with 13 per cent of our population." Because of these statistics, Gittens claims that immigration is slowing the ageing of the Australian population. He also claims that the emphasis on skilled migration also means that the "net benefit to the economy is a lot more clear-cut." Even though Gittens suggests that skilled workers add more to the economy, there are those who acknowledge the importance of unskilled migrants. Treasurer Eric Ripper claims that in Australia "several major capital works projects had to be put on hold because there were not enough skilled and unskilled workers."

Chapman and Cobb-Clark believe that "immigrant spending from past savings will increase the demand for labour and create job vacancies". However, immigration also increases the supply of labour and the number of people applying for job vacancies.

Using regression analysis, Addison and Worswick found that "there is no evidence that immigration has negatively impacted on the wages of young or low-skilled natives." Furthermore, Addison's study found that immigration did not increase unemployment among native workers. Rather, immigration decreased unemployment. The evidence from the Economic Record runs counter to the common view that immigration adds only to labour supply and reduces wages. Economic empirical data show that immigrants not only add to labour supply but also to labour demand. Whether labour demand increase is greater than labor supply increase after immigration is an empirical issue. When the magnitude of change in aggregate labour supply is much greater than the magnitude of change in aggregate labour demand as a result of increased immigration then immigration can cause wages to decrease. Analysis by Garnaut shows this.

In July 2005 the Productivity Commission launched a commissioned study entitled "Economic Impacts of Migration and Population Growth", and released an initial position paper on 17 January 2006 which states that the increase of income per capita provided by higher migration (50% more than the base model) by the 2024-2025 financial year would be $335 (0.6%), an amount described as "very small". The paper also found that Australians would on average work 1.3% longer hours, about twice the proportional increase in income..

In a study in the Australian Economic Review, J[illegible]ank[illegible] finds that during the 1980s the Hawke Government's decisio[illegible] not to decrease immigration lowered the unemployment rate.

Gittens claims there is considerable opposition to immigration to Australia by "battlers" because of the belief that immigrants will steal jobs. Gittens claims though that "it's true that immigrants add to the supply of labour. But it's equally true that, by consuming and bringing families who consume, they also add to the demand for labour-usually by more."

Infrastructure

Individuals and interest groups such as Sustainable Population Australia filed submissions in response to the Productivity Commission's position paper, arguing amongst other things that immigration causes a decline in wealth per capita and leads to environmental degradation and overburdened infrastructure, the latter creating a costly demand for new infrastructure. However, the Productivity Commission's final research report found that it was not possible to reliably assess the impact of environmental limitations upon productivity and economic growth, nor to reliably attribute the contribution of immigration to any such impact.

Australia is a relatively high-immigration country like Canada (the country with the highest per capita immigration rate in the world, see Immigration to Canada) and the United States, and while other economically developed countries like Japan have historically had negligible immigration, the issue of population decline is forcing a rethink of such policies.

Immigration and Australian Politics

Both major Australian political parties favour a relatively high level of immigration. When John Howard became Prime Minister, net migration was rising, and the upward trend in the number of immigrants has increased over the decade since he took office. According to Banham, Australian political leaders who support higher immigration include Amanda Vanstone, John Howard, Peter Costello, Kim Beazley, and Steve Bracks, with vocal opposition to immigration coming from former New

South Wales premier Bob Carr who cites environmental reasons for his opposition. Peter Costello believes that high population growth in Australia is important for economic growth.

An anti-immigration party, the One Nation Party, was formed by Pauline Hanson in the late 1990s. The party enjoyed significant electoral success for a while, most notably in its home state of Queensland, but is now electorally marginalized. One Nation argued for a zero net immigration policy, asserting that "environmentally Australia is near her carrying capacity, economically immigration is unsustainable and socially, if continued as is, will lead to an ethnically divided Australia."

Commentators such as Ross Gittens, a columnist at The Age accuse John Howard of deception, by appearing "tough" on illegal immigration to win support from the working class while simultaneously winning support from employers with high legal immigration. Phillip Adams has also been critical of Howard's seemingly duplicitous policy.

In 2006, the Labor Party under Kim Beazley took a stance against the importation of increasingly large numbers of temporary migrant workers ("foreign workers") by employers, arguing that this is simply a way for employers to drive down wages. At the same time, it is estimated that a million Australians are employed outside Australia.

Ross Gittens claims that "a central element in John Howard's outstanding political success has been his ability to attract the votes of people in modest circumstances whom you'd normally expect to be Labor voters-Howard's battlers." However, issues of industrial relations and Work Choices before the 2007 election are being blamed for the Liberal Party's slump in opinion polls.

ACNielsen polling in March 2007 showed 53% of respondents preferred Kevin Rudd as Prime Minister compared to John Howard on 39%, and Labor on 61% of the two party preferred vote to the Coalition's 39%. Rudd's personal approval rating of 67% makes him the most popular opposition leader in the poll's 35 year history, with Newspoll two party preferred polling the highest in its history.

Some political commentators believe the Liberal Party's slump in the polls is due to environmental issues (Roy Morgon Research claims that 71% of Australians believe the Government should act immediately to address the consequences of global warming). Gittens points to issues of immigration and industrial relations, claiming that "Howard is under considerable pressure to make changes that advantage business and high-income earners but disadvantage ordinary workers."

Migration Agents

It is possible to employ Migration Consultants or Lawyers to assist with a visa application for Australia. Such professionals who provide immigration assistance are regulated by a governing Authority called the Migration Agents Registration Authority. There is a difference in education and training between Migration Consultants and Lawyers. Migration Consultants are required to complete a post-graduate 18 week course. Most law students of Australia do not specifically study Migration Law as part of their curriculum. Prior to July 2006, Migration Consultants were required to pass a complex examination, but not strictly required to complete post-graduate education. While Migration Consultants are legally required to maintain their knowledge of Migration through Continuous Professional Development (CPD) activities, Lawyers' current knowledge is not administered.

Migration and Settlement Services

There are a variety of community-based services that cater to the needs of newly-arrived migrants, refugees, asylum seekers, some of which receive funding from the Commonwealth Government, such as Migrant Resource Centres. Asylum seekers, however, are denied access to such services and there are only a very small number of specific asylum seeker services catering to their needs.

TOURISM IN BAHRAIN

Bahrain is one of the most popular tourist destinations in the Middle East with over two million tourists a year. Most of the visitors are from Arab Gulf states but there is an increasing number of tourists from outside the region thanks to a growing awareness of the Kingdom's rich heritage and its higher profile with regards to the Bahrain Grand Prix.

The Lonely Planet describes Bahrain as "an excellent introduction to the Gulf" because of its authentic Arab heritage and reputation as relatively liberal and modern. The Kingdom combines authentic Arab culture, contemporary Gulf glitz and the archaeological legacy of five thousand years of civilisation. The ancient civilisation of Dilmun, which dominated trade between Mesopotamia and the Indus Valley Civilization, was centred in Bahrain. The inhabitants of Dilmun left behind settlements and temples and tens of thousands of burial mounds which dot the landscape.

Dilmun prospered because it had fresh water, and it is this resource which has meant that Bahrain has long fought over by regional powers in a predominantly arid region. As a result, the island is home to many castles including the impressive Qalat Al Bahrain which was recently listed by UNESCO as a World Heritage Site.

The Bahrain National Museum has a wide-varied collection of artifacts from the Kingdom's history dating back to the island's first human inhabitation 9000 years ago.

MP Adel Al-Mouwdah criticised the sale of alcohol in hotels and restaurants, saying that the 'poison' was attracting 'the wrong type of tourist' from Saudi Arabia where alcohol is banned.

Tourism Developments

Many new tourist attraction resorts are being planned in Bahrain such as the Al Areen Resort, Dannat Hawar, Durrat Al Bahrain, Amwaj Islands, Lulu Island, Riffa Views, iceberg tower and Bahrain Bay which will be home to the Kingdom's first Four Seasons Hotel.

Durrat Al Bahrain The US$1 billion Durrat Al Bahrain is named after the most perfect pearl and sets out to be a model

21st century city resort. The development will comprise of residential and tourism elements and will cover a 20-kilometre stretch of reclaimed desert and sea.

The project resembles a necklace and will comprise of 13 islands-an arc of six atolls and five pearl-shaped islands; an island for a five-star resort and aqua park and a crescent-shaped island for a residential complex.

Spread over 20 square kilometres, the development will include 13 different islands with over 2,000 villas, more than 3,000 apartments, luxury hotels, restaurants, promenades, shopping centres, spas and a proposed golf course among its many sports facilities. A 400-boat marina set in a lagoon is also planned.

Amwaj Islands Work is continuing at a rapid pace on the Amwaj Islands project, a group of man-made islands less than two kilometres off the coast of Muharraq, which, once complete, promises to offer a combination of world-class residential neighbourhoods, commercial districts and spectacular resorts.

The 2.8 million-square-metre Amwaj Islands will have a unifying architectural theme and will include the following components: o Al Marsa: ready-built canal-front villas; o Zawaya: Beautiful houses perched over the water's edge; o Gateway: Spectacular apartments at the doorstep of the project; o Saraya Al Bahar: Designer villas on common or private beach; o Tala: Town-houses, villas and apartments in an exclusive gated neighbourhood setting, overlooking the tranquil Amwaj lagoon; o Meena 7: Stylish apartments on the seafront in the heart of the trendy Al Marsa village; and o Al Fanar Resort: hotel and recreational area to the west of the islands, which includes a 100-berth marina and retail centre. The first four-plus star beach hotel will have 300 rooms and a spacious banquet hall

The commercial heart of the islands is centered on a lagoon, work on the wall of which is nearing completion, with the casting of concrete bollards to the top of the quay wall, as the final touch. The immediate area will accommodate a landscaped promenade that will offer panoramic views across the lagoon, which will be ringed by stylish waterfront cafes and restaurants.

Design work is also under way on a marina and construction is expected to start in the third quarter of this year.

Al Marsa Floating Island Al Marsa, which means 'jetty' or 'harbour' in Arabic is a floating island that is being built with an investment of US$70 million. On completion later this year, the island will have 274 canal houses, a 150-room hotel, time-share apartments, retail mall, restaurants and a yacht club.

The artificial island, which is part of the Amwaj Islands project, will measure approximately 28,000 square metres and is designed to have a series of canals where boats can cruise and even park beside their own back garden where the level of water is maintained within 50 centimetres 'rise and fall' by a sector-lock gate located at the south entrance of the island adjacent to the proposed Yacht Club.

Tala Island One of the components of the Amwaj Islands project, Tala Islands will encompass 136,000 square metres. The development, which costs US$110 million, will accommodate 48 beachfront villas, 42 two-storey, mid-size villas, as well as 410 apartments in 31 blocks (including 12 penthouses) and another 148 smaller apartments. The development will also include an aqua park, retail areas, a sports centre, tennis club and restaurants and coffee shops.

Bahrain

Built in the 8th Century, Al Khamis Mosque is thought to be the first mosque in Bahrain, and is one of the oldest Islamic relics in the region.

Bahrain, officially the Kingdom of Bahrain, is a borderless island country in the Persian Gulf and is the smallest Arab nation. Saudi Arabia lies to the west and is connected to Bahrain by the King Fahd Causeway (officially opened on November 25, 1986), and Qatar is to the south across the Gulf of Bahrain. The Qatar-Bahrain Friendship Bridge currently being planned will link Bahrain to Qatar as the longest fixed link in the world.

Governorates

Bahrain is split into five governorates. Until July 3, 2002, it was divided into twelve municipalities; see Municipalities of Bahrain. The governorates are:

1. Capital
2. Central
3. Muharraq
4. Northern
5. Southern

Cities, Towns and Villages

Among Bahrain's cities and towns are:

- Al Manama
- Al Muharraq
- Isa Town
- Hamad Town
- Jidhafs
- Sitrah
- Al Riffa
- Um Al Hassam

Bahrain's many small towns and villages include:

- Noaim
- Sanabis
- Karbabad
- Seef District
- Al Dair
- Al Deah
- Askar
- Al Buday'a
- Al Duraz
- Al Jufair
- Karrana
- Jid Alhaj
- Jannusan
- jurdab
- Maqaba
- Tubli
- Meqsha'a
- Al Zallaq
- A'Ali
- Bani Jamrah
- Awali
- Ma'ameer

Geography

Bahrain is a generally flat and arid archipelago, comprising of a low desert plain rising gently to a low central escarpment, in the Persian Gulf, east of Saudi Arabia. The highest point is the 122 m Jabal ad Dukhan. Bahrain has a total area of 688 km^2 (266 mi^2), which is slightly larger than the Isle of Man, though it is smaller than the nearby King Fahd International Airport near Dammam, Saudi Arabia (780 km^2 or 301 mi^2). As an archipelago of thirty-three islands, Bahrain does not share a land boundary with another country but does have a 161-kilometre (100 mi) coastline and claims a further twelve nautical miles (22 km) of territorial sea and a twenty-four nautical mile (44 km) contiguous zone. Bahrain enjoys mild winters and endures very hot, humid summers.

Bahrain's natural resources include large quantities of oil and associated and nonassociated natural gas as well as fish stocks, which is perhaps fortunate as arable land constitutes only 2.82%. Desert constitutes 92% of Bahrain and periodic droughts and dust storms are the main natural hazards for Bahrainis.

Environmental issues facing Bahrain include desertification resulting from the degradation of limited arable land and coastal degradation (damage to coastlines, coral reefs, and sea vegetation) resulting from oil spills and other discharges from large tankers, oil refineries, and distribution stations. The agricultural and domestic sectors' over-utilization of the Dammam aquifer, the principle aquifer in Bahrain, has led to its salinization by adjacent brackish and saline water bodies.

Demographics

The official religion of Bahrain is Islam, which the majority of the population practices. However, due to an influx of immigrants and guest workers from non-Muslim countries, such as India, Philippines and Sri Lanka, the overall percentage of Muslims in the country has declined in recent years. According to the 2001 census, 80% of Bahrain's population was Muslim, 10% were Christian, and 10% practiced other Asian or Middle Eastern religions.

There are no official figures for the proportion of Shia and Sunni among the Muslims of Bahrain, however unofficial sources, such as the Library of Congress Country Studies, BBC, and the New York Times, estimate it to be approximately 30 percent Sunni and 70 per cent Shia. The last official census which included sectarian identification was taken in 1941, which reported 53 percent as Shia.

Recently, Bahrain has transformed into a cosmopolitan society with mixed communities: two thirds of Bahrain's population consists of Arabs, while the rest are immigrants and guest workers largely from Iran, South Asia and Southeast Asia. A Financial Times published on 31 May 1983 found that "Bahrain is a polyglot state, both religiously and racially. Leaving aside the temporary immigrants of the past ten years, there are at least eight or nine communities on the island."

The present communities may be classified as: tribals, Arab tribes allied to Al-Khalifa including the Utoob tribes, Dawasir, etc; Bahranis, indigenous Shia Arabs; the Howala, Sunni Arabs that migrated from the eastern shores of the gulf (in modern day Iran); Ajam ethnic Persian Shia; Najdis, non-tribal urban Sunni Arabs from Najd in central Arabia; Indians who traded with Bahrain and settled before the age of oil; a tiny Jewish community; and a miscellaneous grouping.

Culture

Bahrain is sometimes described as the "Middle East lite" a country that mixes thoroughly modern infrastructure with a definite Persian Gulf identity, but unlike other countries in the region its prosperity is not solely a reflection of the size of its oil wealth, but also related to the creation of an indigenous middle class. This unique socioeconomic development in the Persian Gulf has meant that Bahrain is generally more liberal than its neighbours. While Islam is the main religion, Bahrainis have been known for their tolerance, and alongside mosques can be found churches, a Hindu temple, a Sikh Gurdwara and a Jewish synagogue. The country is home to several communities that have faced persecution elsewhere.

It is too early to say whether political liberalisation under King Hamad bin Isa Al Khalifa has augmented or undermined Bahrain's traditional pluralism. The new political space for

Shia and Sunni Islamists has meant that they are now in a much stronger position to pursue programmes that often seek to directly confront this pluralism, yet at the same time political reforms have encouraged an opposite trend for society to become more self critical with a greater willingness in general to examine previous social taboos. It is now common to find public seminars on once unheard of subjects such as marital problems and sex and child abuse. Another facet of the new openness is Bahrain's status as the most prolific book publisher in the Arab world, with 132 books published in 2005 for a population of 700,000. In comparison, the average for the entire Arab world is seven books published per one million people in 2005, according to the United Nations Development Programme.

Also, Bahrain were and still a place of arts. Ali Bahar is the most famous singer in Bahrain. He performed his music with his Band Al-Ekhwa (The Brothers).

The middle classes tend to have a very cosmopolitan outlook, and with mainstream hip hop music very popular among Bahrain's youth. Of DJing in Bahrain, DJ Whoo Kid said:

> *"Growing up in Queens Village, New York, I really didn't know what to expect upon my arrival in a Muslim country. I expected to see camels, sand homes and vehicles that could handle sand, like Jeep Wranglers or Land Cruisers. To my surprise, I was greeted by teenagers blasting music by Mobb Deep, Jay Z, 2Pac, Biggie Smalls, Eminem and 50 Cent. When I turned on the radio I heard a variety of music that included the Black Eyed Peas, Sean Paul and the Pussycat Dolls. The hottest music-and I hear a lot as a DJ for Eminem's Shade 45 channel on Sirius Satellite Radio-was the Arabic hip-hop remixes and beats I heard on the radio. It made me realize why many producers in the U.S. are sampling them like crazy."*

In addition to their modern outlook, there is a mingling of many of the Bahraini youths with British expatriates, who have a broad community within Bahrain. On October 20, 2005, it was revealed that Michael Jackson intended to leave the

United States permanently in order to seek a new life in Bahrain. Jackson has reportedly told friends that he feels "increasingly Bahraini" after buying a former PM's mansion in Sanad, and is now seeking another property by the seashore. Jackson reportedly moved to Las Vegas, Nevada, in 2006. Other celebrities associated with the Kingdom include singer Shakira and Grand Prix driver Jenson Button, who owns property there.

In the Capital Governate lies the city of Juffair. This is the location of the U.S.Naval Support Activity, Bahrain. The base's effect on the area is evident. The concentration of western restaurants, bars and the prevalence of prostitution, make this city a magnet for U.S. servicemembers and Saudi-Arabians. On weekends the Saudi's cross the causeway in droves to escape the restrictive culture of Saudi.

Language

Arabic is the official language of Bahrain. The two main dialects are Baharna Arabic, spoken by the indigenous Baharna Shia, and Bahraini Arabic spoken by the indigenous Sunnis. Persian, Urdu/Hindi and English are also spoken by sections of the population.

Formula One

Bahrain is the home of Formula One racing in the Middle East. It started hosting the Gulf Air Grand Prix on 4 April 2004, the first for an Arab country. The race was won by Michael Schumacher of Scuderia Ferrari. This was followed by the Bahrain Grand Prix in 2005. Bahrain has successfully hosted the opening Grand Prix of the 2006 season on 12 March. Both the above races were won by Fernando Alonso of Renault. The 2007 event took place on April 13th, 14th and 15th resulting in victory of Ferrari's Felipe Massa.

Tourism

Bahrain is one of the most popular tourist destinations in the Middle East with over two million tourists a year. Most of the visitors are from the Arab, Persian Gulf states but there is an increasing number of tourists from outside the region thanks to a growing awareness of the Kingdom's rich heritage and its higher profile with regards to the Bahrain Formula One Race Track.

The Lonely Planet describes Bahrain as "an excellent introduction to the Persian Gulf" because of its authentic Arab heritage and reputation as relatively liberal and modern. The Kingdom combines authentic Arab culture, contemporary Gulf glitz and the archaeological legacy of five thousand years of civilization. The ancient civilization of Dilmun, which dominated trade between Mesopotamia and the Indus Valley Civilization, was centred in Bahrain. The inhabitants of Dilmun left behind settlements and temples and tens of thousands of burial mounds which dot the landscape.

Dilmun prospered because it had fresh water, and it is this resource which has meant that Bahrain has long fought over by regional powers in a predominantly arid region. As a result, the island is home to many castles including the impressive Qalat Al Bahrain which was recently listed by UNESCO as a World Heritage Site.

The Bahrain National Museum has a wide-varied collection of artifacts from the Kingdom's history dating back to the island's first human inhabitation 9000 years ago.

List of Visitor Attractions in Bahrain

A list of tourist attractions in Bahrain, a small island country in the Persian Gulf.

- Al Fateh Mosque
- Al Khamis Mosque
- Arad Fort
- Bab Al Bahrain
- Manama Souq
- Gold Souq
- Bahrain Fort
- Bahrain Grand Prix
- Bahrain National Museum
- Barbar Temple
- Beit Al Qur'an
- Dilmun Burial Mounds
- Diving
- First Oil Well
- Horse Riding
- Jasra House

- Khalid Al Khajah Fort
- King Fahd Causeway
- Riffa Fort
- Riffa Golf Club
- Shaikh Isa's House
- Siyadi House
- Tree of Life

TOURISM IN BRAZIL

Tourism in Brazil is a growing sector. The country had 5,358,000 visitors in 2005, an increase of 4% since 2004, placing them as the fourth greatest tourist destination in the Americas. Of these, 991,000 were Argentine, 792,000 from the United States and 373,000 from Portugal. The visitors left R$4 billion in the country, making tourism an important economic field for Brazil, generating 678,000 new jobs.

The regions receiving the major share of the tourism were Rio de Janeiro (34,7%), Santa Catarina (25,1%), Paraná (20,3%), São Paulo (22,1%), Amazonas (22%) and Bahia (15,5%). The most visited cities were Rio de Janeiro (31,5%), Foz do Iguaçu (17%), São Paulo (13,6%), Manaus (13,4%), Florianópolis (12,1%) and Salvador (11,5%).

The following is a list of major tourist attractions in Brazil:

In 2006, Rio de Janeiro and Salvador were the most visited cities by international tourists and Rio de Janeiro and Fortaleza by national visitors.

- Rio de Janeiro
- Rio de Janeiro State: Angra dos Reis, Parati, Resende, Visconde de Mauá, Itatiaia National Park, Petrópolis, Vassouras, Teresópolis, Serra dos Órgãos, Nova Friburgo, Saquarema, Arraial do Cabo, Cabo Frio, Búzios, Ilha Grande
- Espírito Santo: Vitória, Guarapari, Anchieta, Piúma, Domingos Martins, Santa Teresa
- Minas Gerais: Belo Horizonte, Sabará, Ouro Preto, Congonhas, Mariana, Lavras, São João del Rei, Tiradentes, Diamantina, Caxambu, São Lourenço, São

Tomé das Letras, Caparaó National Park, Serra do Cipó National Park

- São Paulo
- São Paulo State: São Sebastião, Ilhabela, Boiçucanga, Guarujá, Santos, Iguape, Cananéia, Campos do Jordão
- Paraná: Curitiba, Morretes, Antonina, Paranaguá, Ilha do Mel, Superagüi National Park, Foz do Iguaçu, Iguaçu Falls
- Santa Catarina: Florianópolis, Ilha de Santa Catarina, Joinville, Blumenau
- Rio Grande do Sul: Porto Alegre, Torres, Aparados da Serra National Park, Serra Gaúcha
- Distrito Federal: Brasília
- Goiás: Goiânia, Chapada dos Veadeiros National Park, Pirenópolis, Goiás Velho, Caldas Novas, Emas National Park, Araguaia River
- Mato Grosso: Cuiabá, The Pantanal, Chapada dos Guimarães National Park, Barra do Garças, Alta Floresta, Cáceres, Barão de Melgaço, Poconé
- Mato Grosso do Sul: Campo Grande, Corumbá, Bonito, Ponta Porã, Aquidauana, Coxim
- Bahia: Salvador, Cachoeira, Lençóis, Morro de São Paulo, Ilhéus, Porto Seguro, Arraial d'Ajuda, Trancoso, Chapada Diamantina National Park, Abrolhos Marine National Park
- Sergipe: Aracaju, Laranjeiras, São Cristóvão, Estância, Propriá
- Alagoas: Maceió, Penedo
- Pernambuco: Recife, Olinda, Itamaracá, Igarassu, Caruaru, Fazenda Nova, Nova Jesusalém, Garanhuns, Triunfo, Fernando de Noronha
- Paraíba: João Pessoa, Baía da Traição, Sousa
- Rio Grande do Norte: Natal

- Ceará: Fortaleza, Aracati, Canoa Quebrada, Jericoacoara, Tatajuba, Camocim, Sobral, Baturité, Ubajara National Park, Juazeiro do Norte
- Piauí: Teresina, Sete Cidades National Park, Parnaíba, Serra da Capivara National Park
- Maranhão: São Luís, Lençóis Maranhenses National Park, Alcântara, Imperatriz, Carolina
- Pará: Belém, Ilha de Marajó, Santarém
- Amapá: Macapá, Oiapoque
- Tocantins: Palmas, Ilha do Bananal, Natividade
- Amazonas: Manaus, Parintins, Tefé, Mamirauá
- Roraima: Boa Vista, Monte Roraima
- Rondônia: Porto Velho, Guajará-Mirim, Guaporé Valley
- Acre: Rio Branco, Xapuri, Brasiléia, Assis Brasil

TOURISM IN BURKINA FASO

Tourism in Burkina Faso Burkina Faso is located in West Africa with approximately sixty different ethnicities and more than ten thousand inhabitants, each one having their own culture and traditions. However we can consider four regions of tourist spots in Burkina Faso which can be located in the Central, the Western, the Eastern and the Northern (The Sahel) parts of the country. Burkina Faso conceals a lot of tourist spots and those listed here are the principal ones, the most important and those which welcome visitors in great numbers each year. Each of the spots has its particularity, its history and also its chronology.

THE CENTER

Ouagadougou

The Park of Bangr Weogo: Localized in the middle of Ouagadougou, Fernando, G. and Bachirou, N. March 26, 2006. stated that "the urban park of Bangr Weogo owns at this day more than three hundred and sixty (360) species of plants, more than one hundred and sixty (160) species of birds and more than forty (40) species of animals like antelope, crocodiles, monkeys, squirrel and so on. The Bangr Weogo infrastructure includes a museum entirely dedicates to the animal reign, an area of sport, an area of game play for children named "Faso Park", and one restaurant". The tourists in vacation at Ouagadougou will enjoy a trip over the different infrastructures of the Bangr Weogo Park.

The National museum

The National museum of Ouagadougou, also an important tourist spot. It was created in 1962 and is still completely functional. It welcomes a combination of traditional villages which represent the different cultures and tribes of Burkina Faso; inside the museum a library is available and also sacred items which tell a lot about the culture of the country and its population.

The International Saloon of Arts and Crafts (SIAO) and the Festival of cinema (FESPACO) are the tourist spots that the tourists will enjoy the most at Ouagadougou. Indeed these two festivals take place every two years in Ouagadougou. The International Saloon of Arts and Crafts (SIAO) is a way to promote African craft industry and a better way to learn about African art because all African countries are represented. With the Festival of cinema (FESPACO) which is unique in Africa because it facilitates the screening of all African Films, it is certain that the tourists will enjoy the FESPACO because it is the only one of its kind where African actors, film makers meet together especially in the aim of promoting the African cinema. During this period which lasts for 2 to 3 weeks, the national television and every screen of cinema of the city show African movies.

Ziniaré

The Wildlife Park of Ziniaré: The wildlife park of Ziniaré has an important variety of animals living in captivity. There, you can find elephants, lions, antelopes and many other species; it is a very fine place to visit. If you have extra time you can visit the house of the president Mr. Blaise Compaoré near the wildlife park..

The Sculpture on Granite of Loango

The area of Loango near the town of Ziniaré is the granite sanctuary. Indeed, Loango is well-known in the sculptors' world and they meet there once a year to carve the rocks. It is also the opportunity to learn how to sculpt and meet great sculptors. The exploits made by those sculptors are very surprising and magnificent. The tourists can not regret an excursion there particularly those who like stone carvings.

The Museum of Manega

The most extraordinary tourist spot that the tourists will never forget is the museum of Manega also called the "Land of Rest" located at fifty (50) kilometers at the north of Ouagadougou which has been founded by Master Titinga Frédéric Pacéré, lawyer and a man of culture. Indeed, he stated that "strangely related to the sacred, this museum conceals a lot of items dealing with the domain of the mystery.

There, the tourists is able to find for example 500 sacred masks having all participated in rituals in front of dead men; several tens of YAKOUGA or tombstones with men's effigy dating back to several millennia and whose rocks are aged between 2,600,000,000 and 1,600,000,000 years, elements of the oldest African cultures and many others items". A trip in the museum of Manega is absolutely essential for those who felt in love with the mysteries that the African culture carries.

Koudougou

The sacred crocodiles of Sabou: The town of Koudougou with his sacred crocodiles of Sabou also has a lot of reputation. Indeed, the inhabitants venerate crocodiles in this region and for good reason. The crocodiles are harmless and you can easily sit on them and take memorable pictures. That is what the native population suggests the tourists do when they arrive at Sabou.

The West

Bobo-Dioulasso

The old mosquee of Dioulassoba: At Bobo, there is the old, grand mosque of Dioulassoba built in "eighteen ninety (1890)," which is located in the center of the town; there, visits are only allowed in the early morning. The grand Mosque represents a very good example of Sahel architecture.

The Mausoleum of Guimbi Ouattara: The "Princess Guimbi Ouattara" was a prominent figure in the history of the defense of Bobo Dioulasso against the invaders in the early eighteen hundreds and for those interested about her story, it is possible for them to visit her mausoleum.

The Museum of Bobo-Dioulasso: The museum of Bobo also called the museum of the Houet is located just at the entry of the town and it is a very nice place to visit. Many cultures in Burkina Faso are represented, so it is again a chance to learn a little bit more about the culture of Burkina.

The Old Town: When talking about the town of Bobo Dioulasso, the old town (localized in the quarter of Dioulassoba) comes earlier in next but each visitor of the town should make a stop there if he wants to learn about the story of Bobo. Indeed, it represents the oldest quarter of the town.

The Guinguette: the tourists who want to take a rest in a heavenly place, the area of the Guinguette is opened to the public. In fact it is a very beautiful place where people can swim without being disturbed; the vegetation and the atmosphere are pleasant. A system of restoration where people can eat and enjoy the day is also available.

The National Week of Culture (SNC)

Contrary to Ouagadougou, the town of Bobo Dioulasso got his National week of culture (SNC) where the different cultures of Burkina Faso are represented and try to promote their culture through sketches, traditional songs and exhibitions. The week is entirely dedicated to cultural activities and many personalities go to Bobo during this period for the event.

Banfora

Natural Waterfall of Banfora

Among the surroundings of Bobo Dioulasso is the town of Banfora which conceals the most beautiful tourist spots of the west. Indeed we can find the Natural Waterfall of Banfora which attracts each year over three thousand (3000) tourists. It is a heavenly place and tourists can take the opportunity to relax there.

The Lake of Tengrela

Besides, for those who fall in love for nature, the lake of Tengrela is the adequate place where they can find aquatic animals and enjoy the sun.

The Peaks of Sindou

In Banfora, the last and beautiful place to visit is the "peaks of Sindou". Indeed, classified by the United Nation as a world treasure, the peaks of Sindou are a beautiful sandstorm chain which attracts musicians as well as tourists.

The East

Diapaga

The National Parks of Arly and the W: The East of Burkina Faso is the region of hunting and but it also conceals some tourist spots. There we can cite the national park of Arly and the national park of the W which are able to provide mostly for those who fall in love with the nature and the hunting sport the opportunity to find a large variety of animals and to satisfy their envy of hunting.

The Cliffs of Gobnangou

The cliffs of Gobnangou are also among the tourist spots that guests can visit and they may fill with wonder face to vertiginous view the cliffs offers.

The Reserve and Ranch of Nazinga

Unquestionably, we can state that the Eastern region is really the region of hunting with the ranch of Nazinga localized in this region. There, we can find a lot of wild animals and safaris are organized sometimes for the pleasure of the tourists..

The Sahel

Djibo

The Archeological Museum and the Stone Carvings of Pobé Mengao: In the town of Djibo the archeological museum of Pobé Mengao and the stone carvings of Pobé Mengao are the principal attractions of the town. There are many cultural objects exposed in the museum and available for people interested in viewing and learning the different stories of the land of the "men of integrity".

Gorom Gorom

The Feminine Artisanal Center of Gorom

The second town in the Sahel is Gorom Gorom and has the feminine artisan center of Gorom which is very interesting to visit. Women of the town shown what they are really capable of and the more, they excel in the domain of art, sculpture, pottery and many others disciplines. Cheap souvenir objects can be bought in the center.

The Touristic Camp

The tourist camp of Gorom Gorom is the ideal place to stay for the tourists when arriving in the Sahel and principally at Gorom Gorom. Indeed, the entire structure of that area is planned to welcome tourists in vacation. A comfortable place to take a rest, a service of restoration is also available and many others features are available just for the well being of the tourists.

TOURISM IN CANADA

Canada, as a rich Western country, has both a large domestic and foreign tourist industry. Canada is known for its large, majestic landscapes and several record-holding landmarks. Some of the major attractions of the country include its cities but it is probably better known worldwide for its extensive, lightly populated or unpopulated areas of wilderness and its natural sights.

Canada's Provinces and Territories

British Columbia

British Columbia is Canada's westernmost province, along the Pacific Ocean. The winters are relatively warm compared to the rest of Canada. Skiing is popular within the province. Vancouver is a multi-cultural city, with a large proportion of the population of Asian origin. Being a harbour city, Vancouver enjoys landscapes of mountains and ocean.

Whale watching and and wine tours are common. British Columbia is also a popular location for many of Hollywood's filming locations.

Alberta

Alberta is a province in Canada's western prairies next to the Rocky Mountains. Its two major cities are Calgary and Edmonton, the provincial capital. Edmonton is well-known for West Edmonton Mall, until recently the largest mall in the world. Another world-class attraction is the Royal Tyrrell Museum of Palaeontology in Drumheller, housing the largest collection of dinosaur fossils under one roof in the world. Alberta also contains significant natural scenery, including 5 of Canada's 13 UNESCO World heritage sites. These are Banff and Jasper National Parks, Waterton-Glacier International Peace Park, Wood Buffalo National Park, Dinosaur Provincial Park and Head-Smashed-In Buffalo Jump. Alberta has no provincial sales tax.

Alberta is an important skiing destination for tourists. It boasts several world-class ski resorts. Canada Olympic Park, with its downhill ski and ski jumping facilities, is located in the city of Calgary.

Saskatchewan

Saskatchewan offers two major cities, Regina and Saskatoon. The prairie province also has the most golf courses and water bodies per capita than most provinces. Statistically the warmest summers with the most sunlight hours in Canada occur in Saskatoon as well. Natural attractions include Cypress Provincial Park, the Great Sand Hills, Scottie the Dinosaur (the largest intact Tyrannosaurus Rex found in North America).

Manitoba

A visit to Canada would not be complete without visiting a Manitoba Social. A social is essentially a large party, held in a hall with a DJ playing 80s and 90s hits as well some new hits, cheap drinks, dancing and free food is served. Entry into a social is cheap (usually $10 CAN) and these events are held throughout the year for various reasons, but are mostly a form a fundraising for weddings or charities.

In Manitoba, sports fans can see the American Hockey League's Manitoba Moose or the Winnipeg Blue Bombers play. See the Assiniboia Downs for live horse racing.

- Le Musée de Saint-Boniface is the oldest building in Manitoba, built in the mid-1800s as a hospital
- Louis Riel statue near the Manitoba legislative building. See a figure of Manitoba's leadership.
- Churchill is a popular attraction due to the large polar bear population.

Ontario

Ontario, the most populated province in Canada, is also home to the nation's capital, Ottawa. In addition, Ontario contains Canada's largest city, Toronto, which is the provincial capital and one of the most multicultural cities in the world. Toronto embraces Lake Ontario. Toronto's CN Tower overlooks the harbour. The forests and numerous lakes of Central Ontario and Northern Ontario also provide popular hiking and camping destinations.

Site of Interest in Toronto

- Queen's Park
- Royal Ontario Museum

- Ontario Science Centre
- Rogers Centre (formerly SkyDome)
- Air Canada Centre
- Hockey Hall of Fame

Site of Interest in Ottawa

- Parliament Hill
- National War Memoral (Canada)
- National Art Gallery
- Canadian War Museum
- Canadian Aviation Museum
- Canadian Museum of Nature
- Canadian Museum of Civilization
- Chateau Laurier
- Scotiabank Place

Other Sites of Interest in Ontario

- Science North and Dynamic Earth in Greater Sudbury, Ontario
- Niagara Falls
- Muskoka Lakes

Sites of Interest in the Kingston Area

- Fort Henry
- Kingston's Old Town
- Upper Canada Village
- The Thousand Islands
- Boldt Castle

Quebec

Quebec, a majority francophone province is a major tourist draw. Quebec City is a taste of old France in the new world and a UNESCO World Heritage site. Montreal, the third largest Francophone city in the world, boasts several tourist attractions. Here are some of the main province's attractions:

- Canyon Sainte-Anne
- Château Frontenac
- Juste pour rire
- Old Montreal
- Olympic Stadium
- Montreal Opera
- Redpath Museum
- Saint Joseph's Oratory
- Underground city, Montreal

Montreal is Home to the

- Montreal Alouettes, Canadian Football League
- Montreal Canadiens, National Hockey League

New Brunswick

New Brunswick is renowned for its warm, sandy beaches especially along the Northumberland Strait. Moncton, the province's largest urban centre and known as the Hub of the Maritimes, is home to a number of attractions and popular day trips including,

- Tidal bore
- Magnetic Hill
- Palais Crystal Palace
- Magic Mountain Water Park
- Hopewell Rocks
- Parlee Beach
- Fundy National Park
- Kouchibouguac National Park

Saint John, which is at the mouth of the St. John River, is the site of Reversing Falls, Market Square and welcomes numerous cruise ships in its port every summer and fall. Whale watching and the Confederation Bridge to Prince Edward Island are also draws.

Prince Edward Island

Prince Edward Island (PEI) is the birthplace of Lucy Maude Montgomery's character, Anne of Green Gables, and a recreation of her literary home serves as a museum to the character. PEI is also famous the world round for its potato farms and rich red mud beaches.

Newfoundland and Labrador

Newfoundland and Labrador attracts many tourists because of its icebergs and fjords. It was settled by Leif Ericsson, an Icelandic sailor, in 1000 A.D. Remains of this settlement can still be found in L'Anse aux Meadows, northern Newfoundland. Europeans settled in 1497, headed by an expedition by John Cabot.

The province's capital, St. John's, Newfoundland is the oldest English-founded city in both Americas. It contains many historical locations, such as Cabot Tower, receiver of the first wireless trans-Atlantic message in 1901.

Just outside St.John's lies Cape Race, the most eastern point in the Americas. From this point, London, United Kingdom is closer than Vancouver, British Columbia.

Nova Scotia

Nova Scotia is known for its lovely scenery; most renowned is the Cape Breton Highlands. The historic 18th century Fortress Louisbourg is also a major draw.

Halifax, the provincial capital, has several major attractions, such as the Pier 21 museum, Citadel Hill, and the Public Gardens. The Halifax Metro Centre is home to numerous events both sport-related and otherwise, such as the Nova Scotia International Tattoo. Downtown Halifax is considered the prime tourism district in Halifax, with most historic attractions located here as well as the waterfront harbourwalk, a continuous 3km stretch of boardwalk home to street vendors, entertainers, the Casino Nova Scotia, and the Maritime Museum of the Atlantic. Downtown Halifax is also the location of several major hotels.

Yukon Territory

With its history of the Klondike Gold Rush, First Nations culture and spectacular wilderness, the Yukon Territory has an extensive tourism industry, welcoming over 300,000 visitors a year. Tourist attractions include the gold rush town of Dawson City, Kluane National Park and Reserve and a number of attraction in Whitehorse and other communities. Opportunities for wilderness adventure tourism and ecotourism abound (hiking, canoeing, kayaking, skiing, dog-sledding), but the territory is also served by a well-developed road network, with most places accessible by road.

Northwest Territories

Northwest Territories attractions include:

- Aurora Borealis
- Northern Life Museum
- N.W.T. Mining Heritage Society
- Wood Buffalo National Park
- Tuktut Nogait National Park
- Nahanni National Park Reserve
- South Nahanni River
- Canol Heritage Trail
- Aulavik National Park
- Coppermine River
- Mackenzie River

Nunavut Territory

Nunavut is probably the most expensive of all the tourist destinations in Canada. Attractions in Nunavut include:

- Auyuittuq National Park

- Quttinirpaaq National Park
- Sirmilik National Park
- Ukkusiksalik National Park
- Ovayok Territorial Park

Backpacking in Canada

In Canada, both the backcountry enthusiast and the urban explorer are prominent forms of travel that have gained popularity in recent years.

Urban explorers hover between the trendy hostels and clubs in Vancouver, Toronto and Montreal. Those seeking to explore more rural and extreme terrains, including Crown land, the Rockies and Atlantic Canada may be best suited to the nation's vast system of provincial and national parks offered through Parks Canada.

Hostels

Many hostels offer low-cost, safe and friendly accommodation for those looking for their first taste of life in Canada. Students, extreme travellers and backpackers have come to rely on such facilities to exchange information and experience about global travel. As Canada continues to host international travellers from all across the globe, the hostelling and bed and breakfast industries have adapted to accommodate the needs of tourists from a wide array of different socioeconomic and geopolitical classes. The 2006 election of the Conservative Party of Canada into power in Canada has led some to suggest that an economic boom, largely based on investment in the energy industry, will increase the availability of alternative hospitality services and dormitories across Canada. Central destinations like Fort McMurray (north of Edmonton and close to the Athabasca Oil Sands) have attracted a young migrating population.

Preparation and Equipment

Some styles of Canadian backpacking require intense physical and psychological conditioning. Those wishing to prepare for a long journey through the backcountry can expect to visit retailers such as Mark's Work Warehouse, Mountain Equipment Co-op, Coast Mountain Sports, Army-Navy store and Bass Pro Shops for equipment supplies. Gear reviews can be found at Outdoor Adventure Canada.

Popular Backpacking Destinations in Canada

- Banff National Park
- Jasper National Park
- Stanley Park
- Gatineau
- Underground city, Montreal
- Puslinch.Valens
- Rattlesnake Point
- Kensington Market

TOURISM IN CAMEROON

Tourism in Cameroon is a growing but relatively minor industry. Since the 1970s, the government of Cameroon has cultivated the industry by creating a ministry of tourism and by encouraging investment by airlines, hotels, and travel agencies. The government describes the country as "Africa in miniature", promoting its diversity of climate, culture, and geography. Cameroon's wildlife draws both safari-goers and big-game hunters, as Cameroon is home to many of Africa's iconic animals: cheetahs, chimpanzees, elephants, giraffes, gorillas, hippopotami, and rhinoceroses. Impediments to further growth of the tourism sector include poor transport infrastructure and corrupt officials who may harass visitors for bribes.

Development

Government programmes to increase tourism in Cameroon began on 3 December 1974 when President Ahmadou Ahidjo issued an order that set the tourism industry aside as having special status and established the General Commissariat of Tourism. On 28 June 1975, Ahidjo reconstituted the body as the General Delegation for Tourism, whose purpose was to encourage private investment by airlines, hotels, and travel agencies. The delegation publishes tourist literature and publicises Cameroon through advertising. Ahidjo and his successor, Paul Biya, have set aside several game and forest reserves as further touristic draws. Improving air, rail, and road transportation to popular tourist sites has been another priority.

Tourism infrastructure in Cameroon has steadily improved. The country offered 37 hotels with 599 rooms in 1960. This had risen to 203 hotels with 3,229 rooms in 1976. In 1980, the country offered 7,500 hotel rooms. Nevertheless, the vast majority of these rooms are in two major cities, Douala and Yaoundé. In 1971, 29,500 tourists visited Cameroon. This number had risen to 100,000 tourists in 1975, and 130,000 in 1980. Most visitors to the country come from France, the United Kingdom, and Canada. Business travellers make up one of the largest segments of Cameroon's tourists. The industry has made significant strides since the 1990s. Cameroon is primarily French-speaking, but two provinces, the Northwest and the Southwest provinces, are English-speaking.

Barriers

Tourists face several obstacles in Cameroon. Photography is difficult, since Cameroonians often resent foreigners taking photographs of things that outsiders may consider strange or that may cast Cameroon in a negative light. The government forbids all photography of government buildings and personnel, airports, bridges, and markets.

Treatment of tourists by Cameroonian officials has improved as the role of tourism as a source of revenue has been emphasised by the government. Tourists once faced long, thorough searches upon arrival in the country, but these have become rare. Still, police or gendarmes sometimes accuse foreign tourists of spying or carrying out mercenary activities. This is especially true for tourists who visit sites off the main tourist routes or who opt for cheap accommodation or public transport (e.g., mini-buses) over fancier hotels and rental cars. Police and gendarmes at roadblocks may harass foreign visitors for bribes.

Tourist Sites

The Cameroonian government promotes the country as "Africa in miniature", asserting that the country offers all the diversity of Africa-in climate, culture, and geography-within its borders. Other touristic phrases sometimes used include "the melting pot of Africa" and "Africa in microcosm". Cameroon's tourist destinations are in four general areas: the coast, the major cities, the Western highlands, and the north. The coast offers two major beach resort towns: Limbe is English-speaking with black, volcanic sand; and Kribi is a French-speaking city with white-sand beaches. Mount Cameroon on the coast is the highest mountain in Central and West Africa and draws hikers and climbers. The stepping-off point for climbing Mt. Cameroon is the city of Buea, where guides can be hired and equipment can be rented. There are several tin-roofed huts for hikers to sleep in during their trek up the mountain.

Yaoundé is home to most of Cameroon's national monuments. It also has several museums. The Western highlands offer picturesque mountain scenery, waterfalls and lakes, and the altitude provides a cooler climate. Bamenda is the main city in the western highlands, and is the capital of the Northwest province. This area is known for its traditional culture and crafts. The city of Bafoussam is especially famous for its wood-carving culture and artifacts. In fact, the area produces more crafts than any other in Cameroon. The West is also home to traditional chiefdoms and fondoms, such as the sultanate of Foumban. Each chief typically has his own palace or compound which visitors may visit for a fee.

Cameroon's north is the nation's primary tourist draw. The area has several wildlife reserves, including the largest and best-run in West Africa, Waza National Park. These parks offer both animal viewing and big-game hunting. Animals in this region include cheetahs, elephants, giraffes, hippopotami, and rhinoceroses. Maroua offers a large crafts market and museums.

The Adamawa, East, and South provinces offer a new front for expansion of the tourist industry, but poor transport conditions keep the industry small in these regions. Forest reserves in the south have little tourist-oriented infrastructure, but visitors there may see chimpanzees, elephants, gorillas, and other rainforest fauna.

TOURISM IN CROATIA

Tourism in Croatia is a well-developed industry as Croatia is an attractive tourist destination, particularly because of its extensive coastline and well-preserved coastal Renaissance towns. In 2005, Croatia had 10 million tourist visitors.

The interior of the country, with the exception of the capital Zagreb, the erstwhile Baroque capital Vara□din and a plethora of medieval castles, has fewer tourist attractions. Eight areas in the country have been designated national parks, and the landscape in these areas is afforded extra protection from development.

Several companies run flotillas of yachts along different stretches of the coastline, which is also popular with divers.

The country is currently being advertised under the motto The Mediterranean As It Once Was.

Tourist regions

1: *Istria:* The peninsula of Istria has the best tourist infrastructure in Croatia. Its west coast has several historical towns dating from Roman times, such as Porec (Euphrasian Basilica) and Pula (Amphitheater), surrounded by large hotel complexes, resorts, camps and sports facilities. The interior is quieter, very green and wooded, with dozens of tiny stone towns perched on hills, such as Motovun. The island group of Brijuni is a site of luxury tourism.

2: *Kvarner & Highlands:* This is probably the most varied region. The entire Kvarner gulf provides striking sceneries, with tall mountains right next to the sea, overlooking a dozen large islands. The island of Pag has one of the biggest party zones in Europe in the town of Novalja Tourist resorts range from Opatija and Lovran, with their feel of Austro-Hungarian imperial decadence, to the former Venetian island towns of Rab and Lošinj. The interior regions Gorski kotar, Velebit and Lika have vast stretches of virginal nature, with mountain peaks, forests and fields, many animal species including bears, and the national parks of Plitvice Lakes and Risnjak.

3: *Dalmatia-Zadar:* This region is a yachting paradise. The Kornati National Park has hundreds of mostly uninhabited islands. Aside from Zadar, a Roman town with many monuments, there are many smaller coastal resorts. The interior has mixed plains and mountains, with the impressive Paklenica canyon as the main attraction.

4: *Dalmatia-Šibenik:* This is another popular yachting region, dotted with islands, and centered around Šibenik and its famous cathedral. The interior has the Krka National Park with its waterfalls and religious monasteries, and the city of Knin with its medieval fortress and archeological remains.

5: *Dalmatia-Split:* The large islands of this region, which such pearls as the town of Hvar or the resort of Bol, would be its main attraction if there was not the city of Split and its unique Roman heritage, the Diocletian's Palace. There is also the excellently preserved coastal town of Trogir, which boasts of over ten churches, a cathedral, palaces and a fortress. The small town of Primošten is famous throughout the country for its abundant vineyards and wine.

6: *Dalmatia-Dubrovnik:* Probably the most famous Croatian site, the fortified city of Dubrovnik is a breathtaking sight, but the region has numerous attractive islands, ranging from the historical Korcula to the untouched forests of Mljet.

7: *Central Croatia:* The most interesting part of this large region is the north, with the old city of Vara□din and the hilly area of Zagorje, dotted with castles and spas. The Marian shrine of Marija Bistrica is the largest and most notable pilgramage spot for the faithful in the entire country. The south has some natural highlights, such as the nature park Lonjsko polje, where it covers the area of the former Nazi Jasenovac concentration camp. The southwest area is known for it's forests and wilderness, especially. Baroque churches are found readily throughout the area, along with other cultural architecture. Much rebuilding is being done in the areas destroyed during the Croatian war of independence.

8: *Slavonia:* Tourism in this region is just developing, mostly with spas. The area of Baranja has the national park of Kopacki rit, a large swamp with an incredible variety of fauna, especially birds. The cultural center is the historical city of Osijek, with other notable cities being Đakovo and war-torn Vukovar. Gastronomy specialities are popular, with traditional Slavonian wines and cuisine being a unique part of the region.

9: *Zagreb Like:* Prague or Budapest, Zagreb has a Central European feel to it, with a large and well-preserved old town on the hill and a 19th-century city center. The Croatian capital is also the country's largest cultural center, with many museums and galleries.

UNESCO World Heritage Sites in Croatia

United Nations Educational, Scientific and Cultural Organization (UNESCO) has included the following Croatian sites on its World Heritage List:

- Historical Complex of Split with the Palace of Diocletian
- Old City of Dubrovnik
- Plitvice Lakes National Park
- Episcopal Complex of the Euphrasian Basilica in the Historic Centre of Porec
- Historic City of Trogir
- The Cathedral of St James in Šibenik

TOURISM IN CUBA

Tourism in Cuba attracts over 2 million visitors a year, and is one of the main sources of revenue for the island. With its favourable climate, beaches, colonial architecture and distinct cultural history, Cuba has long been an attractive destination for travelers from around the globe. In the first part of the 20th century Cuba benefited from its close proximity to the United States to gain a reputation as a hedonistic escape for U.S. tourists. As relations between Cuba and the United States deteriorated rapidly after the Cuban Revolution of 1959, the island became cut off from its traditional market by an embargo and travel ban imposed on U.S. citizens visiting Cuba, and the industry declined to record low levels within two years.

Following the collapse of Cuba's chief trading partner the Soviet Union, and the resulting economic crisis known as the Special Period, Cuba embarked on a major program to bolster its tourist industry in order to bring in much needed finance to the island. Schemes to encourage visitors meant that by the late 1990s, tourism surpassed Cuba's traditional export industry, sugar, as the nation's leading source of revenue. Visitors come primarily from Canada and Europe and tourist areas are highly concentrated around Varadero Beach, Cayo Coco, the beach areas north of Holguin, and Havana. The impact on Cuba's socialist society and economy has been significant, leading to complaints that the state has fostered a form of divisive wealth apartheid on the island.

History

Cuba has long been a popular attraction for tourists. Between 1915 and 1930, Havana hosted more tourists than any other location in the Caribbean. The influx was due in large part to Cuba's proximity to the United States, where restrictive prohibition on alcohol and other pastimes stood in stark contrast to the island's traditionally relaxed attitude to leisure pursuits. Such tourism became Cuba's third largest source of foreign currency, behind the two dominant industries of sugar and tobacco.

A combination of the Great Depression of the 1930s, the end of prohibition, and the second world war severely dampened Cuba's tourist industry, and it wasn't until the 1950s that numbers began to return to the island in any significant force. During this period, American organized crime came to dominate the leisure and tourist industries, a modus operandi outlined at the infamous Havana Conference of 1946. By the mid-1950s Havana became one of the main markets and the favourite route for the narcotics trade to the United States. Despite this, tourist numbers grew steadily at a rate of 8% a year and Havana became known as "the Latin Las Vegas".

Immediately upon becoming President of Cuba after the Cuban revolution of 1959, Manuel Urrutia ordered the closing of many bars and gambling halls associated with prostitution and the drug trade, thus effectively ending Cuba's image as a hedonistic escape. A new governmental body, the National Institute of the Tourism Industry (INTUR), was established to encourage more tourism; taking over hotels, clubs, and beaches making them available to the general public at low rates. Tourist board chief Carlos Almonia announced a program of huge investment in hotels and the creation of a new airport. But fears of Cuba's post-revolutionary status amongst Americans, who constituted 8 out of 10 of visitors, meant a rapid decrease in travel to the island.

In January 1961, as relations between the nations deteriorated, tourism travel to Cuba was declared by the U.S. State Department to be contrary to U.S. foreign policy and against the national interest. Tourism that year dropped to a record low of a mere 4180, forcing a dramatic downsizing of Cuba's tourist plans. Visitors to Cuba during the 1960s, 70s and 80s were comparatively rare. The number of tourists to the island did increase slowly, but it wasn't until 1989 that they were to equal pre-Revolutionary numbers.

The collapse of the Soviet Union in 1991 caused a crisis in the Cuban economy. The Soviets were Cuba's chief trading partner, and had effectively sheltered Cuba's sugar industry with large subsidies for 30 years. The lack of economic diversification during this period, and the sudden loss of key markets sent the country into a deep economic depression known in Cuba as the Special Period. The crisis precipitated an urgent need to find new avenues of national income.

Policies were drawn up to satisfy the growing tourist markets of Canada and Europe with an aim to replace Cuba's reliance on the sugar industry and gain much needed foreign currency rapidly. A new Ministry of Tourism was created in 1994, and the Cuban state invested heavily in tourist facilities. Between 1990 and 2000, more than $3.5 billion was invested in the tourist industry. The number of rooms available to international tourists grew from 12,000 to 35,000, and the country received a total of 10 million visitors over that period. By 1995 the industry had surpassed sugar as Cuba's chief earner.

Tourism and the Environment

The Cuban government has established safeguards designed to ensure that tourism and other development do not result in significant environmental impacts. The development of new tourist facilities and related infrastructure in Cuba must, among other things, proceed in accordance with Cuban environmental laws and policies. In 1994 the Cuban government established the Ministry of Science, Technology, and Environment (CITMA) and in 1997 the National Assembly has enacted Law 81 of the Environment, one of the most comprehensive "framework" environmental laws in the region. Pursuant to that Law, the government adopted a number of decree laws and resolutions aimed at ensuring that future development (including tourism development) is sustainable. Of particular importance to tourism development is Decree Law 212,Coastal Zone Management, which establishes setbacks and other siting requirements for new facilities in coastal areas. CITMA Resolution 77/99 requires a thorough environmental assessment of major new construction projects and requires that project developers obtain an environmental license from CITMA.

Health Tourism

As well as receiving traditional tourism revenues, Cuba attracts paying health tourists, generating revenues of around

$40m a year for the Cuban economy. In 2002 more than 5000 foreign patients travelled to Cuba for a wide range of treatments including eye-surgery, neurological disorders such as multiple sclerosis and Parkinsons disease, and orthopaedics. Most patients are from Latin America although medical treatment for retinitis pigmentosa, often known as night blindness, has attracted many patients from Europe and North America.

Some complaints have arisen that foreign "health tourists" paying with dollars receive a higher quality of care than Cuban citizens. Former leading Cuban neurosurgeon and dissident Dr Hilda Molina asserts that the central revolutionary objective of free, quality medical care for all has been eroded by Cuba's need for foreign currency. Molina says that following the economic collapse known in Cuba as the Special Period, the Cuban Government established mechanisms designed to turn the medical system into a profit-making enterprise, thus creating a disparity in the quality of healthcare services between Cubans and foreigners.

Casas Particulares

A "Casa particular" ("private house") is a private residence in Cuba converted to allow paid lodging, usually on a short-term basis, they are akin to the Bed and Breakfast residences elsewhere. Casa particulares are typically operated from a single-family residence and are a very popular choice for tourists. Prices can range between 15 and 30 Euros per night, or less for longer stays, and thus the casas provide a more viable option for young or independent tourists. A stay in a private casa allows tourists more opportunity to mix with local Cubans, and engage in Cuban cultural life. This stands in contrast to accommodation in a state-run hotels, where current regulations mean that foreigners are not permitted to invite Cuban guests to hotel rooms.

Impact on Cuban Society

Cocotaxis" in Plaza de la Revolucíon, Havana. A popular form of transport for tourist sightseers. Due to the rapid growth of tourism in Cuba, taxi drivers can earn more than lawyers and doctors Cuba's tourism policies of the early 90s, which were driven by the government's pressing need to earn hard currency, had a major impact on the underlying egalitarianism espoused by the Cuban revolution. Two parallel economies and societies quickly emerged, their demarkation line was represented by access to the newly legalised dollar. Those having access to dollars through contact with the lucrative tourist industry suddenly found themselves at a distinct financial advantage over professional, industrial and agricultural workers.

Barstaff, hotel receptionists and taxi drivers became the coveted occupations in urban Cuba, and by 2006, permission to operate a private taxi cab service could cost up to $500 in bribes. Musicians have also found a radical shift in their economic status. El Nuevo Herald reported that the $200 a month one band percussionist receives in tips performing to tourists in Old Havana is more than 30 times what he would receive from the Cuban government for the same work.

The support base of the Cuban revolution gradually eroded as tourism led to increases in crime and prostitution, particuarily the form of sex tourism known in Cuba as jineterismo Internationally, the Cuban government appeared to be turning a blind eye in hopes the dollars jineteras earned would help overcome the Revolution's worst economic crisis.

An even graver phenomenon was the appearance of what has been described as a kind of apartheid in Cuban society. This arose after large investments in the exclusive private "enclave resorts" for foreign tourists, which had become a key source of revenue throughout the Caribbean. Native Cubans found themselves excluded from many activities that were reserved solely for foreigners-a development that inverted the revolutionary ethic proclaimed by the first government of 1959. Restrictions on access to hotels, resorts, beaches, and restaurants allocated for the benefit of tourists also appeared to flatly contradict Article 43 of the Cuban constitution, which guarantees all Cubans, 'without regard to race, skin color, religious belief, or national origin,' the right to 'lodge themselves in any hotel,' 'be attended in all restaurants and establishments serving the public, and 'enjoy the same spas, beaches, social clubs, and other centers of sport, recreation, and leisure'. The measures, though not explicately defined by the Cuban penal code, were covered by catch-all laws against the 'harassment of tourists', which were familiar to other Caribbean nations such as neighbouring Jamaica.

In 1992, during the early period of Cuba's tourist boom, Cuban President Fidel Castro defended the newly instituted policies in a speech to the Cuban National Assembly. He described the moves as an economic necessity that would need to be maintained for as long as the country had a need for foreign currency and no other means of acquiring it. According to Castro, the government were "pondering formulas" that would allow Cubans to use some of the tourist facilities as a reward for outstanding work, but believed that giving Cubans access to amenities at the expense of paying foreign tourists would ultimately be a counterproductive move for the economy; "For every five Cubans staying two or three days in one of those hotels, the country would have one less ton of meat to distribute to the people,".

As the policies became more visible to both Cubans and international observers, the term "tourist apartheid" entered common currency. In addition to evidence of the term being used by Cubans, the phrase has been widely used by non-Cuban sources, including the Encyclopædia Britannica, United States Department of State, the United States Agency for International Development, members of the United States Congress opposed to the Cuban government, and political columnists. Human Rights Watch condemned the practice, Paul Hare, British Ambassador to Cuba from 2001 to 2004, viewed "tourist apartheid" as a "particularly distasteful" aspect of Cuban society.

In response to the accusations, Fidel Castro described such analysis as a "perfidious, perverse, cynical" campaign to present the current situation as "a case of discrimination". Raul Taladrid, Cuba's deputy minister for economic collaboration in 1992, said that the style afforded tourists was "a bitter pill for some to swallow, especially the young," but tourism was being promoted because "we have a high, fast rate of return on our investment. Our biggest difficulty is getting foreign exchange so we can reach a new economic equilibrium."

With tourism levels growing rapidly towards the late 1990s, the policy of "enclave tourism", where parts of the island were isolated for tourists, collapsed. Though there were still occasions when tourists bringing male Cubans into certain hotels would be asked to leave their guests outside, on the possible grounds that they may be "pimps extending their network of clients". Members of the nomenclature and the higher echolons of Cuban society also enjoyed open access. By the mid-2000s, with the Cuban economic crisis largely over, many tourist hotels had Cuban guests.

Travel and Emigration

Citizens cannot leave or return to Cuba without first obtaining official permission, which is often denied. Unauthorized travel can result in criminal prosecution. The government also frequently bars certain citizens engaged in authorized travel (primarily medical personnel and other professionals deemed essential to the country) from taking their children with them overseas, which critics see as essentially holding the children hostage to guarantee the parents' return.

Castro opposition leader Oswaldo Payá has been allowed to travel abroad to receive his Sakharov Prize, while independent journalist Yndamiro Restano, permitted to leave Cuba to receive an award, has not been allowed to return.

From 1959 through 1993, some 1.2 million Cubans (about 10% of the current population) left the island for the United States, often by sea in small boats and fragile rafts. In the early years a number of those who could claim dual Spanish-Cuban citizenship left for Spain. Over time a number of Cuban Jews were released to Israel in quiet negotiations; the majority of the 10,000 or so Jews who were in Cuba in 1959 have left. After the collapse of the Soviet Union many Cubans now reside in a diverse number of countries, some ending up in countries of the European Union. A large number of Cubans live in Mexico and Canada. At times the exodus was tolerated by the Cuban government as a "release valve"; at other times the government has impeded it. Some Cubans left for economic reasons, some for political ones, but most departed for a combination of the two. Others emigrated by way of the U.S. Naval Base at Guantanamo Bay, which is blocked on the Cuban side by barbed-wired fences and landmines. It is estimated that only one of every three or four Cubans who have attempted to escape has been successful. Thousands have died in their attempts.

In 1995 the U.S. government entered into an agreement with the Cuban government to resolve the emigration crisis that created the Mariel Boatlift of 1980, when Castro opened the docks to anyone who wanted to leave. The result of the negotiations was an agreement under which the United States was required to issue 20,000 visas annually to Cuban emigrants. This quota is rarely filled; the Cuban government claims that the Bush administration has refused to comply with the act, issuing only 505 visas to Cubans in the first six months of 2003. However, this does not address the blockage of certain visa-carrying Cubans.

On July 13, 1994, 72 Cubans attempted to leave the Island on a World War II era tugboat named the 13 de Marzo. In an attempt by the Cuban Navy to stop the tugboat, patrol boats were sent out to intercept the tug. Crewmen and survivors reported that the interception vessels rammed the tugboat and sprayed its passengers with high pressure fire hoses, sweeping many overboard. A total of 41 men, women and children drowned after being swept off the tug's deck, 11 of these were children under the age of 12.

TOURISM IN EUROPE

Europe attracts many tourists each year from across the world wishing to experience European Culture. There are transport links across the continent, and many European countries have the same currency-the Euro.

Europe encompasses an area of 10,400,000 km^2 (4,000,000 square miles), stretching from Asia to the Atlantic, and from

Africa to the Arctic. Europe's longest river is the Volga, which meanders 3,530 km (2,193 miles) through Russia, and flows into the Caspian Sea. Eastern Europe's highest point is Russia's Mt. Elbrus, which rises to 5,642 m (18,510 feet) above sea level. Western Europe's highest point is Mont Blanc in the French-Italian Alps, which rises to 4,807 m (15,771 feet) above sea level. Europe's climate ranges from subtropical near the Mediterranean Sea in the south, to subarctic near the Barents Sea and Arctic Ocean in the northern latitudes. There is much here for the traveller to enjoy, with a bewildering array of diversity and culture, cosmopolitan cities and spectacular scenery.

Regions

Europe defies easy categorization, with its compact size and complex history. The following are five (loosely defined) regions in Europe:

- Western Europe-Belgium, the Netherlands, Luxembourg, the United Kingdom, the Republic of Ireland and France;
- Northern Europe-Finland, Iceland, Norway, Sweden, and Denmark;
- Central Europe-Austria, Czech Republic, Germany, Hungary, Liechtenstein, Poland, Slovakia, Slovenia, and Switzerland;
- Eastern Europe-Armenia, Azerbaijan, Belarus, Bulgaria, Estonia, Georgia, Latvia, Lithuania, Moldova, Romania, Russia and Ukraine;
- Mediterranean Europe-Albania, Andorra, Bosnia and Herzegovina, Croatia, Cyprus, Greece, Italy, Macedonia, Malta, Monaco, Montenegro, Portugal, San Marino, Serbia, Spain, Turkey and Vatican City.

Get in

By Plane

The largest air travel hubs in Europe are, in order, London (LON: LCY, LHR, LGW, STN, LTN), Frankfurt (FRA, HHN),

Paris (CDG), and Amsterdam (AMS) which in turn have connections to practically everywhere in Europe. However, nearly every European city has direct long-distance flights at least to some destinations elsewhere, and other smaller airports can make sense for specific connections: for example, Vienna (VIE) has a very good network of flights to the Middle East and Eastern Europe, while Helsinki (HEL) is the geographically closest place to transfer if coming in from East Asia.

By Train

The Trans-Siberian Railway from Beijing and Vladivostok to Moscow is a classic rail journey.

By Ship

It is possible to get in to Europe by passenger or freight (cargo) ship. The Man in Seat 61 is a good starting point.

By Thumb

The most easy and cheap way to travel in Europe is Hitchhiking. You can find more information in this site: Hitchhiking in Europe

Get Around

There are no border controls between countries that have signed and implemented the Schengen Agreement. Likewise, a visa granted for any Schengen Agreement signatory country is valid in all other countries that signed and implemented the treaty.

These countries are: Austria, Belgium, Denmark, France, Finland, Germany, Greece, Iceland, Italy, Luxembourg, the Netherlands, Norway, Portugal, Spain, Sweden, and Switzerland (voted in, but not yet formalised, nor implemented). Note that not all EU members have signed the Schengen treaty and not all Schengen treaty countries are members of the European Union.

At some airports, airlines will still insist on seeing your id-card or passport. Travel to and from a Schengen Agreement country to any other country will result in the normal border checks.

By Train

The Inter Rail (for Europeans) and Eurail (for everybody else) passes offer good value if you plan on traveling extensively around Europe (or even a single region) and want more flexibility than cheap plane tickets can offer.

As of 2006, Eurail covers the following countries: Austria, Belgium, Bulgaria, Croatia, Denmark, Finland, France, Germany, Greece, Hungary, Italy, Liechtenstein, Luxembourg, Monaco, Montenegro, Netherlands, Norway, Portugal, Republic of Ireland, Romania, Serbia, Slovenia, Spain, Sweden, Switzerland, Turkey.

The most notable omissions compared to Inter Rail are Republic of Macedonia, Morocco, and the United Kingdom.

The most extensive and most reliable train travel planner for all of Europe is the one belonging to the German railways (DB) and can be found here in English.

Train travel in this continent is explained in full detail on the Rail travel in Europe article.

By Plane

Dozens of budget airlines allow very cheap travel around Europe, often much cheaper than the train or even bus fares for the same journey. Currently the cheapest flights are offered by low cost airlines such as airBerlin, Centralwings, easyJet, HLX, Ryanair, SkyEurope Airlines and WizzAir, with the lowest fares usually found on routes which go to or from cities in the United Kingdom, Germany, Sweden, Ireland, Poland, the Czech Republic, Slovakia, Slovenia and Hungary. All of these flights should be booked on the internet well in advance, otherwise the price advantage may become non-existent. Always compare prices with major carriers like British Airways, LOT or Lufthansa! One should never pay more than □ 80 on any airline when booking a month or more ahead of time (except on very long routes e.g. Dublin-Istanbul). You should also make sure where the airport is located, since some low cost airlines name very small airports by the next major city, even if the distance is up to two hours drive by bus (e.g. Ryan-and Wizzair's Frankfurt-Hahn, which is not Frankfurt/Main International)..

Passengers Rights

European Union (EU) Regulation 261/2004 of 17. February 2005 gives certain rights to passenger on all flights, schedule or charter and flights provided as part of a Package Holiday. It only applies to passengers flying from an EU airport or from an airport outside the EU to an EU airport on an EU carrier.

- European Airline passengers rights

Denied Boarding

If:

- you have a valid ticket
- you have a confirmed reservation
- you have checked in by the deadline given to you by the airline

Then you are entitled to a compensation, which is:

- 250 if the flight is shorter than 1500 km
- but only 125 if it is delayed less than 2 hours
- 400 if the flight is between 1500 km and 3500 km
- but only 200 if it is delayed less than 3 hours
- 600 if the flight is longer than 3500 km
- but only 300 if it is delayed less than 4 hours
- and a refund of your ticket (with a free flight back to your initial point of departure, when relevant)
- or alternative transport to your final destination.

The airline also have to cover the following expenses:

- two telephone calls or emails, telexes or faxes
- meals and refreshments in reasonable relation to the waiting time.
- hotel accommodation if you are delayed overnight.

Usually they will give you a prepaid phone card, and vouchers for a restaurant and a hotel.

Refund for Delayed Flight

If your flight is delayed 5 hours or longer you can get a refund of your ticket (with a free flight back to your initial point of departure, when relevant).

By Bus

Eurolines connects over 500 destinations, covering the whole of the continent and Morocco. Eurolines allows travelling from Sicily to Helsinki and from Casablanca to Moscow.

For longer distances, travelling by bus often isn't any cheaper than flying with a low cost airline. It's only worth considering if you travel at very short notice, have heavy luggage, or are keen on reducing your travel-related CO2 emmisions.

Gullivers and Sindbad are other options.

By Ship

The Baltic sea has several lines running between the major cities (for example Gdansk, Stockholm, Helsinki, Tallinn, Riga etc). Most ships are very large, paralleling Caribbean cruise liners in size and in service. This is also true of the Mediterranean Sea where a large number of ferry's and cruise ships operate of the coast of: Spain, Italy, Croatia, Greece, Southern France to Corsica, and across the English channel.

Besides ferry connections to and from the UK and other countries, there are also various ferries on the larger lakes and for crossing rivers. Furthermore, there are several regularly running cruise-lines on the larger rivers like the Rhine or the Danube.

Boating excursions within Europe, particularly along the scenic rivers and between many of the islands in the Mediterranean, are an excellent way to combine travel between locations with an adventure along the way. Accommodations range from very basic to extremely luxurious depending upon the company and class of travel selected.

By Thumb

Ridesharing (Carpooling, Hitchhiking) is a common way of travelling in some parts of Europe, especially former Soviet countries. It is a pleasant way to meet lots of people, and travel without spending too many euros. Don't forget to check out the tips for hitchhiking.

"Especially former Soviet countries", in these countries you often will have language problems, don't hitchhik in ex-Yugoslavia for Example from Croatia to Serbia (you could get big problems with nationalists). From Croatia to Slovenia it's no problem. It's better to take train or bus in Moldova and the Ukraine. In western Europe specially in the Netherlands and Germany it's easy and fast to hitchhike (trains and buses are very expensive).

Stay Safe

The biggest risks to your safety in Europe like in any major tourist area are pick-pockets and muggings. Using common sense and being aware of your surroundings can help to greatly reduce the risk of these occurrences.

TOURISM IN ALBANIA

Tourism in Albania is still in its infancy. The former communist regime did not allow tourism to become established for a long time. Groups of Western tourists were first permitted to visit starting in the 1980s. It is a country of great natural beauty which includes sandy white Mediterranean beaches, rocky mountains, fertile plains, big and small lakes, natural monuments, and remote, pristine areas.

Albania has an old history dating to the Illyrian and Greek civilization and there are many old ruins and other treasures reflecting the old civilizations. Due to its history, Albania is home to many different styles of architectural, religious and cultural influence.

Some of the most visited cities include:

- Butrint-a UNESCO World Heritage site

- Durrës-the old port city of Dyrrhachium
- Krujë-the balcony over the Adriatic sea
- Tirana-the capital
- Vlorë-beach city of Vlora
- Gjirokastër-stone city of Gjirokastër

Some of the problems keeping foreign tourism from flourishing into this beautiful country stem from the political instability. Pollution from illegal construction is ruining some of the most popular areas. Its proximity to Kosovo on the northeast border means that unexploded ordnance may be hazard for unguided tours into the countryside of that border region. At present the security situation in Albania is thought to be improving.

Furthermore, poor infrastructure greatly limits tourism. Electrical brownouts are still fairly frequent. Albania only has one true highway (connecting the capital city of Tirana to Durrës) and most of the other roads, while improving, are in very poor condition. Independent bus and minibus (furgon) operators provide inexpensive transport between most large communities, but schedules and prices are not fixed. Train service is also limited and sporadic.

Despite the above problems, Albania is making progress. Foreign tourists are not uncommon. International hotel chains are established in Tirana and organised day trips are available from Corfu to Saranda and nearby Butrint. Club Mediteranee has proposed a development between Vlores and Saranda.

South of Durres, there is a long, uncoordinated beach development popular with Albanians. There are other, off-the track beach areas, locally popular, with acceptable food and toilet facilities. There are several five star hotels along the vast beaches of Albania that provide quality service for reasonable prices.

Geography of Albania

Albania has a total area of 28,750 square kilometers. It shares a 287-kilometre border with Serbia and Montenegro to the north, a 151-kilometre border with the Republic of Macedonia to the north and east, and a 282-kilometre border with Greece to the south and southeast. Its coastline is 362 kilometres long. The lowlands of the west face the Adriatic Sea and the strategically important Strait of Otranto, which puts less than 100 kilometers of water between Albania and the heel of the Italian "boot" (links Adriatic Sea to Ionian Sea and Mediterranean Sea). Albania has coastline on the Adriatic Sea and the Ionian Sea.

Borders

With the exception of the coastline, all Albanian borders are artificial. They were established in principle at the 1912-1913 conference of ambassadors in London. The country was occupied by Italian, Serbian, Greek, and French forces during World War I, but the 1913 boundaries were essentially reaffirmed by the victorious states in 1921. The original principle was to define the borders in accordance with the best interests of the Albanian people and the nationalities in adjacent areas. The northern and eastern borders were intended, insofar as possible, to separate the Albanians from the Serbs and Montenegrins; the southeast border was to separate Albanians and Greeks; the valuable western Macedonia lake district was to be divided among the three states--Albania, Greece, and Yugoslavia--whose populations shared the area. When there was no compromise involving other factors, borderlines were chosen to make the best possible separation of national groups, connecting the best marked physical features available.

Allowance was made for local economic situations, for example, to prevent separation of a village from its animals' grazing areas or the markets for its produce. Political pressures also were a factor in the negotiations, but the outcome was subject to approval by powers having relatively abstract interests, most of which involved the balance of power rather than specific economic ambitions.

Division of the lake district among three states required that each of them have a share of the lowlands in the vicinity. Such an artificial distribution, once made, necessarily affected the borderlines to the north and south. The border that runs generally north from the lakes, although it follows the ridges of the eastern highlands, stays sixteen to thirty-two kilometers west of the watershed divide. Because negotiators at the London conference declined to use the watershed divide as the northeast boundary of the new state of Albania, the Albanian population of Kosovo was incorporated into Serbia.

In Albania's far north and the northeast mountainous sections, the border connects high points and follows mountain ridges through the largely inaccessible North Albanian Alps, and further south Bjeshkët e Namunës. For the most part, there is no natural boundary from the highlands to the Adriatic, although Lake Shkodër and a portion of the Buna River south of it were used to mark Albania's northwest border. From the lake district south and southwest to the Ionian Sea, the country's southeast border goes against the grain of the land, crossing a number of ridges instead of following them.

Climate

With its coastline facing the Adriatic and lonian seas, its highlands backed upon the elevated Balkan landmass, and the entire country lying at a latitude subject to a variety of weather patterns during the winter and summer seasons, Albania has a high number of climatic regions for so small an area. The coastal lowlands have typically Mediterranean weather; the highlands have a Mediterranean continental climate. In both the lowlands and the interior, the weather varies markedly from north to south.

The lowlands have mild winters, averaging about 7 °C. Summer temperatures average 24 °C, humidity is high, and the weather tends to be oppressively uncomfortable. In the southern lowlands, temperatures average about five degrees Celsius higher throughout the year. The difference is greater than five degrees Celsius during the summer and somewhat less during the winter.

Inland temperatures are affected more by differences in elevation than by latitude or any other factor. Low winter temperatures in the mountains are caused by the continental air mass that dominates the weather in Eastern Europe and the Balkans. Northerly and northeasterly winds blow much of the time. Average summer temperatures are lower than in the coastal areas and much lower at higher elevations, but daily fluctuations are greater. Daytime maximum temperatures in the interior basins and river valleys are very high, but the nights are almost always cool.

Average precipitation is heavy, a result of the convergence of the prevailing airflow from the Mediterranean Sea and the continental air mass. Because they usually meet at the point where the terrain rises, the heaviest rain falls in the central uplands. Vertical currents initiated when the Mediterranean air is uplifted also cause frequent thunderstorms. Many of these storms are accompanied by high local winds and torrential downpours.

When the continental air mass is weak, Mediterranean winds drop their moisture farther inland. When there is a dominant continental air mass, cold air spills onto the lowland areas, which occurs most frequently in the winter. Because the season's lower temperatures damage olive trees and citrus fruits, groves and orchards are restricted to sheltered places with southern and western exposures, even in areas with high average winter temperatures.

Lowland rainfall averages from 1,000 millimeters to more than 1,500 millimeters annually, with the higher levels in the north. Nearly 95% of the rain falls in the winter.

Rainfall in the upland mountain ranges is heavier. Adequate records are not available, and estimates vary widely, but annual averages are probably about 1,800 millimeters and are as high as 2,550 millimeters in some northern areas. The seasonal variation is not quite as great in the coastal area.

The higher inland mountains receive less precipitation than the intermediate uplands. Terrain differences cause wide local variations, but the seasonal distribution is the most consistent of any area.

Terrain

The 70% of the country that is mountainous is rugged and often inaccessible. The remainder, an alluvial plain, receives precipitation seasonally, is poorly drained, and is alternately arid or flooded. Much of the plain's soil is of poor quality. Far from offering a relief from the difficult interior terrain, the alluvial plain is often as inhospitable as the mountains. Good soil and dependable precipitation, however, are found in intermontane river basins, in the lake district along the eastern frontier, and in a narrow band of slightly elevated land between the coastal plains and the interior mountains.

In the far north, the mountains are an extension of the Dinaric Alps and, more specifically, the Montenegrin limestone plateau. Albania's northern mountains are more folded and rugged, however, than most of the plateau. The rivers have deep valleys with steep sides and arable valley floors. Generally unnavigable, the rivers obstruct rather than encourage movement within the alpine region. Roads are few and poor. Lacking internal communications and external contacts, a tribal society flourished in this area for centuries. Only after World War II were serious efforts made to incorporate the people of the region into Albanian national life. A low coastal belt extends from the northern boundary southward to the vicinity of Vlorë. On average, it extends less than sixteen kilometers inland, but widens to about fifty kilometers in the Elbasan area in central Albania. In its natural state, the coastal belt is characterized by low scrub vegetation, varying from barren to dense. There are large areas of marshlands and other areas of bare, eroded badlands. Where elevations rise slightly and precipitation is regular--in the foothills of the central uplands, for example--the land is highly arable. Marginal land is reclaimed wherever irrigation is possible.

Just east of the lowlands, the central uplands, called Çermenikë by Albanians, are an area of generally moderate elevations, between 305 and 915 meters, with a few points reaching above 1,520 meters. Shifting along the faultline that roughly defines the western edge of the central uplands causes frequent, and occasionally severe, earthquakes.

Although rugged terrain and points of high elevation mark the central uplands, the first major mountain range inland from the Adriatic is an area of predominantly serpentine rock (which derives its name from its dull green color and often spotted appearance), extending nearly the length of the country, from the North Albanian Alps to the Greek border south of Korçë. Within this zone, there are many areas in which sharp limestone and sandstone outcroppings predominate, although the ranges as a whole are characterized by rounded mountains.

The mountains east of the serpentine zone are the highest in Albania, exceeding 2,754 meters in the Mount Korab (Mali Korabit) range at Korabi's Peak (Maja e Korabit). Together with the North Albanian Alps and the serpentine zone, the eastern highlands are the most rugged and inaccessible of any terrain on the Balkan Peninsula.

The three lakes of easternmost Albania, Lake Ohrid (Liqeni Ohrit), Big Prespa Lake (Prespa e Madhe), and Small Prespa Lake (Prespa e Vogël), are remote and picturesque. Much of the terrain in their vicinity is not overly steep, and it supports a larger population than any other inland portion of the country. Albania's eastern border passes through Lake Ohrid; all but a small tip of Prespa e Vogël is in Greece; and the point at which the boundaries of three states meet is in Lake Prespa. Each of the two larger lakes has a total surface areas of about 260 square kilometers, and Prespa e Vogël is about one-fifth as large. The surface elevation is about 695 meters for Lake Ohrid and 855 meters for the other two lakes.

The southern mountain ranges are more accessible than the serpentine zone, the eastern highlands, or the North Albanian Alps. The transition to the lowlands is less abrupt, and the arable valley floors are wider. Limestone, the predominant mineral, is responsible for the cliffs and clear water of the coastline southeast of Vlorë. Erosion of a blend of softer rocks has provided the sediment that has caused wider valleys to form in the southern mountain area than those characteristic of the remainder of the country. This terrain encouraged the development of larger landholding, thus influencing the social structure of southern Albania.

List of Cities in Albania

This is a list of villages, towns and cities in Albania:

- Apollonia
- Bajram Curri
- Ballsh
- Bathorë
- Berat
- Bilisht
- Bulqizë
- Burrel
- Butrint
- Cërrik
- Çorovodë
- Delvinë
- Durrës
- Elbasan
- Ersekë
- Fajze
- Fier
- Fushë-Krujë
- Gjirokastër
- Gramsh
- Has
- Himarë
- Kamzë
- Kavajë
- Këlcyrë
- Klos
- Konispol
- Koplik
- Korçë
- Krujë
- Krumë
- Kuçovë
- Kukës
- Laç
- Lezhë
- Libohova
- Librazhd
- Lushnjë
- Maliq
- Mamurras
- Mavrovë
- Memaliaj
- Patos
- Peqin
- Peshkopi
- Përmet
- Pogradec
- Poliçan
- Pukë
- Roskovec
- Rrëshen
- Rrogozhinë

- Rubik
- Sarandë
- Selenicë
- Shëngjin
- Shijak
- Shkodër
- Tepelenë
- Tirana
- Tropojë
- Valbonë
- Velipojë
- Vlorë

Districts of Albania

Albania is divided into 36 districts, or rrethe. Several districts are then grouped into a counties or prefectures, of which there are 12. The capital city, Tirana, has a special status. The districts are:

1. Berat
2. Bulqizë
3. Delvinë
4. Devoll
5. Dibër
6. Durrës
7. Elbasan
8. Fier
9. Gjirokastër
10. Gramsh
11. Has
12. Kavajë
13. Kolonjë
14. Korçë
15. Krujë
16. Kuçovë
17. Kukës
18. Kurbin
19. Lezhë
20. Librazhd
21. Lushnjë
22. Malësi e Madhe
23. Mallakastër
24. Mat
25. Mirditë
26. Peqin
27. Përmet
28. Pogradec
29. Pukë
30. Sarandë
31. Shkodër
32. Skrapar
33. Tepelenë
34. Tirana
35. Tropojë
36. Vlorë

COUNTIES OF ALBANIA

Albania is divided into twelve counties (Albanian: qarku, sing. qark (official term); but often prefektura, sing. prefekturë, sometimes translated as prefecture). Each contains several districts (sometimes described as subprefectures):

	County	Capital	Districts
1.	Berat	Berat	Berat, Kuçovë, Skrapar
2.	Dibër	Peshkopi	Bulqizë, Dibër, Mat
3.	Durrës	Durrës	Durrës, Krujë
4.	Elbasan	Elbasan	Elbasan, Gramsh, Librazhd, Peqin
5.	Fier	Fier	Fier, Lushnjë, Mallakastër
6.	Gjirokastër	Gjirokastër	Gjirokastër, Përmet, Tepelenë
7.	Korçë	Korçë	Devoll, Kolonjë, Korçë, Pogradec
8.	Kukës	Kukës	Has, Kukës, Tropojë
9.	Lezhë	Lezhë	Kurbin, Lezhë, Mirditë
10.	Shkodër	Shkodër	Malësi e Madhe, Pukë, Shkodër
11.	Tirana	Tirana	Kavajë, Tirana
12.	Vlorë	Vlorë	Delvinë, Sarandë, Vlorë

TOURISM IN ANDORRA

Skiing and Snowboarding

Andorra has several major ski resorts, including Soldeu/El Tarter and Pal/Arinsal. These are very popular with tourists from Spain, France and the UK, particularly because their relatively gentle slopes are ideal for less experienced as families. Andorran ski schools are among the largest in Europe, and English-speaking instructors are readily available.

Shopping

Because it is not a member of the European Union, Andorra is able to sell a wide range of duty free products, including alcohol, perfume and cigarettes. These are much cheaper than in neighbouring countries, and are a lucrative source of revenue for the country.

Mountain Climbing and Walking

There are a number of hiking trails which can be explored during the summer months, when the snow has thawed.

Cafés and Restaurants

Although Andorra is not renowned for its wining and dining, there are a number of good quality establishments for eating out, especially in the capital, Andorra La Vella.

TOURISM IN AUSTRIA

Visits to Austria mostly include trips to Vienna with its Cathedral, its "Heurigenschenken" (wine pubs) and romantic Waltz music flair. Worth a visit are Salzburg, birthplace of Mozart, Innsbruck, capital of Tyrol surrounded by the Alps, and the Danube valley with its vineyards, for example the Wachau or Dunkelsteinerwald, which are between Melk and Krems. In the western part of the country the province Vorarlberg reaches the Lake Constance, in the eastern part Neusiedler See.

Of great touristic importance are the Austrian skiing, hiking and mountaineering resorts in the Alps as well as family-friendly recreation areas (e.g. the Witches's Water in Tyrol). The same applies to the numerous Austrian lakes (e.g. Wolfgangsee and other lakes in the Salzkammergut east of Salzburg or Wörthersee in Carinthia).

For visitors interested in Media Art, there is the Ars Electronica Center in Linz. Since 1979 this center has organized the Ars Electronica Festival and presented the Prix Ars Electronica, the worldwide highest-ranked prize for media art.

Austrian States

- Burgenland
- Lower Austria
- Salzburg (state)
- Tyrol
- Vorarlberg
- Carinthia
- Upper Austria
- Styria
- Vienna (state)

TOURISM IN BELGIUM

Tourism in Belgium is one of Belgium's smaller industries; however the country's easy accessibility from elsewhere in Europe still makes it a popular tourist destination.

6.7 million people travelled to Belgium in 2005. Two thirds of them come from the larger nearby countries-France, The Netherlands, the United Kingdom and Germany.

The tourist industry generates 2.8% of Belgium's Gross Domestic Product and employs 3.3% of the working population (142,000 people).

In 1993, 2% of the total workforce was employed in tourism, less than in many neighbouring countries. Much of the tourism industry is located either at the heavily developed coastline or in the Ardennes. Brussels and the Flemish cities of Bruges, Ghent and Antwerp attract many cultural tourists.

Belgium ranked 21st on the World Economic Forum's 2007 Travel and Tourism Competitiveness Index, lower than all the neighbouring countries. Although the country scored highly for 'natural and cultural resources', it was ranked only 114th in the world for both 'price competitiveness' and 'availability of qualified labor'. In recent years the number of international tourists has stayed relatively stable, but the income they generate has increased to 9.863 billion US Dollars in 2005.

Transport

Because it is such a small country, much can be done in a short time. The highway network is one of densest of the world (comparable to the city of Los Angeles) but big cities are often packed, therefore, the use of train is highly encouraged since the rail network is comprehensive and efficient. Although the country is small, using a bike to travel (like in The Netherlands) is discouraged at some places, as traffic can be overwhelming.

Cities

Every large city has its own Gothic cathedral, church, belfry or town hall.

Brussels

The capital Brussels (French Bruxelles, Dutch Brussel) is renowned for its architecture (mediaeval, Gothic, Art Nouveau and Art Déco), the Grand Place (an old market square surrounded by buildings from 16th-18th centuries), the royal palace, its pubs, gallerias with expensive boutiques (some say the oldest covered shopping arcades in the world) and its lifestyle. The Atomium is built on the Expo '58 site. The heart of Brussels has only a few old buildings, mostly around the Grand Place; the rest of the city was the result of modern architecture, mostly erected in the 1960s when the city's inner ring-road was built using cut and cover.

Flanders

The historic cities of Antwerp, Bruges, Ghent, Leuven, Ypres and Mechelen are a must.

Antwerp is the second largest city of Belgium, and the second largest port of Europe. It has a world renowned diamond stock exchange, a zoo, and holds yearly naval festivities. It's a very important cultural city, reaching its height in the 17th century. A fashion museum in Antwerp, MOMU (Mode Museum), houses the prestigious fashion design department of the Royal Academy of Fine Arts.

Ghent and Bruges (the "Venice of the North") are well known for their medieval cultural heritage. Both cities are criss-crossed by canals, and have retained much of their original medieval architecture and city layout. Ghent is somewhat more trendy than Bruges, which keeps its raw and original atmosphere. Ghent has the SMAK (City Museum for Contemporary Art), a modern art museum while Bruges' Groeningemuseum focuses more on the low countries' art in general: works include Paul Delvaux, René Magritte, James Ensor, Hieronymus Bosch, Jan van Eyck and many more.

Leuven is most famous for its impressive Town Hall and the university, which is one of the oldest in Europe. The Begijnhof (béguinage), a medieval hostel for nuns, is also worth a visit, and presents an island of calm in the centre of this bustling small city. Night life centers on campuses in student cities like Leuven, Hasselt, Ghent or Antwerp. Antwerp and Hasselt are a focus for fashion clothing; Hasselt has a Fashion Museum.

Wallonia

- *Liège:* The old capital of an independent bishopric for more than eight centuries, Liège is now a centre of prestigious art, cultural life and an important student community.

  Like Brussels, Liège was a victim of modern architecture and the remaining architectural interest is in the city's heart. Today, Liège is the largest Walloon metropolis and the third urban centre of Belgium. Thanks to its past, Liège has many impressive churches and a lot of architecture from previous centuries. There are also several unique museums, such as the world's most important museum of weapons and firearms.

  Liège and its inhabitants are known to be very welcoming. One can find many shops in the centre of the city, numerous restaurants, a night life in the bars of "the square" (Le carré), and the biggest market in Europe every Sunday on the river's bank.

- *Namur:* Namur, the capital of Wallonia, is increasingly attracting attention. A medium sized city, Namur has many small fully pedestrian streets where you can find bars and restaurants. The city is dominated by the Citadel, a fortress built on a hill overlooking the city. The site has been used defensively for more than two millennia and the limestone hill is riddled with tunnels. The citadel can be visited and contains small museums of military history.

- *Mons:* Mons is also a small city like Namur but with a totally different heart and architecture. The town is dominated by tall spoil heaps from the area's coal mining history. The coal industry in Belgium is now finished but one of the large mining buildings near Mons has now been converted into a museum of science and technology (PASS).

- *Charleroi:* Charleroi is another mining town, near Mons. Since the decline of the mining industry it has managed to attract other industry, but the main reason to visit is to fly in or out of the airport-Brussels South-which is home to low cost airlines.
- *Durbuy:* Durbuy is known as the smallest city in the world. The medieval atmosphere of the narrow streets and the castle are enough to bring thousand of tourists every year. Durbuy is one of the major tourist places in the Ardennes and home to several outdoor adventure companies, offering canoeing, caving, climbing, mountain biking and other activities.
- *Spa:* Spa is the city of water that gives its name to the word spa. A small town in the middle of the Ardennes, surrounded by forest and rivers, Spa is famous for the mineral springs which have fed the hydro-therapy industry for centuries, and which now fill the well-known Spa mineral water bottles. The town has several hydrotherapy centres around it, although the original baths are now closed, replaced by a modern centre on the hill overlooking the town, accessible by funicular.
- *Bastogne:* Bastogne played a major role during the Battle of the Bulge in World War II. You can now visit many museums about that battle, American war cemeteries or just enjoy the beauty of this small city in the middle of the Ardennes.

Other touristic towns in the Ardennes include La Roche En Ardenne (outdoor activities, castle), Rochefort (caves), Han Sur Lesse (caves, wild park) and Bouillon (castle and museum of Crusades).

Bicycle Racing

Belgium has many internationally famous bicycle races, such as:

- Ronde van Vlaanderen

- Liège-Bastogne-Liège
- La Flèche Wallonne
- Gent-Wevelgem
- Het Volk

For cycling enthusiasts, a visit to Belgium should be combined with watching a cycling race. A famous place to spot cyclists is The Wall of Geraardsbergen (De Muur van Geraardsbergen in Dutch) and the Wall of Huy (Le mur de Huy in French). Belgium is undoubtedly the number one country in cyclo-cross.

Food and Drinks

Belgium is well-known for its food and drink-including chocolate, especially pralines, fries, waffles and beer.

Belgium is a top visit for beer fanatics from all over the world. For more info, see the list of Belgian beers. Belgian "national dishes" are fries with mussels, rabbit with plums, eel in green sauce (Paling in't Groen in Dutch) and meatballs with "rabbit sauce"-also called "hunter sauce"-(literal translation of respectively Boulets sauce lapin and Boulets sauce chasseur in French).

Hasselt, the capital of the province Limburg, is famous for its jenever and speculaas. Liège is also very famous for its jenever, called peket, but also for its waffle (Gaufre de Liège-Luikse waffel).

Prestigious chocolate houses (Neuhaus for example) can be found in Brussels or Galler near Liège.

Relaxation and Special Events

Hydrotherapy and relaxation are available in the natural spas of Spa and Chaudfontaine. Towards the year end, Christmas markets are held in many cities and towns in Belgium. The two most important places for Christmas markets, special food, concerts and other seasonal events are Brussels and Liège, which have both about 200 decorated wooden cottages and a big skating ring.

TOURISM IN BULGARIA

During the winter months, Borovetz, Bansko, Pamporovo and Vitosha are ski resorts. During the summer season tourists visit Bulgaria's resorts along the Black Sea coast. Summer resorts include Sozopol, Nessebur, Golden Sands, Sunny Beach, Sveti Vlas, Albena and St. St. Constantine & Helena.

Bulgaria has enjoyed a growth in income from international tourism over the past decade. Beach resorts are popular with tourists from Germany, Russia and Scandinavia. The ski resorts are a favourite destination for English tourists.

Emerging Forms of Tourism

Besides the traditionally developed forms of tourism new types are also gaining popularity. Ethno tourism is one such kind, where tourists explore living among local people, particularly in small mountain villages far from five star hotels and luxury shops.

Bike tourism and mountain hiking have also shown strong growth in popularity among foreign tourists. The mountains of Rila, Pirin and the Balkan attract climbers. Hikers enjoy the mountains of Vitosha and the Rhodopes. Bicycling is popular, Bulgaria is one of only six countries to annually host official 1200km Randonnees-ultra-marathon bicycle rides patterned after Paris-Brest-Paris.

History Tourism

Historical tourism is undeveloped in Bulgaria. The country is situated at crossroads linking East and West. It has been home to many civilisations, including the Thracians, Slavs, Romans, Byzantines, Proto-Bulgarians, and Ottomans.

Although the country is rich in historical ruins, museums and monasteries those are not properly advertised and maintained. Some are not tourist-accessible due to poor infrastructure. This underdevelopment is regarded as desirable by some tourists who prefer to experience history first-hand rather than look at artefacts behind glass.

Popular Destinations

- Summer Resorts
  * Albena Ahtopol Balchik Dyuni Elenite Golden Sands Kiten Lozenets Nessebar Obzor Pomorie Primorsko Riviera Rusalka Sinemorets Sozopol St. Constantine St. Vlas Sunny Beach Tsarevo
- Winter Resorts
  * Bansko Chepelare Borovetz Pamporovo Uzana Vitosha
- Rural Tourism
  * Arbanasi Bozhentsi Kumani Ethnographic museum Etara Shiroka Laka Tryavna Zheravna Orehovo Madzharovo
- City Tourism
  * Sofia Varna Burgas Plovdiv Rousse Kardzhali
- Hiking
  * Balkan Mountains Pirin Mountains Rila Mountains Rhodopi Mountains Strandzha Mountains Sakar Mountains Vitosha Mountains
- Paragliding
  * Central Balkan Mountains
- Monasteries
  * Rila Monastery Rozhen Monastery Bachkovo Monastery
  * Drianovo Monastery Pomorie Monastery
  * Sokolsky Monastery Troyan Monastery The Assumption Monastery in Kardzhali town
- Most Picturesque Bulgarian Villages (per National Geographic, January 2005)
  * Orehovo
  * Narechen

TOURISM IN CYPRUS

Tourism occupies a dominant position in the economy of Cyprus.

- In 2006 it was expected to contribute 10.7% of GDP.
- in real terms it generated CYP£2,598.2 mn (US$5,445.0 mn) (annual-2006).
- total employment was estimated at 113,000 jobs (29.7% of total employment = 1 in every 3.4 jobs).

Cyprus became a full member of the UNWTO when the organisation was created in 1975.

According to the World Economic Forum's 2007 Travel and Tourism Competitiveness Index, Cyprus' tourism industry ranks 20th in the world in terms of overall competitiveness. In terms of Human, Cultural and Natural Resources (in relation to the tourism industry) Cyprus ranks 3rd in the world.

Tourist Arrivals

Recent figures:

2003	2004	2005	2006	2007
2,303,200	2,349,000	2,470,100	2,400,924	

Distribution

Much of the tourist industry relies on the clean beaches to attract foreign tourists. This reflects in the seasonal distribution of tourist arrivals with a disproportionate number arriving during the summer months. Recently Cyprus has provided incentives for the development of winter and all year round tourism such as in the form of nature, golf and activity holidays. Marinas and casinos are being considered to add to the tourist attractions of the island.

TOURISM IN THE CZECH REPUBLIC

Since the end of the Soviet era in Eastern Europe the Czech Republic, and in particular the Czech capital Prague, has become one of the major tourist destinations in Europe. However there are many more on country destinations, from which Karlštejn, Kutná Hora, Ceský Krumlov and Lednice are definitely worth of seeing. One-day travels are offered in Prague to these sites.

Visiting Places

Nightlife

Prague attracts large amounts of foreign (mostly British and German) tourists due to the exceptionally low costs associated with nightlife, especially beer. The availability of Absinthe, the leniency of law enforcement on drug use and prostitution, and the large number of bars and clubs, located close together and often open late, serve as additional incentive for tourists from Western Europe. Teenagers are increasingly attracted by the Stodolni street in Ostrava, where there are more than 60 pubs, clubs and bars in a single locality.

Hiking

The Czech countryside has much to offer, including the beautiful Ceský ráj (Czech Paradise), Ceský kras (Czech Karst) and Šumava regions. These are less accessible to foreign tourists, and one can discover the numerous natural landmarks and castles scattered throughout the country as a peaceful getaway from the busy streets of Prague.

Mountain Resorts

In Northern Czech Republic there are resorts for skiing and hiking in Krkonoše mountains, which is part of the Sudeten mountain range. Krkonoše includes the tourist centre of Harrachov. In Southern Bohemia are several resorts in Šumava mountains, with many hiking and cross-country skiing possibilities. The nature reserve Rejvíz is a popular destination in Jeseníky Mountains, in Moravian Silesia.

Vineyards

Moravia is famous for its wine. Southern Moravia is particularly notable for its white wines.

Traffic

Prague is served by Ruzyne International Airport. For taxis see taxidrivers in Prague. For travelling within the Czech Republic it is common to use CD's InterCity-trains or overland buses. Roads in the Republic are in good condition and include a highway network. There is good touristic infrastructure in every big city and most tourist resorts. However traffic is sometimes bad mostly around 6pm local time

TOURISM IN DENMARK

Tourists in Denmark mainly consist of people from neighbouring countries Sweden, Norway and Germany. Though the main attractions differ greatly.

Denmark has plenty of sandy beaches which attract mainly German tourists. While Swedish and Norwegian tourists often come for the relative metropolitan Copenhagen, or as for many young Scandinavians the cheap prices and easy access of beer and alcohol is the main attraction.

As the worlds oldest kingdom and the home of Hans Christian Andersen, Denmark is often marketed as a "Fairytale country". Previously this image was aimed mainly toward Asian tourists, but was recently expanded to most of the world in relation with the Hans Christian Andersen anniversary in 2005. This has been a tremendous success and even news networks such as CNN described Denmark as a "Fairytale country" during the Cartoon Controversy in 2006.

Danish Culture

The Danes always emphasize the Danish word "hygge". Not an entirely unique concept but one Danes consider their own and are very proud of. This term means spending quality time with family and friends, in a relaxed atmosphere.

Danish Cities

Copenhagen with more than one million citizens, and more than 3 million people living within one hours drive, is the largest city in Scandinavia. Many Swedes take the trip over

Øresund Bridge to Copenhagen to shop on Strøget, and many cruise ships stop here on their way to Baltic Sea.

In 2004 Copenhagen Region had 136 hotels with a total of 4.9 million nights spend. There were 250 cruise liners calling at at Copenhagen Port with more than 350,000 passengers.

TOURISM IN FINLAND

Finland attracted over 4 million tourists in 2005, with most coming from Sweden. The value added by tourism is about 2.4% of the Finnish GDP, and provides around 60,000 jobs.

The Nature and the Finnish Summer

The summer is marked by long days in Finland, especially in the far north where the sun does not set at all. Tourists can go fishing and canoeing. There are several large lakes, including lakes Saimaa, Inari, and Päijänne. Walking is quite a popular activity in the summer. There are no high mountains in Finland, so climbing is somewhat limited. The highest mountain is Halti near Enontekiö. Halti is 1328 metres high.

Attractions

Finland is famous for its many lakes, nearly 200,000 of them, not including the small ones. Finland is also known to have excellent water quality, and green deep woods and forests around the sea, rivers, and the waterways. In Finland, tourists can sit on the shore of a lake, fishing, watching reindeer or moose and enjoying silence.

Alcoholic drinks form an important part of the Finnish culture. When travelling through Finland it is imperative to try national favourites like: the national vodka Koskenkorva, the liquorice flavored Salmiakki Koskenkorva, and a mixture of vodka and sparkling wine that can be roughly translated into English as the "Bitch slammer".

In wintertime Finland provides excellent opportunities for cross-country skiing and some for alpine skiing too. Many of the popular ski resorts are situated north of the Arctic Circle in Lapland, but there are exceptions like Kuusamo in the northeastern part of Oulu Province. Santa Claus is commonly known to live on Korvatunturi in Finland. In the town of Rovaniemi there is the Santa Claus Village for tourists to visit.

Northern Finland and Winter Sports

In the winter there is a large snowcastle with an Ice hotel built every year in the northern town of Kemi. Rovaniemi is a place from which to see the Aurora Borealis or Northern lights. Tourists in the north of the country in winter often enjoy trips in reindeer sleighs with Sami drivers, or in dog sleighs.

It is also possible to ski, with downhill resorts at Saariselkä and Levi, and many cross country ski tracks throughout the northern part of the country. Ice hockey is a popular sport in winter, and it is possible to go ice yachting, or ice skating on the ice. Most lakes are also frozen, so ice fishing (pilkkiminen) is quite popular.

Language

The Finnish language, a member of the Finno-Ugric language group, is not similar in grammar or vocabulary to any major landuage, and is therefore often claimed to be difficult to understand or learn. Swedish is an official language and therefore widely spoken. As a Germanic language it is easier to understand with knowledge of languages of the same group. English is the most widely spoken foreign language, and many Finns are also articulate in German, Russian or French.

The Cities

Helsinki, Finland's capital and largest city, receives many visitors year-round. During the summertime thousands of tourists approach Helsinki by cruising boats travelling across the Baltic Sea. Helsinki is known as a clean, modern and safe meeting point between the east and west. Helsinki has a reputation as the coolest party city in the Nordic countries.

Other popular tourist destinations within Finland include Tampere, Turku, Oulu, Kuopio and Porvoo.

Transportation

The Finnish rail system is called VR. It offers InterCity and express trains throughout the country, and the faster Pendolino trains connecting the major cities. There are very large discounts (usually 50%) available for children (7-16 yr), students, senior citizens, and conscripts. There are international trains to St. Petersburg (Finnish and Russian day-time trains) and Moscow (Russian over-night train) in Russia. Connections to Sweden are by bus due to rail gauge differences. It's possible to take the Silja and Viking Line ferries from Helsinki to Mariehamn in the Åland archipelago, Stockholm (Sweden), and Tallinn (Estonia).

There are about 25 airports in Finland with scheduled passenger services. Finnair, Blue1 and Finncomm Airlines provide air services both domestically and internationally. Helsinki-Vantaa airport is Finland's global gateway with scheduled non-stop flights to such places as Bangkok, Beijing, Guangzhou, Nagoya, New York, Osaka, Shanghai, Hong Kong and Tokyo. Helsinki has an optimal location for great circle airline traffic routes between Western Europe and the Far East. Hence, many foreign tourists visit Helsinki on a stop-over while flying from Asia to Europe or visa versa. The Helsinki-Vantaa Airport has been ranked as one of the best airports in the world.

TOURISM IN FRANCE

France attracted over 75 million tourists in 2004 (surpassing its population), making it the most popular tourist destination in the world. Recently however, its popularity has been diminishing with the increased convenience of cheaper countries in Eastern Europe. France is one of the classics among tourist countries. It offers mountain ranges, coastlines like in Brittany or along the Mediterranean Sea, cities with a rich cultural heritage, châteaux (castles) like Versailles, countryside, vineyards in Burgundy, Tourism is accountable for 6% of the country's income (4% from French tourists travelling inside France and 2% from foreign tourists), and contributes significantly to the balance of payments.

Paris

Paris, the capital city of France attracts tourists with museums such as the Louvre and Musée d'Orsay, the Eiffel Tower, Arc de Triomphe and cathedral of Notre-Dame and dozens of other attractions, for example, Disneyland Paris.

Eastern France

In the eastern parts of France there are skiing resorts in the Alps. Other notable cities are Avignon with the Popes' palace, Arles, Aix-en-Provence, Marseille, Nice, Orléans on the Loire River, Saint-Benoît-du-Sault, Toulouse on the Garonne, Strasbourg on the border with Germany, and Lyon.

France's tourist industry, however, is not limited to the towns and cities, Paris and the Alpine ski resorts. All over France rental accommodations and hotels are available. For example, the English like to spend their summers in the Dordogne valley, the Spanish vacation in Biarritz and St Jean de Luz on the Basque coast, and the Irish often visit Lourdes.

South Beaches: French Riviera, Languedoc-Roussillon, or Corsica, are famous. The great touristic potential of Polynesia (especially Tahiti), Caribbean islands (Martinique, Guadeloupe...) are very attractive.

France offers a high-speed train service called TGV (train à grande vitesse) as well as regional services, both operated by the SNCF.

TOURISM IN GERMANY

The Federal Republic of Germany has a prospering tourism industry. Tourism in Germany has expanded since the end of World War II, and many tourists visit Germany to experience a sense of European history. The countryside exhibits a pastoral aura, while its cities exhibit both a modern and classical feel.

Places

The places in Germany with the most domecstic and international trade are:

- Berlin
- Ruhrgebiet
- Baltic Sea
- Heidelberg
- Bavarian Alps
- North Sea
- Bamberg
- Munich
- Cologne
- Hamburg
- Schwarzwald
- Dresden
- Brandenburg
- Rothenburg ob der Tauber

TOURISM IN EAST GERMANY

Tourism in the German Democratic Republic (GDR) was tightly controlled by the communist government, though it was nonetheless possible to enjoy a holiday in East Germany.

Types of Travel

Tours

A traveller would first have to book his or her trip at a travel agent that was accredited by the Reisebüro der DDR, the East German state tourist organisation. The travel agent would then offer the traveller one of the several package tours that the Reisebüro offered.

Individual Travel

It was indeed possible to travel relatively independently in the GDR. Motoring or taking a railway trip through the country was the most feasible possibility, although other types of visit were possible. Everything, including the itinerary, would have to be arranged through the Reisebüro. Simple and straightforward visits could be arranged at border posts and other Reisebüro offices in the GDR. More complicated excursions would have to be arranged before arrival, possibly involving a large and confounding amount of bureaucracy.

The formalities involved with a holiday in the GDR (such as the visa, any hotel bookings, advice on currency exchange, etc) would be taken care of by the Reisebüro. This made the usually tedious and complicated border crossing between East and West Germany much smoother. Once inside the GDR, the traveller would be closely watched, and any GDR citizens having contact with the traveller would also be carefully monitored. This made staying with East German friends or family difficult, as both the reluctance of the authorities to permit it and the knowledge that the Stasi were almost certainly watching made it both dangerous and uncomfortable for the East German hosts.

Formalities

All foreigners from non-socialist countries were required to have visas to enter or exit the GDR. Of all the Warsaw Pact nations, the GDR probably had the most foreign visitors at any one time. The one exception involved military and civilian personnel of the United States, the United Kingdom and France based in West Germany and West Berlin, who were under the jurisdiction of the Soviet military and not the East German government. There were four basic types of visas:

- Non-stop transit visa (for example, for travellers transiting between West Germany and West Berlin)
- Transit visa (with 72-hour stopover)
- Standard entry and exit visa (Visum zur Ein-und Ausreise)
- Day visa (Tagesvisum) for tourists from West Berlin wanting to visit East Berlin.

There were other types available to West Germans as well. Journalists and other non-tourists were also dealt with separately. All of these four basic types of visa could, in theory, be arranged at the Reisebüro offices at the main border crossings. In practice, to avoid the formidable bureaucracy in obtaining an entry visa either at the frontier or outside the country, it was simply easier to enter East Berlin on a day visa and then have an extension arranged at a Reisebüro office in the city. Visitors to East Germany could only enter the country by car, bus or train-not by bicycle or on foot. The exceptions to this were international airports, as well as Checkpoint Charlie. A special case involved the Friedrichstraße train station in East

Berlin, which one could reach from West Berlin by U-Bahn, S-Bahn or long-distance train.

Visitors not on non-stop transit visas were required to change a minimum of DM25, or its equivalent in other hard currency, into GDR marks every day of their stay at the (unrealistic) official rate of 1:1. An exception was made for persons booking overnight hotel stays in the GDR, as the hotel charges were payable in hard currency and almost always exceeded the minimum daily exchange amount. The visa fee itself was an additional DM5-DM15 (depending on the type of visa).

In addition to visas, travellers to the GDR staying overnight (or longer) were required to register with the Volkspolizei. The police would place an "Aufenthaltsberechtigung" (residence entitlement) stamp in the traveller's passport; the names of each city or Bezirk (district) where the traveller was registered would be entered in the appropriate space.

Customs

Many foreigners who travelled to East Germany had difficult experiences with customs. The strict regulations enforced by the communist government meant that no spare parts for cars could be brought into East Germany without special permission, VHS tapes were expressly forbidden and compact discs and vinyl records could only be brought if they were of "cultural significance", a requirement that resulted in the confiscation of much pop music from Westerners. Any Western newspapers or magazines would also be confiscated.

Gifts up to the value of 200 East German Mark could be imported. This was not based on the price the traveller would have paid for them at home, but rather the price the item would sell for in East Germany.

Accommodation

Hotels

Visitors to the GDR were effectively obliged to stay in hotels belonging to the state-run Interhotel network. Contrary to the expectations of Westerners who envisioned the GDR as run down, Interhotels (especially the Metropol and Grand Hotels in East Berlin, the Bellevue in Dresden and the Merkur in Leipzig) met or exceeded international standards for hotel accommodations.

There were four classes of hotel room:

- Deluxe-a minimum of 100 GDR marks per night per person
- Expensive-90 to 100 GDR marks
- Moderate-70 to 90 GDR marks
- Inexpensive-40 to 70 GDR marks

A room with a bath would cost an extra 5 or 10 GDR marks.

Camping

Thirty campsites run by Intercamp dotted the GDR in the following areas:

- East Berlin
- Baltic coast
- Mecklenburg lake district
- Dresden and surrounding area
- Erfurt
- Leipzig
- Harz Mountains

Equipped with electricity, sanitation, running water and other facilities, these camps were not cheap and had to be booked in advance.

Intercamp sites were open from May 1 to September 30.

Youth Hostels

East German youth hostels were not officially open to Westerners, but sometimes Westerners were allowed to use them if space was available.

Tipping

Tipping was officially abolished by the communist government, which viewed it as distinctly bourgeois (receiving extra money without actually doing anything extra). However, most people in the GDR service industry knew that Western tourists carried valuable West German marks, or US dollars, and were grateful when tipped in either of these.

Things to See

East Berlin

East Berlin was rebuilt as a modern socialist capital after World War II. The hub of the city was Alexanderplatz, a pedestrian square. Tourist attractions included the television tower (Fernsehturm), the Palast der Republik and the Brandenburg Gate.

The Baltic Coast

The East German government developed a series of beach resorts for Western tourists along the coast.

Erzgebirge Ore Mountains and Thuringia Forests

The Erzgebirge Ore Mountains contained the GDR's highest point, Fichtelberg (1,214 m). Oberhof, a resort town in the Thuringia Forests, contained the country's only artificial luge/ bobsled run.

TOURISM IN GREECE

Greece attracts well over 16 million tourists a year contributing 15% of the Gross Domestic Product (GDP) of the nation's Economy. The country has been an attraction for international visitors since antiquity for its rich and long history and more recently for its glorious Mediterranean coastline and beaches. 2005 saw 6.088.287 tourists in the capital city of Athens alone.

In 2004, the country welcomed over 16.5 million tourists. At the same time, tourism consumption increased considerably since the turn of the millennium, from US$ 17.7 bn. in 2000 to US$ 29.6 bn. in 2004. The number of jobs directly or indirectly related to the tourism sector were 659,719 and represented 16.5% of the country's total employment for that year.

In 2006 the Greek Ministry of Tourism invested more than 38 million euro in promoting the tourism industry, up from the 30 million spent in 2002 by the previous government. In addition, the government intends to promote winter tourism in Greece, which could potentially increase international arrivals even further.

Tourism in Greece is run by the Greek National Tourism Organisation (GNTO) who use Helena Paparizou, a famous Greek singer who won Eurovision song contest in 2005 as an ambassador.

The World Travel & Tourism Council (WTTC) expects Greece to gain US$54.12 billion in economic activity through tourism in 2007, a 4% increase over 2006.

General

According to a survey conducted in China in 2005, Greece was voted as the Chinese people's number one choice as a tourist destination. Furthermore, Greece has been actively trying to secure a large share of Chinese tourists per year, highlighted by the large presence of Greek tourist informatives at the 2006 Beijing International Tourism Expo. Greece had the largest single country participation with a total exhibition space take-up of more than 1,152 m², more than any other nation.

In November 2006, Austria, like China, announced that Greece was the favourite destination for tourism giving optimistic hopes for the future.

Cities

- Athens, Attica-Capital of Greece. Historically significant as the birthplace of democracy among other things.
- Thira, Santorini-One of the most photographed towns in the world. Famous for its sunset.

- Hora, Mykonos-Hora is the main town of Mykonos. There is a large gay scene on this island.
- Rhodes, Rhodes-Rhodes is famous for its legendary Colossus of Rhodes, one of the Seven Wonders of the World.
- Heraklion, Crete-Crete is one of the most visited islands in the world. Heraklion is its capital.

Tourism Infrastructure

Although Greece has always been a popular tourist destination, It has been criticised many times for lagging behind other Western European nations interms of tourism infrastructures and amenities. This has been greatly improved however since the 2004 Athens Olympic Games.

Hotels

According to the Hellenic Chamber of Hotels, the number of hotels in Greece was, by classification (beds):

- AA 155 (56,888),
- A 944 (173,431),
- B 1,712 (233,315),
- C 4,496 (233,315) and
- other 1,729 (59,065).

Marinas

Greece has 51 marinas and 14,661 mooring places that provide such services as berths, fuel, water and electricity, telephony, and repairs. Some of the most developed and busiest marinas in Greece are just a few kilometres from the centre of Athens. The marinas of Alimos and Flisvos, on the south coast of Athens, have an aggregated capacity of more than 1,800 vessels.

Spas and Thermal Springs

Greece has 752 thermo-metallic springs. Many have been classified as therapeutic by the National Institute for Geographical and Mineral Research.

Conference Facilities

Conference tourism, targeted at academic, business, or cultural markets is a cornerstone of the Greek national tourism policy. As a result, the Greek Government, with strong support from local authorities, has been offering lucrative cash grants, leasing and employment subsidies and tax allowances to establish new conference facilities and expand existing ones. In a recent report in Meeting and Incentive Travel, Greece was ranked eighth in the world in overnight stays for conferences. Figures from Tourism Satellite Accounting Research, conducted by WTTC (World Travel & Tourism Council), project a worldwide increase in revenues in business travel to Greece from US $1.51 bn. in 2001 to US $2.69 bn. in 2011. In 1998, the figure stood at US $1.18 bn.

TOURIST DESTINATIONS IN IRELAND

Destinations

- Armagh-ecclesiastical capital of all Ireland.
  - St. Patrick's Cathedral, Armagh-seat of the Church of Ireland Archbishop of Armagh.
- Clare
  - The_Burren
- Cork
- Dublin
  - Dublin Castle-seat of British rule, now a major tourism centre.
  - Dublin Zoo
  - Howth Head
  - Phoenix Park-"largest inner city park in the world."
  - Áras an Uachtaráin-residence of the President of Ireland.
  - Glasnevin Cemetery-burial location of Éamon de Valera, Michael Collins, Roger Casement, Timothy Healy, Seán T. O'Kelly, memorial to Irish war dead in First World War, Republican Plot, etc.

  * National Botanic Gardens, Glasnevin, Dublin
  * St. Mary's Pro-Cathedral-seat of the Roman Catholic Archbishop of Dublin.
  * Smithfield, Dublin
  * Trinity College Dublin (also called the University of Dublin) Ireland oldest university, founded by Queen Elizabeth I and home of the Book of Kells and the Book of Durrow. (The film Educating Rita was made on the campus.)
  * Georgian Dublin-view of eighteenth century streetscape of Dublin.
- Galway
  * Aran Islands-Irish gaeltacht speaking islands in Galway bay.
  * Connemara-Irish gaeltacht (gaelic speaking area).
- Kildare
  * Maynooth-ecclesiastical capital of the Republic of Ireland.
- Kilkenny-Ireland's most characterful medieval city
  * Kilkenny Castle-meeting place of the Confederate Ireland government in the 1640s.
  * Rothe House
- Meath
  * Newgrange-a monument older than the pyramids.
  * Knowth-a similar monument even more impressive than Newgrange that has only recently been opened for visitors.
  * Boyne Valley-location of the above two and other monuments.
  * Hill of Tara-seat of Ireland's ancient High Kings.
  * Kells-after which the Book of Kells is named.
- Limerick A quickly improving modern city in the midwest.

- Kerry Scenic rural county in the south west.
  * Dingle
  * Valentia Island, Europe's most western point.
  * Tralee Home of The Rose of Tralee.
- Westmeath Centre of Ireland-attractive lakes.
  * Athlone Castle-old castle in Athlone Town
  * Belvedere House and Gardens-Historic Gardens near Mullingar
  * Lough Owel and Lough Ennell-beautiful lakes

TOURISM IN ITALY

With more than 38.9 million tourists a year, Italy is the fourth most visited country in the world, behind France (77 million), Spain (51.7 million) and United States (41.9 million).

Ancient Resorts

The tone or style of this article or section may not be appropriate for Wikipedia.

Specific concerns may be found on the talk page. See Wikipedia's guide to writing better articles for suggestions.

Italy has some of the world's most ancient tourist resorts, dating back to the time of the Roman Republic, when destinations such as Pompeii, Naples Ischia, Capri and especially Baiae were popular with the rich of Roman society.

Popular Destinations

Rome, Venice, and Florence are the top three destinations for tourism in Italy. Other major tourist locations include Turin, Milan, Naples, Bologna, Perugia, Genoa, Sicily, Sardinia, and Cinque Terre. Two factors in each of these locations is history and geography. The Roman Empire, middle ages, and renaissance have left many cultural artifacts for the Italian tourist industry to use. Many northern cities are also able to use the Alps as an attraction for winter sports, while coastal southern cities have the Mediterranean Sea to draw tourists looking for sun. Italy is home to forty one UNESCO World Heritage Sites, more than any other country, including many entire cities such as Verona, Siena, Vicenza, San Gimignano, and Urbino. Ravenna hosts an unprecedented eight different internationally recognized sites.

Grand Tour

The Grand Tour was a European travel itinerary that flourished from about 1660 until the arrival of mass rail transit in the 1820s. It was popular amongst young British upper-class men and served as an educational rite of passage for the wealthy. Similar trips were made by the wealthy of other Northern European nations. Its primary value lay in the exposure both to the cultural artifacts of antiquity and the Renaissance and to the aristocratic and fashionable society of the European continent. A grand tour could last from several months to several years.

Travel Itinerary

The most common itinerary of the Grand Tour began in Dover, England, and crossed the English Channel to Calais in France. From there the tourist, usually accompanied by a tutor and if wealthy enough a league of servants, acquired a coach-which would be resold on completion-and other travel and transportation necessities, such as a French-speaking guide, and set off for Paris. In Paris the traveller might undertake lessons in French, dancing, fencing and riding. The appeal of Paris lay in the sophisticated language and manners of high French society, including courtly behavior and fashion. Ostensibly this served the purpose of preparing the young British nobleman for a leadership position at home, often government-related or diplomatic in nature.

From Paris he would typically go to Geneva and experience Switzerland for a while. Then a difficult crossing over the Alps into Northern Italy (such as at St. Bernard Pass), which included dismantling the carriage and luggage, and if wealthy enough he might be carried over the hard terrain by servants. Once in Northern Italy the tourist might spend a few months in

Florence and Pisa studying Renaissance art, then move on to Bologna and Venice to do the same. From Venice it was on to Rome to study the classical ruins, with perhaps a visit to Naples for music, and to appreciate the recently discovered archaeological sites of Herculaneum and Pompeii and for the adventurous thrilling ascent of Mount Vesuvius. Later in the period the more adventurous, especially if provided with a yacht, might attempt the Greek ruins of Sicily or Greece itself. But Naples, or later Paestum a little further south, was the usual terminus; from here it was back north through the Alps to the German speaking parts of Europe. The traveller might stop first in Innsbruck before visiting Berlin, Dresden, Vienna and Potsdam, with perhaps some study time at the universities in Munich or Heidelberg. Then it was on to Holland and Flanders, with more gallery-going and art appreciation, before returning across the channel to England.

History

The idea of traveling for the sake of curiosity and learning was a developing idea in the 18th century. With John Locke's Essay Concerning Human Understanding (1690) it was argued, and widely accepted, that knowledge comes entirely from the external senses, that what one knows comes from the physical stimuli to which one has been exposed, thus, one could "use up" the environment, taking from it all it offers, requiring a change of place. Travel, therefore, was an obligation for the person who wanted to further develop his or her mind and so expand his or her knowledge of the world. The typical 18th century sentiment was that of the studious observer traveling through foreign lands reporting his or her findings on human nature for those unfortunate to have stayed home. Traveling observation became a duty, an obligation to society at large to increase its welfare. The Grand Tour flourished in this mindset.

The Grand Tour not only provided a liberal education but allowed those who could afford it the opportunity to buy things otherwise unavailable at home, and it thus increased participants' prestige and standing. Grand Tourists would return with crates of art, books, pictures, sculpture, and items of culture, which would be displayed in libraries, cabinets, gardens, and drawing rooms; The Grand Tour became a symbol of wealth and freedom. Artists who especially thrived on Grand Tourists included Pompeo Batoni the portraitist, and the vedutisti such as Canaletto, Pannini and Guardi. The less well-off could return with an album of Piranesi etchings.

Critics of the Grand Tour derided its lack of adventure. "The tour of Europe is a paltry thing", said one 18th century critic, "a tame, uniform, unvaried prospect". The Grand Tour was said to re-enforce the old preconceptions and prejudices about national characteristics, as Jean Gailhard's Compleat Gentleman (1678) observes: "French courteous. Spanish lordly. Italian amorous. German clownish."

After the arrival of mass transit, around 1825, the Grand Tour custom continued, but it was of a qualitative difference-cheaper to undertake, safer, easier, open to anyone. During much of the 19th century, most educated young men of privilege undertook the Grand Tour. Later, it became fashionable for young women; a trip to Italy, with a spinster aunt chaperon, was part of the upper-class woman's education, as in E.M. Forster's A Room with a View.

Thomas Coryat's travel book Coryat's Crudities (1611) was an early influence on the Grand Tour. According to the Oxford English Dictionary, the first recorded use of the term (perhaps its introduction to English) was by Richard Lassels in his book An Italian Voyage (1670).

Some contemporary sociologists view the Grand Tour as the prototype for modern tourism.

TOURISM IN LITHUANIA

Lithuania attracts many tourists form neighbouring countries and all the world.

Statistics

Lithuania experiences a constant increase of foreign visitors. As of the first half of 2006 the number of visitors (except from the EU Member States and EFTA Member States) has risen 11.1 percent compared to 2005 and reached 985.7 thousand. Lithuania attracts most foreign visitors from Russia, Germany, Poland, Latvia, Belarus, the United Kingdom, Estonia and Finland. Druskininkai and Birštonas resorts experienced around 50 percent increase of occupiers in 2005 compared to 2004; while the increase of arrivals staying in Neringa and Palanga averaged 22 percent. The majority of visitors staying in hotels and lodging houses come from Germany, Poland, Latvia, the United Kingdom, Russia, and Finland.

From January to September of 2006, Lithuanian hotels have experienced a 13,7 percent increase of occupiers compared to 2005, 51 percent of them being foreign visitors (nearly 620 000). Among them, a number of foreign occupiers in Druskininkai has increased 25,7 percent and 27,5 percent in Palanga. Almost a half of the foreign visitors were staying in the capital, Vilnius, that experienced an increase of 10,6 percent. More than twice as many foreigners had stayed in Birštonas' sanatories, compared to 2005.

Agrotourism has also gained extreme popularity in the country among the locals as well as foreigners.

Major Cities

- Vilnius-capital of Lithuania
- Kaunas-temporary interbellum capital of Lithuania with prominent Functionalism architecture
- Klaipeda-sea port with an attractive old town and heritage of the German culture
- Paneve□ys-capital of Aukštaitija
- Šiauliai-famous for nearby Hill of Crosses
- Kedainiai-city in central Lithuania with prominent Renaissance architecture monuments

National Parks

- Aukštaitija National Park

- □emaitija National Park
- Kuršiu Nerija National Park
- Dzukija National Park
- Trakai Historical National Park

UNESCO World Heritage Sites

- Kernave-a complex of historical hillforts and an archeological site, nicknamed "Lithuanian Troy"
- Curonian Spit
- Vilnius Old Town-the old capital of the Grand Duchy of Lithuania, is among the largest in the Eastern Europe

Resorts

Seaside Resorts

- Palanga-the summer capital of Lithuania with sandy beaches
- Nida-a world heritage site with unique heritage and nature
- Juodkrante-a former German luxury resort

Spa Towns

- Birštonas
- Druskininkai-a developed spa town with the largest water park in the Eastern Europe.

Fishing Resources

- Rusne

List of national parks of Lithuania

There are 5 national parks in Lithuania. They were established in 1991 after Lithuania declared independence from the Soviet Union in 1990. Lithuanian SSR National Park established in 1974 was reorganized and renamed Aukštaitija National Park. Now they cover about 2.3 percent of Lithuania's territory.

Name	Established	Territory (km²)	Municipalities	Ethnographic region
Aukštaitija National Park	1974	406	Ignalina, Utena, and Švencionys	Aukštaitija
Dzukija National Park	1991	559	Varena	Dzukija
Kuršiu Nerija National Park	1991	264	Neringa	Lithuania Minor
Trakai National Historic Park	1991	82	Trakai	Dzukija
□emaitija National Park	1991	217	Plunge	Samogitia

List of regional parks of Lithuania

Lithuania has 30 regional parks. They were all established in 1992.

#	Name	Area (km²)	Area rank	Municipality
1	Anykšciai Regional Park	140.80	10	Anykšciai
2	Asveja Regional Park	109.70	17	Moletai, Švencionys, Vilnius
3	Aukštadvaris Regional Park	153.50	7	Trakai, Prienai, Kaišiadorys
4	Birai Regional Park	140.30	11	Birai, Pasvalys
5	Dieveniškes Regional Park	87.94	23	Šalcininkai
6	Dubysa Regional Park	89.00	22	Raseiniai, Kelme
7	Graute Regional Park	242.30	4	Zarasai, Ignalina
8	Kaunas Lagoon Regional Park	96.00	21	Kaunas district, Kaišiadorys, Kaunas city
9	Krekenava Regional Park	86.80	25	Paneve□ys, Kedainiai
10	Kurtuvenai Regional Park	150.90	8	Kelme, Šiauliai

Contd...

#	Name	Area (km²)	Area rank	Municipality
11	Labanoras Regional Park	553.43	1	Švencionys, Moletai, Utena, Ignalina
12	Meteliai Regional Park	177.29	6	Lazdijai, Alytus
13	Nemunas Delta Regional Park	288.70	3	Šilute
14	Nemunas Loops Regional Park	240.80	5	Prienai, Birštonas, Alytus, Kaišiadorys
15	Neris Regional Park	99.00	19	Vilnius, Elektrenai, Trakai
16	Pagramantis Regional Park	144.20	9	Taurage, Šilale
17	Pajuris Regional Park	58.70	26	Klaipeda district, Palanga, Klaipeda city
18	Panemuniai Regional Park	11,5.63	15	Šakiai, Jurbarkas, Kaunas
19	Pavilniai Regional Park	20.10	30	Vilnius
20	Rambynas Regional Park	45.20	28	Pagegiai
21	Salantai Regional Park	136.30	13	Kretinga, Skuodas, Plunge
22	Sartai Regional Park	136.50	12	Rokiškis, Zarasai
23	Sirveta Regional Park	86.80	24	Švencionys, Ignalina
24	Tytuvenai Regional Park	114.30	16	Kelme, Raseiniai
25	Varniai Regional Park	338.00	2	Telšiai, Šilale, Kelme
26	Veisiejai Regional Park	122.00	14	Lazdijai
27	Venta Regional Park	106.30	18	Akmene, Ma□eikiai, Šiauliai
28	Verkiai Regional Park	27.31	29	Vilnius city, Vilnius district
29	Vištytis Regional Park	97.00	20	Vilkaviškis
30	Zagare Regional Park	49.30	27	Joniškis

List of Castles in Lithuania

Most of Lithuanian early castles were wooden and didn't survive until nowadays.

All remaining castles have been constructed of stone and brick starting from the 13th century.

List of Castles and Castle Ruins in Lithuania

- Biliunai Castle-nothing remains
- Bir□ai Castle-rebuilt
- Dubingiai Castle-ruins
- Kaunas Castle-partially rebuilt
- Kaunas Fortress
- Klaipeda Castle, Klaipeda-visible ruins
- Kruonis Castle-visible ruins
- Liškiava Castle-visible ruins
- Medininkai Castle-partially rebuilt
- Merkine Castle-nothing remains
- Norviliškes Castle-rebuilt
- Panemune Castle
- Raudondvaris Castle
- Raudone Castle
- Rokantiškes Castle-visible ruins
- Siesikai Castle-under restoration
- Trakai Castles
    - Senieji Trakai Castle-ruins
    - Trakai Island Castle-rebuilt
    - Trakai Peninsula Castle-partially rebuilt
- Vilnius Castle Complex
    - Upper Castle with remaining Gediminas Tower-partially rebuilt

* Lower Castle with Royal Palace-partially rebuilt
* Crooked Castle-nothing remains

List of Landmarks in Lithuania

- Europos Parkas
- Gediminas Castle
- Geographical Center of Europe
- Grutas Park
- Hill of Crosses
- Palanga Amber Museum
- Rambynas
- Stelmu□e Oak
- Three Crosses
- Trakai Island Castle
- Trakai Peninsula Castle

TOURISM IN MONTENEGRO

Tourism in Montenegro is in a rapid expansion. The location of this small Mediterranean country, rich architectural and cultural heritage, and the diversity of landscapes and climates makes Montenegro a desirable tourist destination.

In 2005 820,000 tourists visited Montenegro, of which some 272,000 were from abroad. This represents nearly a 17% increase over the previous year, and Montenegro is considered the fastest-growing tourist destination in recent years.

The biggest problem of Montenegrin tourism is inadequate infrastructure, most notably obsolete road network and difficulties with water and electricity supply in coastal area. For that reason, main investments of the Government is building new and reconstuction of the current road infrastrucutre.

Main Points of Interest

Coastal Region

This region is of main interest to tourists. Montenegrin Adriatic coast is 295 km long, with 72 km of beaches, and with many well-preserved ancient old towns. The main attractions are:

- Old town of Kotor, listed with UNESCO world heritage sites.
- Boka Kotorska (Bay of Kotor), some say most beautiful bay in Europe, with ancient small town of Perast and its islets.
- Old town of Budva, very well preserved old town.
- Sveti Stefan, a small hamlet on an island turned into a luxury hotel. Most picturesque resort on the coast.

Besides these, every other coastal town, sepecially south of Budva, is very popular among tourists, primarily because of sandy beaches and vibrant nightlife.

Central Region

Although it is most densely populated area of Montenegro, it has fewer tourist attractions. Notable are:

- Ostrog monastery, a famous pilgrimage site,
- Archeological remains of Duklja (Doclea) from Roman times outside Podgorica.
- Skadar lake, a popular wildlife reserve.
- Cetinje, historical capital of Montenegro.

Northern Region

Northern region is centre of Montenegrin mountain tourism. It has ski resorts, and is popular for its untouched nature. Destinations in the north are:

- Town of □abljak on mountain Durmitor, the most popular mountain tourism destination in Montenegro.
- Town of Kolašin, also popular destination, near national park Biogradska Gora, mountain Bjelasica and ski-resort Bjelasica
- Tara River Gorge, second-longest canyon in the world. Tara river is a popular rafting destination.

- Biogradska Gora, with Biogradsko Lake, a national park and untouched virgin forest.

The entire area of Durmitor mountain and Tara river canyon is protected as a national park, and listed with UNESCO world heritage sites.

Budva Riviera (Region)

The Budva Riviera is a 35 km long strip of the Adriatic coast surrounding the town of Budva in Montenegro. Historically it was part of the Albania Veneta. It is located roughly along the middle of the Montenegrin coast, and is a center for Montenegrin beach tourism. There are 12.5 km of beaches which lie along the Budva Riviera.

Settlements

The best known and most popular settlements along the Budva Riviera are:

- Budva
- Milocer
- Sveti Stefan
- Becici
- Rafailovici
- Petrovac

Beaches

The best known feature of the Budva Riviera is its beaches. They are listed here, from north to south.

Trsteno

Trsteno beach is 100 metres long, deeply pulled in the dry land. It has perhaps the finest sand on the Budva Riviera. It is accessible by the same road which leads to Jaz beach.

Jaz

Jaz beach lies with Mrcevo Polje and its hinterlands. The beach is 2,5 km away from Budva in the direction of Tivat. It consists of two parts, one 500 m long and the other, formerly a nudist beach, 300 m long. It is a pebble beach, with a campground along the greater part of the beach (capacity 2,000 lots). The beach is a protected natural heritage site.

Mogren

Mogren one or two beaches stretch from the cape called Mogren to the Avala Hotel belvedere. Their natural environment place Mogren into the category of most attractive beaches, with sand of medium particle size, both on the beach itself and in water. The beach is well exposed to sun and southerly wind. From the back, it is protected by the hill of Spas covered in dense pine and oak woods.

The beach is accessible by a narrow path going through Avala hotel complex. It is not more than 150 m away from Budva's old town. Mogren consists of two sandy beaches of total length of 350 m, connected with a tunnel in the rock. They were named after the Spanish sailor Mogrini, who landed on the beaches after a shipwreck, As a sign of gratitude, he built St. Anthony's church.

A small fee (one euro as of 2005) is collected at Mogren's entrance, to keep the beaches not too crowded for guests at Avala hotel.

On the narrow path which leads to the beach, there is one section completely dedicated to divers and risk takers. Almost at the half point of the path, there is a little outlet into the sea, sandwiched between rocks, giving risk takers about 3 meters of width to dive safely into the water. This area is called by people from Budva, Kanal, which has no meaning but in english it means literally Canal. These divers have built up quite a reputation in Budva because of their rambunctious and hilarious acts.

Slovenska

Slovenska beach stretches from the Budva marina to the Park hotel, 1,600 m in total length. It was declared a beach from as early as 1920, and the Czechs who spent their summer holidays in Budva in 1935 gave it its present name Slovenska Pla□a, (Slavic beach). It is a pebble beach, and has a large hotel complex of the same name at it's backside. Budva's main promenade, where most of the nightlife and shopping takes place, goes alongside this beach.

Guvance

Guvance is a small sandy beach located below the walking path near the tunnel leading to Becici. It is 80 m long.

Becici

Becici beach is one of the largest and most beautiful beaches in the South Adriatic. It is a sandy beach, 1,950 m long and stretches from Zavala to Djevištenje. In 1935 it won the "Grand Prix" in Paris as the most beautiful beach in Europe. It is perhaps the best equipped beach on the riviera, with sport fields and all other amenities.

Kamenovo

Kamenovo beach is the first in a series of 16 smaller beaches lying between the town of Becici and "Perazica do". It faces southesat and has a large number of hours of sunshine. This 730 m long sandy beach is easily accessible from the main road towards Petrovac.

Prno

Prno beach is located in front of the picturesque Mediterranean settlement of the same name. It stretches for 350 m between Prno cape and Milocer cape. It is surrounded by olive groves of exceptional value, which is why the entire area is enlisted as a protected nature reserve. In the vicinity of the beach is "Maestreal hotel", and a string of taverns and cafes.

Milocer

Milocer beach is located near the former summer residence of the royal family Karadordevic, built in 1934. The beach is 280 m long, surrounded by woods covering the area of 18 ha, with rare exotic tree species like the Lebanon Cedar, tropical mimosas, loquats, cacti, agavas and others. Milocer beach belongs to high category of sandy beaches.

Kraljicina

Kraljicina beach is located next to Milocer beach. It is a 200 m long beach surrounded by cypress and olive trees. Its name derives from the fact that it was a favourite spot of Queen Marija Karadordevic.

This beach may not be open to the general public at all times, or its entrance may be charged, because this is the favourite resort of Montenegrin officials.

Sveti Stefan

The beaches of Sveti Stefan are formed on both sides of the strip that connects the town-hotel of Sveti Stefan with the coast. Those are two sandy beaches of 1,170 total length. Onde side is reserved for famous guests of this de-luxe hotel.

Drobni Pijesak

Drobni Pijesak is a secluded 250 m long beach and is accessible only from the sea. It is has the appearance of a real tropical beach.jar

Perazica Do

Perazica Do beach is in immediate vicinity of Re□evici monastery, below the highway. This little sandy beach is hidden in a deep valley.

Petrovac

Petrovac beach is a sandy beach of some 600m of length, with the sand of reddish colour. The beach is bordered by Petrovac promenade, filled with cafes, restaurants and shops.

Lucice

Lucice is a popular beach located some 500 m south from town of Petrovac. This sandy beach is shaped like a little bay, and is 220 m long.

Buljarica

Buljarica is possibly the greatest development potential along the Montenegrin coast. Buljarica field and the slopes of Dubovica hill are well suited for the development of all types of tourism. Buljarica cove stretches from "Resovo brdo" cove to

Dubovica, and is a largest beach of the Budva Riviera. It is 1 km from Petrovac in the direction of Bar, and is 2,250 m long.

Sveti Nikola Island

The Sveti Nikola island is the main excursion site in Budva area. The island has three sandy beaches whose combined length is 840 m. The island itself is about one km away from Budva. There are many small beachs around the island, accessible only by boat.

TOURISM AND RECREATION IN THE NETHERLANDS

Tourism is an important economic sector in the Netherlands. The country receives some 10 million foreign visitors every year, primarily from Germany, the United Kingdom, the United States and Belgium.

The Netherlands is a densely populated country with famous cities like Amsterdam known for its many canals, red light district (De Wallen) and cannabis coffee shops. One can purchase and use cannabis legally in the Netherlands, which is rare for most western countries, and has led to a large number of "drug tourists" from abroad. Amsterdam is also a city of rich culture and history with popular attractions like the Van Gogh Museum, Rijksmuseum (national museum), Rembrandt House Museum and Anne Frank House.

Other tourist destinations in the Netherlands are cities like the royal seat The Hague with its elegant downtown, beaches and Madurodam miniature city; modern Rotterdam with its harbour, shopping and skyline; and Delft and Utrecht-formerly rich trading cities. In the south you have one of the oldest (Roman) cities, Maastricht and a very old village called Valkenburg lying in a romantic landscape with old castles and hills.

Many tourists seeking to experience the typically Dutch tulips and windmills visit the Keukenhof flower gardens, the windmills of the Zaanse Schans and Kinderdijk, and the traditional fishing villages of Volendam and Marken. Popular souvenirs from the Netherlands are flower bulbs, delftware and clogs (wooden shoes). But the Netherlands also has to offer a great coastline along the North Sea, the IJsselmeer and the Wadden Sea-great resorts for sailing with picturesque little typical Dutch towns like Elburg or Harderwijk. The Netherlands is a great country for cycling, sailing or ice skating in winter. They have mainly flat landscapes with many canals, windmills, little villages, rivers like the Rhine or IJssel, Maas or Schelde.

TOURISM IN NORWAY

Norway is a country that attracts tourists mostly by virtue of its impressive and varied landscapes that extends far north across the Arctic Circle. It is famous for its fjord-indented coastline and its mountains, ski resorts, lakes and woods. Famous cities in Norway include the capital Oslo with its castle, its cathedral, its picturesque landscape and interesting architecture.

On the west coast there are the cities of Bergen (the Hanseatic city) and Stavanger, each of them set alongside a fjord. Preikestolen is located in Lysefjorden right outside Stavanger. It is a cliff hanging 604 metres directly above the water. In the south you find the city of Kristiansand which is the fith largest in Norway, and to many it is the favourite holiday city. Trondheim, Norway's first capital, is home to the largest medieval cathedral in Scandinavia, Nidaros Cathedral. Tromsø, gateway to the arctic, is situated 400 km north of the arctic circle in the midst of a stunning landscape of mountains and fjords.

Transportation to Norway

Norway is accessible via several routes:

- *By car:* With the opening of the Oresund Bridge and the Great Belt Fixed Link, there is a continuous highway connection between Norway and the European continent, taking drivers through Germany, Denmark, and Sweden.
- *By sea:* There are car ferry connections to various points in Southern Norway from Kiel in Germany, Copenhagen, and the United Kingdom.

- *By air*-there are daily non-stop connections from many European cities to Oslo Airport, Gardermoen, as well as connections to other airports
- *By rail:* the Norwegian railroad system has connections through the Swedish railroad system.

Transportation and Accommodations within Norway

Norway has a well-developed transportation infrastructure that includes:

- A highway system, covering more than 90,000 kilometers, of which more than 67,000 is paved. The highway system includes ferry transit across waterways, numerous bridges and tunnels, and several mountain passes. Some of these mountain passes are closed during the winter months, and some may close during winter storms.
- A domestic air travel network that includes airports in all major cities, covered by several domestic airlines.
- Rail transportation, 4,058 km rail network that connects most of the major cities south of Bodø
- Waterway transportation, especially Hurtigruten, that connects cities on the coast between Bergen to Kirkenes. Several cruise lines also make port calls in the fjords of Norway.

Most population and vacation centers in Norway offer tourist accommodations, in the form of:

- Hotels, of varying standards. Chains such as Rica Hotels, Choice Hotels, Rainbow Hotels, and Radisson SAS have a number of hotels, and in addition there are privately owned hotels. A unified portal for all hotels in Norway is Hotell.no. Historic Hotels of Norway offers an overview of the unique and historic hotels in Norway
- Cabin rentals, typically these are offered through local services
- Shared cabin accommodations, in the mountains-the Norwegian Mountain Touring Association offers simple accommodations for trekkers across the mountains.

Activities

Norway has a rich cultural heritage that has evolved as a result of its sparse population, harsh climate, and relative isolation from the rest of Europe. See History of Norway, Geography of Norway, and Demographics of Norway to gain a better understanding of the country's characteristics.

As a tourist destination it is therefore distinct from other countries in Europe in that it has fewer opulent palaces and castles, smaller agricultural areas, and longer travel distances. On the other hand, interested visitors can find unique architecture, a rich ethnological heritage, and vast areas of undisturbed and dramatic natural scenery.

Culture and the Arts

View of the Vigeland Sculpture Park, Probably the most Famous Park in Norway

Both by virtue of governmental policy and public interest, cultural expression in Norway is taken very seriously. Many artists sustain their livelihood through grants and fellowships from the Norwegian government, and local and national governments are among the biggest buyers of art.

The Norwegian cultural outlook is characterized by both a wish to be cosmopolitan and to be distinctly Norwegian. The growing cultural diversity in recent years has added impulses to the various cultural scenes. Some of the most noted cultural events and attractions in Norway include:

- Visual arts-in Oslo, the National Gallery, the Munch Museum, and the Henie-Onstad Art Centre offer classical and contemporary art pieces for viewing by the public
- Music:
    - Classical-the Oslo Philharmonic Orchestra and Bergen Philharmonic Orchestra offer regular programs, as does the Norwegian Chamber Orchestra. The Risør Festival of Chamber Music is a week-long event held in late June/early July in the southern town of Risør

* Jazz-most cities in Norway have jazz clubs, and the Moldejazz festival is held in mid-to late July in Molde

- Dramatic arts-laying claims to playwrights such as Ludvig Holberg and Henrik Ibsen, there are several theaters that offer high quality fare. In addition, there are numerous historical reenactments, especially during the summer months.

Outdoor Life

Much of Norway remains untouched by human hands and lets hikers experience the mountainous, harsh and beautiful landscapes the country is known for. Norway has lots of skiing resorts and parks, although the country's free nature offers the best skiing experience.

The modern Jotunheimen national park is central in southern Norway, and remains a completely unspoilt wilderness with no roads or permanent residences within the park boundaries, making it an emerging destination for walking holidays.

The Lofoten Islands are a popular destination, with majestic, towering landscapes, and allowing visitors to experience the midnight sun during summer months. The island Røst is with 2.5 Mio seabirds Norway's largest bird rock.

The island of Runde near Ålesund is known as Norway's largest bird rock south of the Arctic Circle. Runde is conected with a bridge to the mainland.

List of Most Visited Tourist Attractions

Innovation Norway, a state-owned promotion company also being in charge of tourism affairs, makes annual reports of the country's most visited tourist attractions, both cultural and natural.

The 2006 report lists 50 cultural and 20 natural attractions, below are listed the top ten of each category.

Rank	Cultural Attraction	Location	Visitors, 2006
1	Holmenkollen Ski Jump and Ski Museum	Oslo	686 857
2	World Heritage Site Bryggen	Bergen	583 510
3	Kristiansand Zoo and Amusement Park	Kristiansand	532 044
4	Amusement park Tusenfryd	Ås/Oslo	501 235
5	Railroad Flåmsbanen	Flåm	457 545
6	Hadeland Glassverk	Jevnaker	431 400
7	Local rail Fløibanen	Bergen	422 297
8	Fredrikstad Fortress, Old Town of Fredrikstad	Fredrikstad	372 360
9	Viking Ship Museum	Oslo	314 560
10	Amusement park Hunderfossen Familiepark	Øyer/ Lillehammer	270 500

Rank	Natural Attraction	Location	Visitors 2006
1	Vøringsfossen waterfall	Eidfjord	655 000
2	Scenic road Trollstigen	Åndalsnes	563 331
3	Kjosfossen waterfall	Flåm	457 400
4	World Heritage Site Geirangerfjorden	Geiranger	423 643
5	Låtefossen waterfall	Odda/ Hardanger	420 000
6	Steindalfossen waterfall	Norheimsund/ Hardanger	300 000
7	World Heritage Site Nærøyfjorden	Aurland	297 038
8	Briksdalsbreen glacier	Olden/Stryn	280 000
9	National Tourist Road Sognefjellsvegen	Lom-Luster	253 953
10	Scenic road Atlanterhavsvegen	Averøy/ Kristiansund	237 316

Norwegian World Heritage Sites

Bryggen, the old wharf of Bergen, is a reminder of the town's importance as part of the trading empire Hanseatic League from the 14th to the 16th century. Many fires, the last in 1955, have ravaged the beautiful wooden houses, although its main structure has been preserved.

Urnes Stave Church, a stavkirke in Luster municipality, wooden church by the Sognefjorden. Stave churches were built from the 11th to the 13th century, and is a great example of traditional Scandinavian wooden architecture.

Røros, a mining town in southern Sør-Trøndelag county. The copper mines were active from 1744 to 1977, and the town was destroyed by Swedish troops in 1679. After this, Røros was rebuilt and has about 80 wooden houses which gives the town a medieval appearance due to the dark pitch-log facades.

Rock carvings at Alta are petroglyphs in the Alta fjord, in Finnmark county, north of the Arctic Circle. Thousands of paintings and engravings into rocks gives us the impression of what it must have been like living in the Far North before 4200-500 B.C.

Vegaøyan/The Vega Archipelago in Nordland county, just south of the Arctic Circle is the name of a dozen islands, where fishermen and farmers have been living since the Stone Age. There are fishing villages, quays, warehouses, eider houses (built for eider ducks to nest in), farming landscapes, lighthouses and beacons.

Struve Geodetic Arc is a chain of survey triangulations stretching from Hammerfest in Norway to the Black Sea. These are points of a survey, carried out between 1816 and 1855 by the astronomer Friedrich Georg Wilhelm Struve, and it represented the first accurate measuring of a long segment of a meridian.

West Norwegian Fjords-Geirangerfjord and Nærøyfjord is the most recent addition to the list, these are typical Norwegian fjord landscapes. Nærøyfjord is in Sogn og Fjordane county and Geirangerfjord is in Møre og Romsdal county, 200 kilometres north. The village of Geiranger is a popular destination for cruise ships.

TOURISM IN POLAND

Poland is interesting for everyone who wants to visit old cities, pubs, culture and a picturesque landscape varying from sea shores to mountains for an affordable price.

Sightseeing

Tourism in Poland includes visits to big and old cities like the capital of Warsaw with its castle and its Old Town, its parks and boulevards. Other famous and old cities are Kraków with its cathedral and its old town, the medieval Hanseatic city of Gdansk, the old city of Wroclaw with its famous cathedral, Lublin with its impressive Jewish history, or Medieval Torun, the birthplace of Copernicus.

The memorial museums in Auschwitz, a UN world heritage site, and other holocaust related sites are also of interest. The bigger Polish cities are especially interesting for backpackers because of their young population, affordable cultural events and many pubs.

The Mazury lake district in northeastern Poland with its picturesque villages and Malbork castle is also worth a visit. South of Bialystok one can find the Bialowieza Forest, a UNESCO Heritage Site and nature preserve where European bison (wisent) may be found.

Sea Resorts

There are several sea resorts on the coast of Baltic Sea like Wolin island, which is located close to the German border, and the coast of Pomerania. Other include Swinoujscie, Kolobrzeg, Leba, Hel, Jurata, Sopot, Krynica Morska to name just a few.

Mountain Resorts

In southern Poland there are resorts for skiing and hiking in the Karkonosze mountains, which is part of the Sudetes mountain range and in Carpathian Mountains. Karkonosze includes the touristical centres of Karpacz and Szklarska Poreba. Other famous resorts for skiing and hiking include Zakopane in the Tatra mountains, Szczyrk, Krynica in Beskides or Szczawnica and Kroscienko in Pieniny mountains.

Transportation

Most major Polish cities have airports with connecting services with the Frederic Chopin International Airport in Warsaw. For travelling in Poland the PKP's intercity or eurocity train, PKS's overland bus service are both comfortable options. Alternative options include slower PKP longdistance or local trains or numerous coach services.

Since the fall of communism roads in Poland are slowly improving. There is acceptable tourist infrastructure, especially in larger cities and in major tourist resorts.

List of Airports in Poland

List of airports by IATA and ICAO airport codes:

IATA code	ICAO code	City	Airport	Website
BZG	EPBY	Bydgoszcz	Bydgoszcz Ignacy Jan Paderewski Airport	[1]
GDN	EPGD	Gdańsk	Gdańsk Lech Wałęsa Airport	[2]
IEG	EPZG	Zielona Góra	Zielona Góra International Airport	[3]
KRK	EPKK	Kraków	John Paul II International Airport Kraków-Balice	[4]
KTW	EPKT	Katowice	Katowice International Airport in Pyrzowice	[5]
LCJ	EPLL	Łódź	Łódź Władysław Reymont Airport	[6]
POZ	EPPO	Poznań	Poznań-Ławica Airport	[7]
RZE	EPRZ	Rzeszów	Rzeszów-Jasionka Airport	[8]
SZY	EPSY	Szczytno	Szczytno-Szymany International Airport	[9]
SZZ	EPSC	Szczecin	Szczecin-Goleniów "Solidarność" Airport	[10]
WAW	EPWA	Warsaw	Warsaw Frederic Chopin Airport	[11]
WRO	EPWR	Wrocław	Copernicus Airport Wrocław	[12]

By Traffic Size

List of airports by traffic size in 2005, with % change since 2004:

City	IATA Code	ICAO Code	Passengers	Cargo in tonnes	Aircraft movements
Warsaw	WAW	EPWA	7 071 667 (+16.21%)	48 535 (+2.70%)	120 271 (+11,10%)
Kraków	KRK	EPKK	1 564 338 (+94.77%)	3 255 (?01.04%)	21 951 (+53.27%)
Katowice	KTW	EPKT	1 083 517 (+86.85%)	5 619 (+11.52%)	11 316 (+24.50%)
Gdańsk	GDN	EPGD	677 946 (+46.16%)	3 433 (+10.73%)	12 658 (+21.78%)
Poznań	POZ	EPPO	399 255 (+13.74%)	2 166 (+41.72%)	8 983 (?02.38%)
Wrocław	WRO	EPWR	454 047 (+27.75%)	1 378 (?07.39%)	20 556 (+11.06%)
Szczecin	SZZ	EPSC	100 847 (+11.05%)	655 (+12.63%)	3 050 (?02.84%)
Rzeszów	RZE	EPRZ	91 499 (+30.53%)	488 (?14.84%)	2 091 (+03.57%)
Bydgoszcz	BZG	EPBY	38 682 (+52.57%)	338 (+26.47%)	1 359 (?42.39%)
Łódź	LCJ	EPLL	18 063 (190.12%)	0 (0%)	1 456 (?10.84%)
Zielona Góra	IEG	EPZG	427 (?89.19%)	0 (0%)	163 (?59,25%)
Szczytno	SZY	EPSY	0 (0%)	0 (0%)	0 (0%)
Total	-	-	11 501 242 (+30.18%)	65 867 (+04.34%)	204 060 (+13,80%)

Source: Poland's Office of Civil Aviation (Urzad Lotnictwa Cywilnego)

PTTK

Polskie Towarzystwo Turystyczno-Krajoznawcze (Polish Tourist-Sightseeing Society, Polish Tourist Country-Lovers' Society) is a Polish non-governmental tourist society. It is one of the oldest tourist societies in Europe, founded in 1950 from the merger of the Polish Tatry Society (Polskie Towarzystwo Tatrzanskie) (1873) and Polish Sightseeing Society (Polskie Towarzystwo Krajoznawcze) (1906). It plans and marks tourist trails in Poland (as well as cycling, horse and river trails). It also has a network of tourist hotels and camps, museum, libraries and runs several courses and workshops; it trains and recognizes travel guides. It publishes various maps and guidebooks. It has over 80,000 members.

It is a member of international organizations: Alliance Internationale de Tourisme, Naturfreunde Internationale,

Federation of Nature and National Parks of Europe and Confédération Mondiale des Activités Subaquatiques.

TOURISM IN PORTUGAL

Portugal attracts many tourists each year. In 2006, the country was visited by 12,8 million tourists. Tourism is playing an increasingly important role in Portugal's economy contributing with about 5% of the the Gross Domestic Product (GDP).

The main tourist areas are, by order of importance, the Greater Lisbon (Lisboa), the Algarve, Portuguese Islands (Ilhas Portuguesas: Madeira and Azores), Greater Porto and Northern Portugal (Porto e Norte) and Alentejo.

Lisbon is, after Barcelona, the European city attracting most tourists, with 7 million tourists sleeping in the city's hotels in 2006, the number grew 11.8% compared to previous year. Lisbon in recent years surpassed the Algarve as the leading tourist region in Portugal. Porto and Northern Portugal, especially the urban areas north of Douro River, was the tourist destination which grew most in (11.9%) in 2006. Today, most tourists in Portugal are British, Spanish or German, travel in low cost airliners, and are not only in search of the beach and the sun, but mostly searching culture, city breaks, gastronomy, nautical tourism or travel in business.

Tourism Regions

Tourist hotspots in Portugal are Lisbon, the Algarve and Madeira, but the Portuguese government is currently developing new destinations: the Douro Valley, Porto Santo Island, and Alentejo.

Portugal has several other tourism regions such as Douro Sul, Templários, Dão-Lafões, Costa do Sol, Costa Azul, Planície Dourada, etc. Most of them are unknown to tourists and locals alike. As of 2007, these are being reorganized.

All these regions are grouped in tourism reference areas, which are widely known due to the fact that these are the traditional regions:

- Costa Verde-The Portuguese green coast comprises all the northern coast of Portugal from the estuary of the Minho River to the city of Porto.
- Costa da Prata-Silver coast. The coast of central Portugal from Porto to Lisbon.
- Costa de Lisboa-Lisbon coast. The coast of the capital city and its important suburbs.
- Montanhas-Mountainous and interior regions of northern and central Portugal, namely Serra da Estrela and Trás-os-Montes.
- Planícies-The Portuguese plane region of Alentejo in the south.
- Algarve-The southern coast of Portugal.
- Madeira-The Madeira islands.
- Açores-The Azores islands.

TOURISTS BY COUNTRY

Tourist nationalities in 2005 (excluding nationals):

1. United Kingdom 21.8%
2. Spain 19.0%
3. Germany 12.3%
4. France 7.0%
5. Italy 5.2%
6. Netherlands 5.0%
7. USA 4.0%
8. Brazil 3.0%
9. Ireland 2.5%
10. Belgium 2.2%

TOURISM IN ROMANIA

Tourism in Romania focuses on the country's natural landscapes and its rich history. The number of tourists is growing every year and tourism is becoming an increasingly important source for Romania's GDP with 6-7 million people now visiting yearly. Romania's economy is characterized by a huge potential for tourism. Tourism in Romania attracted 880 million in investments in 2005.

Activities & Must Sees

- camping and hiking in the Carpathian Mountains
- skiing at Poiana Brasov and on Valea Prahovei
- the Black Sea Romanian resorts (see also Mamaia)
- the medieval churches and monasteries of Moldavia and Bukovina
- the Danube Delta, the best preserved delta of Europe
- Sighisoara town and medieval festival
- the medieval Castles of Transylvania
- the folklore and traditions of Maramures (see also Wooden churches of Maramures)
- rural tourism
- spas and health resorts
- visiting the cultural cities of Sibiu, Iasi, Brasov, Cluj-Napoca, Bucharest and Alba Iulia
- the Iron Gates (Danube Gorge)

Unique Places

- Berca Mud Volcanoes, in Buzau County
- Scarisoara Cave
- Merry Cemetery, in Sapânta, Maramures County
- Palace of the Parliament, Bucharest

Protected Areas of Romania

This is a list of protected areas of Romania. About 5.18% of the area of Romania has a protected status (12,360 km^2), including the Danube Delta, which makes half of these areas (2.43% of Romania's area).

Biosphere Reserves

Name	Area (km²)	Counties
Danube Delta	5,800.00	Tulcea, Constanta

National Parks

Name	Area (km²)	Counties
Calimani	240.41	Bistrita-Nasaud, Harghita, Mures, Suceava
Ceahlau	83.96	Neamt
Retezat	380.47	Hunedoara
Rodna	463.99	Bistrita-Nasaud, Maramures, Suceava
Cheile Bicazului-Hasmas	65.75	Harghita, Neamt
Cheile Nerei-Beusnita	371.00	Caras-Severin
Cozia	171.00	Vâlcea
Domogled-Valea Cernei	601.00	Caras-Severin, Mehedinti, Gorj
Muntii Macinului	113.21	Tulcea
Piatra Craiului	148.00	Arges, Brasov
Semenic-Cheile Carasului	366.64	Caras Severin

Natural Parks

Name	Area (km²)	Counties
Muntii Apuseni	757.84	Alba, Bihor, Cluj
Balta Mica a Brailei	175.29	Braila
Bucegi	326.63	Arges, Brasov, Dâmbovita, Prahova
Gradistea Muncelului-Cioclovina	100.00	Hunedoara
Portile de Fier	1,156.55	Caras-Severin, Mehedinti
Vânatori Neamt	308.18	Neamt
Putna-Vrancea	382	Vrancea

TRANSPORT IN ROMANIA

Railways

The national railway operator is Caile Ferate Române.

- Total track: 11,385 km (3,888 km electrified)
- Standard gauge: 10,898 km
- Narrow gauge: 487 km (1996)

Bucharest is the only city in Romania with an underground railway system, comprising both the Bucharest Metro and the light rail system Regia Autonoma de Transport Bucuresti.

Rail Links with Adjacent Countries

- Ukraine-yes-Break-of-gauge 1435mm/1524mm
- Moldova-yes-Break-of-gauge 1435mm/1524mm
- Hungary-yes
- Serbia-yes
- Bulgaria-yes

Highways

More detail can be found at Roads in Romania.

- Total: 153,359 km
- Paved: 103,671 km (including 264 km of motorways-April 2007)
- Unpaved: 49,688 km (1998 est.)

Waterways

- 1,724 km (1984) of navigable waterways.

Pipelines

- Crude oil: 2,800 km
- Petroleum products: 1,429 km
- Natural gas: 6,400 km (1992)

Ports

- Black Sea ports:
    * Constanta (the biggest port and shipyard in the Black Sea)

  * Mangalia
  * Sulina
  * Navodari
- Ports on the Danube:
  * Galati
  * Braila
  * Tulcea
  * Giurgiu
  * Drobeta-Turnu Severin
  * Oltenita
- Ports on the Danube-Black Sea Canal:
  * Cernavoda
  * Poarta Alba
  * Constanta Sud
  * Agigea

Merchant Marine

- Total: 142 ships (1,000 GRT or over) totaling 1,154,127 GRT/1,612,314 DWT
- Ships by type estimated as of 1999:
  * bulk 16
  * cargo 110
  * container 1
  * passenger 1
  * passenger/cargo 1
  * petroleum tanker 5
  * rail car carrier 2
  * roll-on/roll-off 6
  * specialized tanker 1

Airports

There are 62 airports in Romania (estimated as of 1999). For more information, see Aviation in Romania.

- Airports-with paved runways: 25
    * Runways over 3,047 m: 4
    * Runways from 2,438 to 3,047 m: 9
    * Runways from 1,524 to 2,437 m: 12
- Airports-with unpaved runways: 37
    * Runways from 1,524 to 2,437 m: 2
    * Runways from 914 to 1,523 m: 12
    * Runways under 914 m: 23
- Heliports 1

TRANSPORT IN RUSSIA

Rail Transport

- total: 87,157 km
- broad gauge: 86,200 km 1.520-m gauge (40,300 km electrified)

Note: an additional 30,000 km of non-common carrier lines serve industries (2003)

- narrow gauge: 957 km 1.067-m gauge (on Sakhalin Island)

Russian, CIS and Baltic Railway Map (with place names in Russian, but legend in English).

Rapid-transit Systems

- Moscow Metro-12 lines, 172 stations, 278.8 km
- Saint Petersburg Metro-4 lines, 60 stations, 105.5 km
- Nizhny Novgorod Metro-1 line, 13 stations, 15.3 km
- Novosibirsk Metro-2 lines, 12 stations, 14.3 km
- Samara Metro-1 line, 8 stations, 10.3 km

- Yekaterinburg Metro-1 line, 8 stations, 8.5 km
- Kazan Metro-1 line, 5 stations, 7.0 km

Also there is a Metrotram system in Volgograd and three more cities with metro systems under costruction:

- Omsk
- Chelyabinsk
- Krasnoyarsk.

Rail Links with Adjacent Countries

Voltage of electrification systems not necessarily compatible.

- Japan-no-But Proposed Rail Tunnel to Sakhalin & Then Another Tunnel To Japan-break of gauge 1524mm// 1067mm
- Alaska (United States)-no-But Proposed Rail Tunnel or Bridge Under or Over Bering Straits From Trans-Siberian Railway-break of gauge 1524mm/1435mm
- Norway-no-But Proposed Via Finland & Sweden-break of gauge 1524mm/1435mm
- Finland-Yes-same gauge 1524mm
- Estonia-Yes-same gauge 1524mm
- Latvia-Yes-same gauge 1524mm
- Lithuania-Yes-same gauge 1524mm
- Poland-Yes-Via Kaliningrad Oblast-break of gauge 1524mm/1435mm
- Belarus-Yes-same gauge 1524mm
- Ukraine-Yes-same gauge 1524mm
- Georgia-Yes-same gauge 1524mm
- Azerbaijan-Yes-same gauge 1524mm
- Kazakhstan-Yes-same gauge 1524mm
- China-Yes-break of gauge 1524mm/1435mm
- Mongolia-Yes-same gauge 1524mm
- North Korea-Yes-suspended-link proposed-break of gauge 1524mm/1435mm

Highways

total: 948,000 km (including 416,000 km which serve specific industries or farms and are not maintained by governmental highway maintenance departments)

paved: 336,000 km

unpaved: 612,000 km (including 411,000 km of graveled or some other form of surfacing and 201,000 km of unstabilized earth) (1995 est.)

Waterways

total navigable routes in general use 101,000 km; routes with navigation guides serving the Russian River Fleet 95,900 km; routes with night navigational aids 60,400 km; man-made navigable routes 16,900 km (January 1994 est.)

Pipelines

crude oil 48,000 km; petroleum products 15,000 km; natural gas 140,000 km (June 1993 est.)

Ports and Harbours

Arkhangelsk, Astrakhan, Baltiysk, Kaliningrad, Kazan, Khabarovsk, Kholmsk, Krasnoyarsk, Moscow, Murmansk, Nakhodka, Nevelsk, Novorossiysk, Petropavlovsk-Kamchatsky, St. Petersburg, Rostov-on-Don, Sochi, Tuapse, Vladivostok, Volgograd, Vostochny Port, Vyborg.

Merchant Marine

total: 695 ships (1,000 GRT or over) totaling 3,920,923 GRT/4,867,676 DWT

ships by type: barge carrier 1, bulk 19, cargo 379, chemical tanker 4, combination bulk 21, combination ore/oil 3, container 25, multi-functional large load carrier 1, passenger 35, passenger/cargo 3, petroleum tanker 149, refrigerated cargo 26, roll-on/roll-off 22, short-sea passenger 7 (1999 est.)

Airports: 2,743 (2002)

Airports with paved runways

total: 630

over 3,047 m: 54

2,438 to 3,047 m: 202

1,524 to 2,437 m: 108

914 to 1,523 m: 115

under 914 m: 151 (1994 est.)

Airports with unpaved runways

total: 1,887

over 3,047 m: 25

2,438 to 3,047 m: 45

1,524 to 2,437 m: 134

914 to 1,523 m: 291

under 914 m: 1,392 (1994 est.)

Transport in San Marino

San Marino is a small European republic, with limited public transport facilities.

Railway

San Marino's railway network consisted of a single line, connecting the country with the Italian rail network at Rimini. Unable to access the capital, San Marino City (which has a mountain-top location), the terminus station was located at the village of Valdragone. The railway was opened on 12 June 1932.

It was an advanced system for its time, being an electric railway, powered by overhead electric cables. The trains drew power from these cables by means of a pantograph system. The railway was well built and well used, and in all probability would have been a long-term feature of Sammarinese public transport, but it was almost completely destroyed during the fighting in this region during World War Two. Today there is no operational railway in San Marino.

Aerial Tramway

There is a 1.5 km aerial tramway connecting the city of San Marino on top of Monte Titano with Borgo Maggiore, a major town in the republic, with the second largest population of any Sammarinese settlement. Indeed, for the tourist visitor the aerial tramway gives the best available views of Borgo Maggiore, as the cars sweep low over the rooftops of the main town square. From here a further connection is available to the nation's largest settlement, Dogana, by means of local bus service.

Two aerial tramway cars, known as gondolas, and numbered '1' and '2', operate in opposition on a cable, and a service is provided at roughly fifteen minute intervals throughout the day. A third vehicle is available on the system, being a service car for the use of engineers maintaining the tramway.

Taxi and Private Road Vehicles

There are 220 km of highways in the country, the main road being the San Marino Superhighway. Roads are well used by private car drivers. Sammarinese authorities license private vehicles with distinctive licence plates which are white with blue figures, usually a letter followed by up to four numbers. To the left of these figures is printed the national Coat of Arms of San Marino. Many vehicles also carry the international vehicle identification code (in black on a white oval sticker), which is "RSM".

A limited licensed taxi service operates nationwide. There are seven licensed taxi operating companies in the republic, and Italian taxis regularly operate within San Marino when carrying passengers picked up in Italian territory.

Buses

There is a regular bus service between Rimini and the city of San Marino, popular with both tourists and tourist industry workers commuting to San Marino from Italy. This service stops at approximately twenty advertised locations in Rimini and within San Marino, with its two terminus stops at Rimini railway station and San Marino coach station, respectively. San Marino also has its own small local bus system within the republic. This can be a useful means of transport for a visitor staying more than one day in San Marino, and therefore having the opportunity to explore the wider country and some its smaller communities. It is worth noting that tourists who are resident in a Sammarinese hotel are usually entitled to a discount on local bus fares (though not on the international service to Rimini, Italy).

Air Transport

There are no airports in San Marino, but there is an international heliport located in Borgo Maggiore. Most tourists who arrive by air land at Rimini's international airport in Italy, and then make the transfer by bus.

Waterways

Two rivers flow through San Marino, but there is no major water transport, and no major port or harbour.

TOURISM IN HONG KONG

The tourism industry has been an important part of the economy of Hong Kong since it shifted to a service sector model in the late 1980s and early 90s. There has been a sharp increase of mainland Chinese tourists due to the introduction of the Individual Visit Scheme in 2003.

Background

The total tourism expenditure associated to inbound tourism reached HK$117.3 billion in 2006. Overall visitor arrivals to Hong Kong in 2006 increased by 8.1% to 25.25 million, which was lower than what the Hong Kong Tourism Board (HKTB) had expected. The HKTB had initial expectations of 27 million visitor arrivals. Visitor arrivals from Mainland China exceeded 13.5 million. Arrivals in December 2006 exceeded 2.4 million, setting an outright record for a single month. Along with the strong growth in the number of Mainland visitors, most other long and short-haul markets are also performing healthily with double-digit growth over 2006. Among long-haul markets, Europe, Africa and the Middle East took the lead with arrivals of 1,916,861, an 11.1% increase that made this Hong Kong's best-performing market region in 2006. While facing increasing competition from Mainland cities and Macau, The Hong Kong Tourism Board work closely with authorities and trade to make Hong Kong an essential component in all combo and multi-destination itineraries. Tourism, along with import/export and financial services are the three main sources of income for Hong Kong.

Accommodation and Length of Stay

In December 2006, there were 612 hotels and tourist guest houses in Hong Kong, with 52,512 rooms. The average occupancy rate across all categories of hotels and tourist guesthouses was 87% for the whole of 2006, an one-percentage-point growth compared with 2005 regardless of the 7.4% increase in Hong Kong's room supply between December 2005 and December 2006. During 2006, 62.7% of all visitors stayed one night or longer, which is a trend reflecting Hong Kong's increasing importance as a regional transport hub.

Tourism Commission

The Tourism Commission was established in May 1999 to promote Hong Kong as Asia's premier international city for all visitors. A Tourism Strategy Group, comprising representatives from the Government, the HKTB and various sectors of the tourism industry has been established to advise the Government on tourism development from a strategic perspective.

Attractions and Facilities

Almost any districts of Hong Kong can be considered a tourist destination. The following items are areas generally marked as main attractions.

Hong Kong Island

- Victoria Peak
- Stanley

- Repulse Bay
- Ocean Park
- Victoria Harbour
- Aberdeen Harbour
- Lan Kwai Fong
- Soho

Kowloon

Including New Kowloon

- Hong Kong Art Museum
- Avenue of Stars
- Chungking Mansions
- Clock Tower
- Hong Kong Cultural Centre
- Hong Kong Heritage Discovery Centre
- Hong Kong History Museum
- Hong Kong Observatory
- Kowloon Park
- Nathan Road
- Ocean Terminal
- The Peninsula Hotel
- Hong Kong Science Museum
- Hong Kong Space Museum
- Star Ferry
- Wong Tai Sin Temple

New Territories

Including the Outlying Islands

- Che Kung Temple
- Cheung Chau

- Hong Kong Disneyland Resort
- Hong Kong Heritage Museum
- Hong Kong Railway Museum
- Hong Kong Wetland Park
- Ngong Ping 360
- Ping Shan
- Tai O
- Tian Tan Buddha
- Ting Kau Bridge
- Tsing Ma Bridge
- Tung Chung Fort

Festivals

- Tin Hau Festival
- Cheung Chau Bun Festival
- Buddha's Birthday celebrations at Po Lin Monastery.
- Dragon boat Festival

Accessing Hong Kong

To facilitate entry of visitors, various measures were introduced in 2002. The quota of the Hong Kong Tour Group Scheme of Mainland visitors has been abolished since January 2002.

The number of Mainland travel agents authorised to organise such tours has also increased significantly. Nationals from some 170 countries can visit Hong Kong visa free for period from seven days to 180 days.

The Individual Visit Scheme (IVS) was introduced on July 28, 2003. The Scheme has been gradually extended and now covers Guangdong province, Shanghai, Beijing, Chongqing, Tianjian and nine cities in Fujian, Jiangsu and Zhejiang. In 2006, over 6.6 million Mainland citizens travelled to Hong Kong under the IVS, which is 20.2% more than 2005.

Shopping in Hong Kong

Shopping in Hong Kong have been categorized from "social activity" to a "serious sport". It is an important part of the culture and a way of life. Few cities in the world can rival the experience from an economic, business or social standpoint.

Hong Kong's culture is very much dominated by consumerism. In the early Colonial Hong Kong period, the territory served as a middleman that sold far more than it consumed. Goods were largely sold via mobile hawker units or independent shops, with the majority of trade, utilities, shipping and manufacturing handled by the Hongs. The establishment of banks and deposit institutions allowed people to accumulate savings, and expand their personal finance.

With significant manufacturing outputs, the economy turned around in the 1960s, setting the mall trends in motion. One of the first recognized modern shopping centre was Ocean Terminal. Daimaru opened the flood gate of Japanese goods to Hong Kong in 1966. Deng Xiaoping's 1978 Open Door Policy also made Hong Kong the definitive gateway to China. The people's mindset then begin to change from buying necessity to buying luxury.

Food and clothing supplies were always available for sale, but complex goods did not come about until the arrival of major brand name franchises. In the 1970s and 80s, items like air-conditioners, fans and refrigerators were popular items that eased the hot climate. Major increase in consumer spending continued due to the period of explosive economic growth.

In the late 1970s, one of the first modern shopping development was The Landmark in Central above the MTR station. In 1984 Cityplaza in Taikoo Shing was also redeveloped. A large architectural project at the time was also to connect Ocean Centre to Harbour City shopping mall in Tsim Sha Tsui. The large mall construction movement continued into the 1990s with Pacific Place, Dragon Centre, Time Square, Plaza Hollywood and Festival Walk. Developments also expanded into the New Territories.

Shopping Highlights

- Hong Kong is renowned for its cuisine.
- Custom tailors
- The latest models of Japanese and European watches and electronics.
- Hong Kong is the 4th largest exporter of jewelry in the world specializing in Jade and Gold (Chuk Kam).

Shopping Locale

Antiques-Upper Lascar Row, Hollywood Road

Video Games (regular or mod)-Wan Chai, Sham Shui Po

Computers-Wan Chai, Sham Shui Po, Tsim Sha Tsui, Causeway Bay, Kowloon

Modern Fashion-Time Square

Leather Goods-Tsim Sha Tsui

Fortune Advice-Wong Tai Sin Temple

Japanese Items-Sogo

Bargain-Stanley, Shenzhen

Jewellery

Cars-Gloucester Road, Hong Kong

Advantage

Economic

Basic items for sale do not include duty, sales tax or import taxes. Only specific import goods like alcohol, tobacco, perfumes, cosmetics, cars and petroleum products have taxes associated. For companies, there is a 17.5% corporate tax, which is lower than international standards.

Its close proximity to manufacturing plants in China as well as being a free port provide the territory with significant advantages. Large quantities of goods could be manufactured and transported in short periods of time. Imports from Europe, Japan, US and Taiwan also add international flavor to the mix.

Culture of Hong Kong

The culture of Hong Kong can best be described as a foundation that began with China, and then leaned West for much of the 20th century under constructive British colonialism. Despite the 1997 transfer of sovereignty with the mainland, Hong Kong continues to hold an identity of its own. It can best be summarized as an upbeat, hi-tech and fashionably conscious culture in a super city.

People in the Culture

Chinese people naturally lean toward eastern culture, since demographically they are the majority. Many have adopted western ways with substantial numbers still adhere to traditional Chinese traditions. On various social aspects, the bottom-line Chinese values of "family solidarity", "courtesy" and "saving face" carry significant weight in the culture. Heavy influence are derived from Cantonese culture from the neighbouring province of Guangdong.

There are also substantial communities of Hakka, Fukien, Teochiu and Shanghainese people. On the contrary, people have long been referred to by their origin in China. It wasn't until 1970 when terms like "Hongkongese" were invented. Overall the background of Hong Kong Chinese born after 1945 can be classified as westernized, since they have been influenced by liberal western cultural symbols.

Social

Structurally one of the first law to define people's relationship is the 1972 "Hong Kong Matrimonial Ordinance". The law set the precedence to ban concubinage and same sex marriages with a strict declaration for heterosexual relationships with one partner only.

Other economic changes include families in need of assistance due to both working parents. In particular, foreign domestic workers have become an integral part of the household since the late 1980s.

Languages

Cantonese is the most widely spoken language in Hong Kong. Since the 1997 handover, the government has adopted the "biliterate and trilingual" policy. Under the principle, Chinese and English must both be acknowledged as official languages, with Cantonese being acknowledged as the de facto official spoken dialect of Chinese in Hong Kong, while also accepting the use of Standard Mandarin.

Superstition and Beliefs

Given the relatively modernized way of life, Chinese superstition still plays an integral part of the culture. Concepts like Fung shui are taken quite seriously. Expensive construction projects often include the hiring of consultants, that are believed to make or break a business. Other objects like bagua mirror are still used regularly to shield evils. Numbers in Chinese culture also play a role in people's everyday life. Numbers like "4" are avoided at all cost. Other rituals like not using scissors on Chinese New Year are still around.

Holidays

There are some distinctive holidays celebrated by Hong Kong as part of the eastern culture, not participated in the west except in select overseas Chinese communities. The most well known is Chinese New Year, which occurs after every regular New Year. Other events include Dragon Boat Festival where zongzi is made by the millions at home as part of the tradition. Dragon boats also compete for regional awards. Mid-Autumn Festival is another highly celebrated event with massive purchase of mooncake around Chinese bakery shops.

Pop Culture

Because of years and decades of cantopop dominance in Hong Kong, music in general has been synonymous with the genre. While many other forms of music exist, young cantopop fans continues to be the biggest driver of the market. The influx of mandarin influence has been changing the style. Most artists are essentially multi-language singers, singing in Cantonese and Mandarin nowadays.

Food

Food holds an important place in Hong Kong culture. Restaurants are available in a level of convenience and variety unmatched by anywhere in the world. The fusion of east and west makes Hong Kong unique, especially in the close proximity where one can find any style any time. From dim sum, da been lo, fast food to the most rare of delicacies, Hong Kong carries the reputable label of "Gourmet Paradise" and "World's Fair of Food".

Shopping

Hong Kong is well identified by its materialistic culture and high levels of consumerism. Shops from the lowest end to the most upscale pack the streets in close proximity. The mild weather, low tax and convenience makes Hong Kong a premiere international shopping center. Some popular shopping destination include Mongkok, Tsim Sha Tsui, and Causeway Bay.

Cinema

The industry has been one of the most successful worldwide, especially during the second half of the 20th century. It remains prominent despite a severe slump starting in the mid-1990s. Martial artists and stars such as Jackie Chan and Bruce Lee are known globally, especially in Chinese settlements overseas. Many have transitioned over to Hollywood, including Chow Yun Fat and John Woo.

Mass Media and Publishing

Hong Kong has two broadcast television stations, ATV and TVB. The latter, launched in 1967, was the territory's first free-to-air commercial station, and is currently the predominant TV station in the territory, often garnering more than 90% share of the viewing population. Paid cable and satellite television have also been widespread. The production of Hong Kong's soap drama, comedy series and variety shows have reached mass audiences throughout the Chinese-speaking world.

Magazine and newspaper publishers distribute and print in numerous languages like Chinese and English. The media lean heavily on sensationalism and celebrity gossips. While the practice is criticized, it continues to sell papers. The media is relatively free from government interference compared to that of mainland China, and newspapers are often divided along political lines of support or show skepticism toward the Chinese government in Beijing.

Manhua

Manhua are Hong Kong based comic books that have provided an avenue of expression long before the arrival of television. While readership has fluctuated throughout different decades, the art is one of the most consistent in terms of providing highly affordable entertainment. Manhuas are regularly available at news stands in most street corners. Characteristics of Old Master Q, Chinese Hero and many others have undoubtedly showcased Chinese artwork and stories. Japanese manga have also been translated and fused into local manhua libraries.

Animation

While Hong Kong have had an endless supply from Japanese anime and US disney animations. China have been trying hard to revitalize the industry. Hong Kong have made contributions in recent years with productions like A Chinese Ghost Story: The Tsui Hark Animation and DragonBlade. Most notably companies like Imagi Animation Studios located directly in the territory are now pushing 3D-CG animations to the market.

Cantonese Opera

Cantonese opera is one of the major categories in Chinese opera, originating in southern China's Cantonese culture. The art carries a national identity that goes as far back as the first wave of immigrants to arrive from Shanghai in the 1950s. Sunbeam Theatre is one of the places that hold the tradition. Like all versions of Chinese opera, it is a Chinese art form involving music, singing, martial arts, acrobatics, and acting.

Sports

With limited land resource available, Hong Kong continues to offer recreational and competitive sports. Locally sports in Hong Kong is described as "Club Life". Internationally, Hong Kong have participated in Olympic Games, and numerous other Asian Games events. Major multipurpose venues like Hong Kong Coliseum are found. Others include regular citizen facilities like Macpherson Stadium.

Martial Art

Martial arts in Hong Kong is accepted as a form of entertainment or exercise. Tai chi is one of the most popular, especially among the elderly. There are groups of people practicing the motion in every park at dawn. Many forms of martial arts were also passed down from different generations of Chinese ancestry. Styles like praying mantis, snake fist and Crane are some of the more recognized. The atmosphere is also distinct as people practice outdoor in peaks next to ultra modern high rise buildings.

Leisure

Much time is spent on leisure games like Mahjong. The popularity of the game is apparent when family and friends play for hours together. The image of elderly men playing Chinese chess, surrounded by crowds in observation is common. Checkers are also enjoyed by people of all ages. Today video games is one of the main forms of entertainment among all ages. Japan remains to be the leading importer for software and hardware. Titles like Super Street Fighter II has been highly respected. In the past, Hong Kong had some of the most up-to-date arcades games available outside of Japan. Associations have been made between triad gang hang outs and arcade arenas. Improvement of home console also diminished arcade culture.

Gambling

Hong Kong Jockey Club provides an avenue for horse racing and gambling to mostly middle-aged locals. The club was established in 1844 by the British with the first racecourse built in Happy Valley. The club closed for a few years during World War II due to the Japanese occupation of Hong Kong. In 1975, lottery Mark Six was introduced. And in 2002, the club offered wagerings for soccer world championship games including the English FA Premier League and the World Cup.

Games like mahjong can be played in relaxation or with sizeable money at stake. Plenty of Mahjong shops and parlors are available. Since Hong Kong do not have the space for large scale casinos, its close distance to Macau casinos is the next best thing. All variations of card games are found in Hong Kong. Street smart and gambling tactics have been valued by Hong Kong culture, much to the credit of movies like God of Gamblers in the 1980s.

Transport in Hong Kong

Hong Kong has a highly developed and sophisticated transportation network, encompassing both public and private transport. Over 90% of the daily travels are on public transport, making it the highest in the world.

Travelling on public transport is facilited through use of the Octopus card, an "anonymous" stored value smart card which can be purchased at Mass Transit Railway (MTR) and Kowloon Canton Railway (KCR) stations. It can be used to pay fares on most trains, buses and ferries, and is even accepted at parking meters.

Automated Pedestrian Transport

Escalators and Moving Sidewalks

Hong Kong Island is dominated by steep, hilly terrain, which required the development of unusual methods of transport up and down the slopes. In Central and Western district there is an extensive system of free escalators and moving sidewalks. The Mid-levels Escalator is the longest outdoor covered escalator system in the world, operating downhill until 10 am for commuters going to work, and then operating uphill until midnight.

The Mid-levels Escalator consists of 20 escalators and 3 moving sidewalks. It is 800 meters long, and climbs 135 vertical meters. Total travel time is 20 minutes, but most people walk while the escalator moves to shorten the travel time. Due to its vertical climb, the same distance is equivalent to several miles of zigzagging roads if travelled by car. Daily traffic exceeds 35,000 people. It has been operating since 1993 and cost HK$ 240 million (USD $30 million) to build.

Rail Transport

Hong Kong has an efficient train network. Public transport trains are operated by two companies, the MTR Corporation Limited (MTR) and the Kowloon-Canton Railway Corporation (KCRC). The MTR operates the metro network within inner urban Hong Kong, Kowloon Penisula and northern part of Hong Kong Island with newly developed areas, Tsuen Wan, Tseung Kwan O, Tung Chung, Hong Kong Disneyland and the Hong Kong International Airport, while the KCR network connects the northeastern and northwestern parts of the New Territories with the urban areas of Hong Kong. The Hong Kong Tramways operates a tram service exclusively on northern Hong Kong Island. The Peak Tram connects Central, Hong Kong's CBD, with the Victoria Peak.

Kowloon Canton Railway

There are four systems under the KCR, namely East Rail, West Rail, Ma On Shan Rail and Light Rail. There are several extensions planned or under construction, including the Lok Ma Chau Spur line, the Kowloon Southern Link, the Sha Tin to Central Link and the Northern Link. Note that the Light Rail possesses many characteristics of a tramway, including running on streets with other traffics (at grades) on some of its tracks and providing services for the public in New Territories West, including Tuen Mun and Yuen Long.

Mass Transit Railway

There are altogether seven lines in the MTR system, with a total of 53 stations. The seven lines are Kwun Tong Line,

Tsuen Wan Line, Island Line, Tseung Kwan O Line, Tung Chung Line, the Airport Express and the Disneyland Resort Line. The former 5 lines provide ordinary metro services, whereas the Airport Express provides a direct link from the Hong Kong International Airport into the city centre, while the Disneyland Resort Line exclusively takes passengers to Hong Kong Disneyland.

All trains and most KCR/MTR metro stations feature air conditioning which allows the visitor intimidated by Hong Kong's tropical heat to literally shop and work all day without having to experience outside temperatures.

Tramways

The Hong Kong Tramways is the tram (streetcar) system run exclusively with double deckers. The electric tram system was proposed in 1881; however nobody was willing to invest in a system at the time. In August 1901, the Second Tramway Bill was introduced and passed into law as the 1902 Tramway Ordinance. Hong Kong Tramway Electric Company Limited, a British company, was authorised to take the responsibilities in construction and daily operation. It was soon taken over by another company, Electric Tranction Company of Hong Kong Limited and then the name was changed to Hong Kong Tramways Company Limited in 1910.

The rail system is 13 kilometres (8 miles) long, with a total track length of 30 km (18.6 miles), and it runs together with other vehicles on the street. Its operation relies on the 550V direct current (d.c.) from the overhead cables, on 3'6" gauge (1067 mm) tracks. The trams provide service to only part of Hong Kong Island: they run on a double track along the northern coast of Hong Kong Island from Kennedy Town to Shau Kei Wan, with a single clockwise-running track of about 3 kilometres (1.9 miles) around Happy Valley Racecourse.

Funicular Railways

The Peak Tram is a funicular railway service which was inaugurated in 1888. It carries both tourists and residents to the upper levels of Hong Kong Island. It provides the most direct route to Victoria Peak and offers scenic views over Victoria Harbour and the skyscrapers of Hong Kong.

Road Transport

Buses

Bus services have a long history in Hong Kong. In 2005, five companies operate franchised public bus services. There are also a variety of non-franchised public buses services, including feeder bus services to railway stations operated by the railway companies, and residents' services for residential estates (particularly those in the New Territories).

The five franchised bus companies are:

- Kowloon Motor Bus Company (1933) Limited;
- Citybus Limited;
- Long Win Bus Company Limited;
- New World First Bus Services Limited; and
- New Lantao Bus Company (1973) Limited.

Founded in 1933, the Kowloon Motor Bus Company (1933) Limited (KMB) is one of the largest privately-owned public bus operators in the world. KMB's fleet consist of about 4,300 buses on 420 routes and a staff of over 13,000. In 1979, Citybus began its operation in Hong Kong with one double-decker, providing shuttle service for the Hong Kong dockyard. It later expanded into operating a residential bus route between City One, Shatin and Kowloon Tong MTR station. New World First Bus Services Limited was established in 1998, taking over China Motor Bus's franchise to provide bus services on Hong Kong Island together with Citybus. NWFB's owner company later bought Citybus, but the two companies have basically been operating independently.

Public Light Buses

Public light buses (widely referred to as minibuses, or sometimes maxicabs, a de facto share taxi) run the length and breadth of Hong Kong, through areas which the standard bus lines cannot or do not reach as frequently, quickly or directly. Minibuses carry a maximum of 16 passengers; no standees are allowed.

The Hong Kong Transport Department (HKTD) allows and licenses the operation of two types of public light buses-(1) green minibuses that have route numbers, stop at designated stops and whom have their fares, service and frequency regulated by the HKTD; and (2) red minibuses that may or may not have regular routes, may or may not be numbered, may or may not have fixed stops and whose fares and service levels are not regulated by HKTD.

Red minibuses do often provide more convenient supplementary transportation services for riders which aren't serviced by green minibuses or other public buses, and are thus quite popular to use. Where green minibus drivers are paid fixed wages to drive their routes, red minibus drivers often rely on their pick-up fares for a living and thus are often seen to be more aggressive drivers. The prevalence of aggressive driving has resulted in the HKTD making it mandatory for Hong Kong minibuses to be equipped with large read-out spedometers which allow passengers to track the speed at which minibus drivers operate. At the current moment, minibuses are not allowed to travel in excess of 80km/h before the spedometer makes delivers and audible warning signal to the driver and passengers.

The HKTD has also regulated, after a series of minibus accidents, that all new minibuses brought into service after August 2005 have safetybelts installed, and riders use these safety belts when riding in a minibus.

Taxis

As of 2005, there were 18,138 taxis in Hong Kong, 15,250 of which were urban taxis, 2,838 New Territories taxis, and 50 Lantau taxis. Every day, they serve 1.1 million, 207,900, and 1,400 passengers respectively. Taxis carry an average of one million passengers each day, occupying about 12% of the daily patronage carried by all modes of public transport in Hong Kong.

Most of the taxis in Hong Kong run on LPG (liquified petroleum gas) for protection of the environment. In August 2000 a one-off cash grant was paid to taxi owners who replaced their diesel taxi with an LPG one. By the end of 2003, over 99.8% of the taxi fleet in Hong Kong ran on LPG. Since August 2001, all newly purchased taxis run on LPG.

Taxi fare is charged according to the taximeter; however, additional charges on the faretable may apply, such as road tolls and luggage fees. Red urban taxis are the most expensive, while blue Lantau taxis are the cheapest. The standard of service among different kinds of taxis is mostly the same. The reason for having three types of taxis is to ensure service availability in less populated regions, as running in the urban centre is considered to be more profitable.

Private Cars

There are 517,000 cars licensed in Hong Kong, 64% of which are private cars. In terms of private car ownership, the number of cars per capita is half that of Singapore and one-third that of Taiwan. Private cars are most popular in newly developed areas such as Lantau and areas near the boundary with mainland China, as there are fewer public transportation options, and more parking spaces compared to other areas of Hong Kong.

Most cars are right hand drive models, from Japanese or European manufacturers. Hong Kong does not allow left hand drive vehicles to be primarily registered in Hong Kong. However, Hong Kong registered vehicles may apply for secondary mainland Chinese registration plates, and these can be driven across the boundary to mainland China; likewise, left hand drive cars seen in Hong Kong are usually primarily registered in mainland China and carry supplementary Hong Kong registration plates.

Cars are subjected to a first-time registration tax, which varies from 35% to over 100%, based on the size and value of the car. The level of vehicle taxation was increased swingeingly by a law passed on June 2, 1982 to discourage private car ownership, and also as an incentive to buy cars to buy smaller, more efficient cars, as these have less tax levied on them. First-time registration tax was doubled, annual licensing fees were increased by 300%, and $0.7 duty was imposed on each litre of on light oils.

In addition to the heavy traffic at times, parking may be problematic. Due to high urban density, there are not many filling stations; Petrol in Hong Kong averages around US$1.55 per litre, of which around half the cost is taxes. It was suggested in the news that that the government had deliberately impeded the use of new environmentally friendly diesel engines by allowing only light goods vehicles to be fuelled by diesel.

While it cannot be determined why exactly the government does not allow private cars to be fuelled by diesel, it has been pointed out that the government does receive a tax that is 150% of the actual fuel cost. This is mostly to discourage car ownership for environmental reason.

There is a waiting list for local driving tests, while a full (private car) driver's license valid for 10 years costs around US$115. Residents of Hong Kong holding foreign licenses can be issued a Hong Kong drivers license, provided that they present a valid license from a "recognised" country. Private car owners often provide transport service for a nominal fee as if it was a taxi, hence the cultural term white card was created to describe these drivers.

Maritime Transport

Internal Routes

Most ferry services are provided by licensed ferry operators. As of September 2003, there were 27 regular licensed passenger ferry services operated by 11 licensees, serving outlying islands, new towns and inner-Victoria Harbour. Two of the routes operated by the Star Ferry are franchised. Additionally, 78 "kai-to" ferries are licensed to serve remote coastal settlements.

The following companies operate ferry services in Hong Kong:

Star Ferry:

- Central to Tsim Sha Tsui
- Wanchai to Tsim Sha Tsui
- Central to Hung Hom
- Wanchai to Hung Hom
- Harbour Tour (Circular between Tsim Sha Tsui, Central, Wan Chai, and Hung Hom)

New World First Ferry:

- Central to Cheung Chau, Mui Wo, and Peng Chau
- Tsim Sha Tsui, Mui Wo, Cheung Chau (Weekends Only)
- Peng Chau, Mui Wo, Chi Ma Wan, and Cheung Chau
- North Point to Hung Hom and Kowloon City
- Tuen Mun to Tung Chung

Hong Kong & Kowloon Ferry:

- Lamma Island to Central and Aberdeen

HKR International Limited:

- Discovery Bay Transportation Services-Discovery Bay to Central

Park Island Transport Company Ltd.:

- Ma Wan to Central
- Ma Wan to Tsuen Wan

Fortune Ferry

- North Point to Kwun Tong

Coral Sea Ferry

- Sai Wan Ho to Kwun Tong

External Routes

Fastferry hydrofoil and catamaran service is available at all times of the week between Hong Kong and Macau. TurboJet provides 24-hour services, connecting Central and Macau. Its highest frequency is 15 minutes. It also provides the following regular services:

- Hong Kong International Airport to Shenzhen Airport/ Macau/Guangzhou (East River Guangzhou Ferry Terminal)
- Tsim Sha Tsui to Guangzhou
- Macau to Shenzhen Airport
- Tsim Sha Tsui to Macau

New World First Ferry (Macau) provides an 17-hour service daily between Tsim Sha Tsui and Macau, with the highest frequency of 30 minutes.

Chu Kong Passenger Transport (CKS) connects Hong Kong to cities in Guangdong province, including Zhuhai (Jiuzhou), Shenzhen (Shekou), Zhongshan, Lianhua Shan (Panyu), Jiangmen, Gongyi, Sanbu, Gaoming, Heshan, Humen, Nanhai, Shunde, Doumen, Zhaoqing.

Other

Gondola Lifts

This image has an uncertain copyright status and is pending deletion. You can comment on the removal.

There are two gondola lift systems in Hong Kong:

- Ocean Park, Hong Kong Island-A 1.5 km in-park cable car system between Nam Long Shan Headland and Wong Chuk Hang, opened in 1977.
- Ngong Ping Skyrail on Lantau Island, a 5.7 km cableway between Tung Chung MTR station and Ngong Ping Terminal near Po Lin Monastery, opened on September 18, 2006.

Infrastructure

Ports and Harbours

The port of Hong Kong has always been a key factor in the development and prosperity of the special administrative region, which is strategically located on the Far East trade routes and is in the geographical centre of the fast-developing Asia-Pacific Basin. The sheltered harbour provides good access and a safe haven for vessels calling at the port from around the world. In terms of tonnage of shipping using its facilities, cargo handled and the number of passengers carried, Hong Kong is undoubtedly one of the major ports of the world.

The Victoria Harbour is one of the busiest ports in the world. An average of 220,000 ships visit the harbour each year, including both oceanliners and river vessels, for both goods and passengers. The container port in Hong Kong is one of the busiest in the world. The Kwai Chung Terminal operates 24 hours a day. Together with other facilities in Victoria Harbour, they handled more than 20 million TEUs in 2003. Some 400 container liners serve Hong Kong weekly, connecting to over 500 destinations around the world.

Airports

Hong Kong only has one active international airport. The famous former Hong Kong International Airport at Kai Tak was retired in favour of the recently constructed Hong Kong International Airport, also known as Chek Lap Kok International Airport. The airport now serves as a transport hub for East Asia, and as the hub for Cathay Pacific Airways, Dragonair, Hong Kong Express, Hong Kong Airlines (former CR Airways) and Air Hong Kong. Ferry services link the airport with several piers in Pearl River Delta, where immigrations and customs are exempted.

The airport is the third busiest airport for passenger traffic in Asia, and the world's second busiest airport for cargo traffic in 2003. In terms of international traffic, the airport is the third busiest for passenger traffic and the busiest for cargo since its operation in 1998. It is popular with travellers-from 2001 to 2005 Hong Kong International Airport has been voted the world's best airport in an annual survey of several million passengers worldwide by Skytrax.

According to the Guinness World Records, the passenger terminal of the HKIA is the world's largest airport terminal building, with a covered area of 550,000 m^2 and recently increased to 570,000 m^2. The Airport Core Programme was the most expensive airport project in the world.

Shek Kong Airfield, located near Yuen Long, is a military airfield for the People's Liberation Army, which is of limited operating capabilities due to surrounding terrains. The only aircraft operating on the airfield are PLA's Z-9 helicopters, which is the license-built version of the Eurocopter Dauphin.

Heliports

Hong Kong has three heliports. Shun Tak Heliport (ICAO: VHST) is located in the Hong Kong-Macau Ferry Terminal, by the Shun Tak Centre, in Sheung Wan, on Hong Kong Island. Another is located in Southwest Kowloon, near Kowloon station. The other is located inside Hong Kong International Airport.

Heli Express operates regular helicopter service between Macao Heliport (ICAO:VMMH) on the Macau Ferry Terminal in Macau and the Shun Tak Helipot. There are around 16 flights daily. Flights take approximately 20 minutes in the eight-seater aircraft. There are also a number of helipads across the territory, including the roof of the Peninsula Hotel (which is the only rooftop helipad in the territory, excluding the rooftop heliport of Shun Tak Centre and those in hospitals) and Cheung Chau Island, between Tung Wan Beach and Kwun Yam Beach.

Highways

There are a total of 1,831 km of paved highways in Hong Kong. These roads are built to British standards with maximum of three lanes with hard shoulders.

There are 9 roads classified as highways in Hong Kong and re-numbered from 1 to 9 in 2004. Route 1 to 3 are in north-south direction and crossing three Cross-Harbour Tunnels while others are in east-west direction:

- Route 1: Southern District <> Causeway Bay <> Tsim Sha Tsui <> Mong Kok <> Sha Tin
- Route 2: Eastern District <> Kwun Tong <> Wong Tai Sin <> Sha Tin

- Route 3: Central & Western District <> Tai Kok Tsui <> Sham Shui Po <> Kwai Tsing <> Tsuen Wan <> Yuen Long
- Route 4: Eastern District <> Wan Chai <> Causeway Bay <> Central & Western District
- Route 5: Kowloon City <> Wong Tai Sin <> Sham Shui Po <> Kwai Tsing <> Tsuen Wan
- Route 7: Tseung Kwan O <> Kwun Tong <> Wong Tai Sin <> Sham Shui Po <> Kwai Tsing
- Route 8: Kwai Tsing <> Lantau Island North <> Tung Chung <> Airport (Extension to Sha Tin in the future)
- Route 9: Circular Route linking the whole New Territories (Sha Tin, Tai Po, Northern District, Yuen Long, Tuen Mun, Tsuen Wan)

Route 6 (Hong Kong) is an unbuilt and proposed highway.

There are 120 CCTV cameras monitoring traffic on these highways and connecting roads.

Bridges and Tunnels

There are 15 vehicular tunnels (3 currently under construction) in Hong Kong. They include three cross-harbour tunnels and nine road tunnels.

The other road tunnels and bridges which are proposed or under construction are:

- Nam Wan Tunnel (under construction)
- Eagle's Nest Tunnel (under construction)
- Sha Tin Heights Tunnel (under construction)
- Stonecutters Bridge (under construction)
- Hong Kong-Zhuhai-Macau Bridge (Proposed)

Bank of China Tower

The Bank of China Tower (abbr. BOC Tower; Traditional Chinese) is one of the most recognized skyscrapers in Central, Hong Kong. It houses the headquarters for the Bank of China

(Hong Kong) Limited. Designed by Pritzker Prize-winning Chinese American architect I. M. Pei, the building is 315 meters (1,034 feet) high with two masts reaching 369 meters (1,209 feet) high. The 70 story building was built in 1989 and is located near Central MTR station. This was the tallest building in Hong Kong and Asia from 1989 to 1992, and it was the first building outside the United States to break the 305 m (1,000 foot) mark. That also means it was the tallest outside America from its completion year, 1990. It is now the third tallest skyscraper in Hong Kong, after Two International Finance Center and Central Plaza.

The structural expressionism adopted in the design of this building resembles growing bamboo shoots, symbolising livelihood and prosperity. The whole structure is supported by the five steel columns at the corners of the building, with the triangular frameworks transferring the weight of the structure onto these five columns.

The building has been criticised by some practitioners of Feng Shui for its sharp edges and its negative symbolism by the numerous 'X' shapes in its original design, though Pei modified the design to some degree before construction following this feedback. The building's profile from some angles resembles that of a cleaver. In Feng Shui, this is described as a cleaver building and it is not difficult to observe that it is facing the HSBC Hong Kong headquarters building in this guise.

A small observation deck on the 43rd floor of the building is open to the public; visits to the main observation deck on the 70th floor are by appointment only.

The BOC Tower's bold futuristic design has made it into popular culture. It is the only Hong Kong landmark included in the city-building/simulation computer games SimCity 3000 and SimCity 4. The digitally modified facade of the building is featured in the science fiction television series Star Trek: Voyager as the Starfleet "Communications Research Center".

The formal address of the building is: 1 Garden Road, Central, Hong Kong.

City Hall, Hong Kong

The Hong Kong City Hall is a building located at Edinburgh Place, Central, Hong Kong Island, Hong Kong. Since Hong Kong does not designate itself or any part of itself as a city, there is no mayor or city council; therefore, the City Hall does not hold the offices of a city government, unlike most city halls around the world. Instead, it is a complex providing municipal services, including performing venues and libraries. The City Hall is managed by the Government's Leisure and Cultural Services Department. The Urban Council managed the City Hall (through the Urban Services Department) and held its meetings there prior to its dissolution in December 1999.

History

First Generation

The first City Hall of Hong Kong, which existed from 1869 to 1933, was located at the current site of the HSBC Hong Kong headquarters building.

Design and Function

The City Hall was built on Government land, and funds were raised for its construction, which started in 1866, from public subscriptions. The two-storey hall was designed by Maître Hermite, a French architect, in a magnificent renaissance style, with cupolae, colonnades and arches. The facilities available for use by the local community included a theatre, library, museum and assembly rooms. A fountain, sponsored by Dent & Co. was located at the front (south side) of the Hall. The building was inaugurated by HRH Prince Alfred, Duke of Edinburgh on June 28, 1869 on his visit to the colony. The land was acquired by the Hong Kong Bank in 1933 for its 3rd generation headquarters, so that the western part of City Hall was pulled down. The remaining part was demolished in 1947 to make way for the Bank of China Building.

Second Generation

The City Hall complex was built in the late 1950s on a 10,000-square-metre plot of land on the newly reclaimed seafront, and was officially opened on March 2, 1962 by then Governor Robert Brown Black. It was placed under the responsibility of the Urban Council.

Design

It was designed in 1956, by British architects Ron Phillips and Alan Fitch. With its clean lines and stark geometric forms, the new Hall is an example of the International style fashionable at the time. The structure was constructed using steel and concrete, and much of the equipment was of steel, glass and anodised aluminium.

The two separate blocks and gardens were laid out as a cohesive whole, along a central axis. The entrance to the lower block (exhibition hall) of the City Hall formed an axis with Queen's Pier to lend a sense of occasion to visiting dignatories. One major consideration was juxtaposing the city bustle whilst maximising public access to the surrounding area. Thus, the out-sized public areas of the Memorial Gardens and the piazza in front were conceived as a natural extension to promote the "freedom of movement and a sense of unlimited space".

Function

The most important civic function performed by City Hall was as the ceremonial location for swearing in of successive Governors since it was inaugurated.

City Hall's Concert hall and theatre have been an important home to the performing arts in Hong Kong since its inauguration. A number of culture events, including the Hong Kong Festival, Hong Kong Arts Festival in 1973, Asian Arts Festival in 1976, the Hong Kong International Film Festival in 1977, and the International Arts Carnival in 1982 were hosted there. The conference room of the former Urban Council was also at the lower building of the City Hall.

The High block once housed Hong Kong's principal public library, until a new Central library was opened in 2001; the Hong Kong art gallery (which became the Hong Kong Art Museum in 1969) began life there on the tenth and eleventh floors. The Hong Kong Museum of History relocated in 1975, and the Hong Kong Museum of Art also moved out of City Hall in 1991. The City Hall Memorial Garden at the north-western quadrant is a walled garden. It is a popular spot and obligatory backdrop for photographs of couples who celebrate their marriage in the City Hall Registry. Within the garden is a regular dodecagon shrine with a embedded memorial (Roll of Honour and Plaque) to those killed in Hong Kong during the World War II (1941-1945).

Summary of Facilities

The complex has two buildings and a garden.

The High Block, a 12-storey building, is in the south-western end and houses a number of government facilities, including:

- City Hall Library, an eight-storey building., which in the past served as the central library of Hong Kong (on the 9th-11th floors)
- Exhibition Gallery, 260-square feet.
- Recital Hall with 111-seats.
- Committee Rooms: two 40-seat committee rooms (on the 7th floor)
- Marriage Registry (on the 1st floor)

The 3-storey Low Block is at the eastern end, with the following facilities:

- Concert Hall, with 1,434 seats and 60 standees at the mezzanine level.
- Restaurants and a cafe-continental (Deli and Wine), Chinese (City Hall Maxim's Palace) and European (Maxim's Restaurant) cuisines
- The URBTIX Box Office
- Exhibition Hall, 590-square metres.
- Theatre with 463 seats.
- Performing Arts Shop
- an enquiry counter

Venue for 2009 East Asian Games

To organize the 5th East Asian Games that will be hosted in Hong Kong in 2009, Hong Kong Stadium will be one of the venue of HKEAG.

Hong Kong Convention and Exhibition Centre

The Hong Kong Convention and Exhibition Centre is one of the two major convention and exhibition venues in Hong Kong, along with AsiaWorld-Expo. It is located in Wan Chai North, Hong Kong Island. Built along the Victoria Harbour, it is linked by covered walkways to nearby hotels and commercial buildings.

Construction

The original building was built on reclaimed land off Gloucester Road in 1988. The glass curtain was the world's largest at the time, overlooking the Victoria Harbour on three sides.

The second phase of the centre, located on an artificial island, was constructed from 1994 to 1997, and features a bird-like rooftop (also referred to as a turtle by some critics). It is connected to the old phase with an atrium link-a sky bridge, and to Convention Road with two road bridges. The project took only 48 months from reclamation to completion, which is extremely fast for a building project of this size. The main constructor of the extension was a joint venture named Hip Hing Construction Co Ltd Dragages et Travaux Publics. The atrium link will be rebuilt and expanded.

The complex's construction was financed by New World Development, with the Renaissance Harbour View Hotel, Grand Hyatt and Harbour View Apartments on top of it.

The HKCEC has a total internal exhibition area of more than 28,000 square metres with 16-metre headroom and spans ranging from 26 m to 81 m. Its multi-curved steel roof has a total area of 40,000 m^2, while the 7,000 m^2 fully glazed main entrance foyer has a clear headroom of about 60 metres.

Convention Facilities Statistics

- 5 exhibition halls: 46,600 m^2
- 2 convention halls: 6,100 m^2; total seating for 6,100
- 2 theatres: 800 m^2; total seating for 1,000
- 52 meeting rooms: 6,900 m^2
- Pre-function areas: 8,000 m^2
- 7 restaurants: total seating for 1,870
- Business centre: 150 m^2
- Carpark spaces parking: for 1,300 cars and 50 vans
- Total available rental space: 63,580 m^2
- Capacity: 140,000 visitors per day

Functions held at the Site

Numerous functions are held at the HKCEC each year, including exhibitions, conventions/meetings, banquets and other special events.

The centre hosts more than 45 international trade fairs for buyers from more than 100 countries each year, including the world's largest leather fair and watch and clock fair. The regular international fairs for giftware, toys, fashion, jewellery, electronics and optical products are Asia's largest.

The HKCEC also includes provisions for video-conferencing, teleconferencing, satellite links, simultaneous interpretation in up to eight languages, audio-visual equipment, foyer registration space, and event signage.

It also served as the site of the Hong Kong handover ceremony, which signified the end of British colonial rule.

Awards

The centre has won a number of awards, including "Best Convention and Exhibition Centre in Asia Pacific" in the Competitive Enterprise Institute (CEI) Asia Pacific annual survey by organizers of exhibitions and conferences.

2005

- Golden Bauhinia Cantonese Restaurant Sous Chef Lui Yau Wing won Gold Award
- Distinction Award in 'Deep-fried Dish Category' in the Best of the Best Culinary Awards 2005 by the Hong Kong Tourism Board
- Voted Best Convention & Exhibition Centre" in 16th TTG Travel Awards 2005
- Voted Asia Pacific's Leading Conference Centre for the third consecutive year at the 11th World Travel Awards by tens of thousands travel agents from around the world.

2004

- "The CIM Accolade Award 2004"
- Voted "Best Convention and Exhibition Centre"

2002

- Golden Bauhinia Cantonese Restaurant won Gold Award in 'Lobster Category' and 'Bean Curd Category' in the Best of the Best Culinary Award
- Voted "Best Exhibition Centre" in Asia Pacific for the second consecutive year by exhibition organisers in the annual exhibition venue survey
- Voted "Best Overseas Centre, Meetings Category" for the ninth consecutive year
- Second Prize in the 53rd Sapporo Snow Festival

The HKCEC had also won awards in previous years.

Restaurants and Bars

Gaddi's

Gaddi's has long been regarded as one of the finest and most elegant French cuisine French restaurants in Hong Kong. It is known for establishing one of the first Chef's Tables in Hong Kong which allows the diners to have their meals in a special table set outside the restaurant's kitchen, where diners can watch their meals being prepared.

Felix

The bar-restaurant Felix, located on the 28th floor, was designed by Philippe Starck. One of the more unusual and considered notable design features of the hotel is the layout of the 28th floor men's washrooms, which feature urinals facing the window, offering a wide panoramic view to the male guests.

Felix was ranked 47th and 49th in Restaurant magazine's best 50 restaurants in the world in 2004 and 2005 respectively.

The Lobby

The Peninsula Lobby Lounge also serves traditional English-style high tea, reminiscent of Hong Kong's colonial era.

Awards

The Peninsula Hotel Hong Kong has been recognized as an internationally leading hotel in many areas. It has received awards from Condé Nast Traveler magazine, Travel + Leisure, and other industry organizations.

In Popular Culture

The Peninsula is featured in several movies, including:

- Soldier of Fortune(1955)
- The Man with the Golden Gun (1974)
- Gorgeous(1999)

The hotel is also featured in the following TV programs:

- The Luxury Travel Show
- The Love Boat
- Dynasty
- China Rose(1983)
- I Spy
- Noble House

TOURISM IN JAPAN

Tourists visit spots in all prefectures in Japan. Among these are quiet national parks, centuries-old Buddhist temples and shrines, and the high-technology shopping areas of Akihabara. These spots can be reached by trains, buses, walking, and taxi.

Traveling Tips

Customs

There are no stringent religious obligations nor criminal punishments because of them. Most Shinto shrines and Buddhist temples permit photography, though the use of tripods and flash might be restricted both there and at castles, gardens, museums, and elsewhere.

Language

All Japanese people speak Japanese, but older people in some areas speak only the local dialect, which may not be mutually comprehensible with standard Japanese. English is by far the most widely known foreign language, but relatively few Japanese people speak English well. Major tourist spots and trains have displays in both Japanese and English. The Japan National Tourist Organization provides free travel guides, and books are available on how to travel in Japan. When one gets lost, it would be helpful to find a koban (police box) or a large store and ask for help. Police officers will attempt to be helpful and are good at giving directions, but except in areas popular with tourists may not be able to speak English or other foreign languages. If one is unable to communicate verbally, then it may prove useful to carry a pen and paper around, as Japanese are generally better at reading English than speaking it. Even if their English is poor, all Japanese people learn to read and write Japanese in Roman letters in Grade 5.

Directions

Be aware that Japanese maps are not necessarily oriented to the North or, especially in the case of sketch maps, in any particular direction. With the exception of the city of Sapporo, Japanese addresses are not based on a rectangular grid but on a series of hierarchical units, ending in the block and the lot within the block. Lot numbers are not sequential as they are in many other countries but are assigned when the lot is developed. It is therefore fairly easy to locate the general part of the city you want to go to but sometimes difficult to find the specific address. Especially in residential and small-scale shopping neighbourhoods, there are often maps of the surrounding area, showing blocks and lots, by the side of the road.

Money

The yen (pronounced [en]) is the currency in use throughout the country. Exchange services are available at the airport, larger post offices, and banks. Automatic teller machines in Japanese post offices accept check and debit cards in the PLUS and Cirrus networks. Most larger stores and hotels that deal with a lot of foreign tourists accept credit cards, but in smaller stores and in the countryside credit cards are generally not accepted. Tipping is not customary in Japan. Japanese people may actually be insulted by tipping as they interpret it as implying that they will not do their jobs properly unless bribed. Tipping is however not unknown in hotels that cater to foreign tourists. Carrying around large amounts of money is generally safe, as crime rates are low, and it is perfectly normal to make relatively large payments, such as those for airline tickets and hotel bills, in cash. Few establishments accept personal checks.

Shopping

Major department stores and gift shops wrap items for little or no fees. Electronics are available for Japan's 100 volt electric supply as well as for overseas specifications; buyers should ask sales personnel whether an item can be used in any particular country. Models made for the international market have worldwide warranties; others may have warranties valid only within Japan. The national 5% consumption tax on all products can be waived for large purchases which will be taken out of the country.

Trouble

Even with a rising crime rate, Japan remains one of the safest countries in the world. There is only a small chance of being a victim and it is generally safe to walk around at night. It is best to avoid yakuza (professional gangsters), even if they seem friendly, as they may attempt extortion on foreigners. The emergency telephone numbers are 110 for the police department and 119 for the fire and ambulance services. The police have a reputation for being strict, sometimes a little rough, with suspected criminals whom they have arrested but otherwise can be expected to behave very correctly. Do not be surprised if a police officer comes to attention when approached.

Popular Sightseeing Spots in Japan

- Hiroshima Prefecture:
  - Hiroshima Peace Memorial-The remains of the Hiroshima Prefectural Promotion Hall after the atomic bombing.
  - Hiroshima Castle
  - Hiroshima Municipal Stadium, home of the Carp
  - Itsukushima Shrine, a World Heritage Site
- Hyogo Prefecture:
  - Himeji Castle-One of the finest surviving 17th century Japanese castles.
  - Kobe-Port, Chinatown, Western influence, cruise on Inland Sea
- Kyoto Prefecture:
  - 1600 Buddhist temples, 400 Shinto shrines
  - Nijo Castle
  - Kyoto Imperial Palace
  - Various Japanese gardens
  - Uji, including the Byodo-in
  - Amanohashidate, one of the Three Views of Japan

- Nara Prefecture:
    * Todai-ji-The world's largest wooden building hosting the world's largest gilded bronze Buddha; part of UNESCO World Heritage Site
    * Horyu-ji-The world's oldest wooden building hosting 115 of the National Treasures and 1,955 of the important cultural properties; the 1st UNESCO World Heritage Site of Japan.
    * Other Buddhist temples and Shinto shrines including Kasuga Shrine
    * The remains of the Heijo Palace
- Traditional towns:
    * Tsumago, Magome-Nakasendo is one of the roads from Old Tokyo (Edo) and Kyoto passes through the Nagano prefecture. Some of the post towns (shuku) along this road have been preserved and show the lifestyles of both the commoners and the high ranking officials.
    * Gassho-zukuri are traditional style houses from the mountain region of Gifu prefecture. A visit to Shirakawago and Takayama are well worth the effort. In Takayama be sure to visit Hida No Sato, an outdoor museum that allows you to walk around the inside of the houses, visit the tea house for free tea and senbei, and enjoy walk around the village.
- Tochigi Prefecture:
    * Nikko-Nikko Tosho-gu, mausoleum and shrine to Shogun Tokugawa Ieyasu; other nearby temples and shrines
- Miyagi Prefecture:
    * Matsushima, one of the Three Views of Japan
- Mie Prefecture:
    * Ise Grand Shrine

Other common spots to visit:

- Three Views of Japan-Japan's most famous scenic spots.
- Tokyo:
    * See Tourism in Tokyo
- Kanagawa Prefecture:
    * Yokohama-The first city that opened to foreigners in the Edo period.
- Mount Fuji

Famous events in Japan:

- Hokkaido
    * Sapporo Snow Festival

Sports

Professional, company, university, and amateur athletes compete in sports throughout Japan.

- Sumo, especially six annual Grand Sumo tournaments at Tokyo's Ryogoku Kokugikan and in Nagoya, Osaka, and Fukuoka
- Baseball at stadiums such as the Tokyo Dome and other locations for Nippon Professional Baseball
- Soccer, especially the professional J. League
- The Studio Ghibli museum.

Japan National Tourist Organization

The Japan National Tourist Organization, or JNTO, is provided so that visitors who do not speak Japanese can enjoy traveling in Japan more easily.

National Treasures of Japan

The Ministry of Education, Culture, Sports, Science and Technology of the government of Japan designates the most famous of the nation's cultural properties as National Treasures (??: kokuho). Examples of the types of works that receive this designation are:

- Buildings such as castles, temples, shrines
- Paintings, scrolls, sutras, and works of calligraphy

- Statues in stone, bronze, wood, lacquer or other materials
- Crafts, such as pottery, lacquer ware, carvings, metals, netsuke, swords and textiles
- Archeological and historical artifacts, including burial objects, documents, and letters
- People, called "living treasures"

Many of Japan's national treasures are in museums such as the national museums in Tokyo, Kyoto, and Nara. The prefectural and city governments also operate public museums, and these and private museums also house national treasures. Many Buddhist temples and Shinto shrines, castles and similar installations also open their buildings and grounds to the public, and some have museums as well. The Imperial Household of Japan holds many national treasures. Kyoto boasts about one in five national treasures. The term Living National Treasure is an informal designation for a person whom the government has recognized as exemplary in carrying on Japanese traditions. Performing artists in genres including noh, bunraku, and kabuki, and artists and artisans in traditional crafts, have received this distinction.

Former and Present National Treasures

The word "National Treasure" has been used since 1897. However, the term "National Treasure" is different before and after 1950. Before 1950, all the nation-designated cultural properties were called "National Treasure." At that time, 5824 art works and 1059 buildings were National Treasures. On August 29, 1950, the Law for the Protection of Cultural Properties were enforced and all National Treasures were regarded as "Important Cultural Properties". Some of them have been designated as new "National Treasures" since June 9, 1951.

TOURISM IN INDONESIA

Tourism in Indonesia is an important component of the Indonesian economy and an important source of foreign exchange revenues. With a vast archipelago of more than 17,000 islands, the second longest shoreline in the world, 300 different ethnic groups and 250 distinct languages, and tropical climate throughout the year, nature and culture are two major components of Indonesian tourism.

Tourism in Indonesia is currently overseen by the Ministry of Culture and Tourism. International tourist campaigns have been focusing largely on tropical destination with white sand beaches and blue sky imageries. Beach resorts and hotels were developed in some Indonesia islands, with Bali island as the primary destination. Cultural tourism is also an important part of Indonesia tourism industry. Toraja, Prambanan and Borobudur temples, Yogyakarta and Minangkabau are popular destinations for cultural tourism, apart from many Hindu festivities in Bali. About 5 million foreign tourists have visited Indonesia annually since 2000.

However, tourism development had sometimes clashed with local people, that has created criticism over Indonesia's tourism industry. Most of the disputes were related over land possession, local traditions (adat) and the impact of tourism development to the local people. In another area, tourism industry in Indonesia faces major threats. Since 2002, several warnings have been issued by some countries over terrorist threats and ethnic/religious conflicts in some areas, which significantly reduces the number of foreign visitors.

Statistics

Indonesian Tourism Statistics

Year	International visitors	Average stay (days)
2000	5,064,217	12.26
2001	5,153,620	10.49
2002	5,033,400	9.79
2003	4,467,021	9.69
2004	5,321,165	9.47
2005	5,002,101	9.05

As with most countries, domestic tourists are by far the largest market segment. The biggest movement of domestic tourists is during the annual Eid ul-Fitr, locally known as "lebaran". During this period, which is a 2 week holiday after the month of Ramadan fasting, many city-dwelling Muslim Indonesians visit relatives in their home towns. Intercity traffic is at its peak and often an additional surcharge is applied during this time.

Over the 5 years up to 2006, attention has been focused on generating more domestic tourism. Competition amongst budget airlines has increased the number of domestic air travellers throughout the country. Recently, the Ministry of Labour legislated to create long weekends by combining public holidays that fall close to weekends, except in the case of important religious holidays. During these long weekends, most hotels in popular destinations are fully booked.

Since 2000, there have been, on average, 5 million foreign tourists each year, who spend an average of US$ 100 per day (see table). With an average visit duration of 9-12 days, Indonesia gains US$ 4.6 billion of foreign exchange income annually. This makes tourism Indonesia's third most important non-oil/gas source of foreign revenue, after timber and textile products.

Three quarters of Indonesia's visitors come from the Asia Pacific region, with Singapore, Malaysia, Australia, Japan and South Korea among the top five markets. The United Kingdom, France, Germany and the Netherlands are the largest sources of European visitors. Although Dutch visitors are at least in part keen to explore the historical relationships, many European visitors are seeking the tropical weather at the beach resorts.

Historical Context

During the colonial era, tourism was regulated carefully by the government administration of the Dutch East Indies, with international tourists encouraged to travel in groups, and to visit the more significant 'landmark' destinations of Java, Bali and Sumatra. Much of the international tourism of the 1920s and 1930s was by international visitors on oceanic cruises. The

1930s did see a modest but significant influx of mainly European tourists and longer term stayers to Bali. Many came for the blossoming arts scene in the Ubud area, which was as much a two-way exchange between the Balinese and outsiders as it was an internal phenomenon.

Tourism more or less disappeared during World War II, and in the early years of the Sukarno era. National pride and identity in the late 1950s and early 1960s was incorporated in the monumentalism of Sukarno in Jakarta-and this included the development of international standard hotels. The political and economic instability of the mid-1960s saw tourism decline radically again. Bali, and in particular the small village of Kuta, was however, in the 1960s, an important stop over on the overland hippy trail between Australia and Europe, and a "secret" untouched surf spot. In the early to mid 1970s high standard hotels and tourist facilities began to appear in Jakarta and Bali, and from this period to the end of the Suharto era, governmental manipulation of the tourism industry included an array of policies and developments to encourage increasing numbers of international tourists to both visit Indonesia and stay longer.

Sometimes tourism development clashed with local people, particularly in Bali. In 1994, an open demonstration against the new Tanah Lot development project were held and simply halted by military intervention. In 1997, mounting anger of local people reached boiling point over a strip of a beach in front of the Bali Beach Hotel.

There were a number of years that were declared 'Visit Indonesia Year'-with different themes. In a number of cases, where international events interfered, some years in the "Visit Indonesia" decade were considerable disasters. Considerable cynicism on the part of some poor local communities in Java led to the appearance of graffiti on water tanks and abandoned buildings proclaiming "obyek wisata", in reference to local government authorities enthusiasm to attract interest to locations with very limited interest to international tourists who tended to tread the well-worn path between the larger, and in some cases, over-promoted "tourism objects" as they were called. With the advent of the internet and the enthusiasm for promotional websites, tourism in the twenty first century has seen the style of street vendors in busy tourist locations of the past extend to website creators-cluttered, chaotic and of varying quality.

Tourists Attractions

Nature Tourism

Indonesia has well-preserved natural ecosystem such as rainforests that stretch over about 57% of Indonesia's land (225 million acres) and about 2% of them are mangrove. One reason why the natural ecosystem in Indonesia is still well-preserved is because only 6,000 islands out of 17,000 are permanently inhabited. Forests on Sumatra and Java are examples of popular tourists destinations. Moreover, Indonesia has one of longest coastlines in the world, measuring 54,716 km, with a number of beaches and island resorts, such as those in southern Bali, Lombok, Bintan and Nias Island. However, most of the well-preserved beaches are those in more isolated and less developed areas such as Karimunjawa, the Togian Islands, and the Banda Islands.

Dive Sites

With more than 17,000 islands, Indonesia presents ample diving opportunities. Bunaken at the northern tip of Sulawesi, claims to have seven times more genera of coral than Hawaii, and has more than 70% of all the known fish species of the Indo-Western Pacific. Moreover, there are over 3,500 species living in Indonesian waters, including sharks, dolphins, manta rays, turtles, morays, cuttlefish, octopus and scorpionfish, compared to 1,500 on the Great Barrier Reef and 600 in the Red Sea. Tulamben Bay in Bali boasts the wreck of a 120 meter (400 foot) US Army commissioned transport vessel, the USAT Liberty Glo. Beside Bunaken and Bali, Lombok, with three Gilis (Gili Air, Gili Meno and Gili Trawangan), Thousand Islands and Bangka are some of the most popular diving sites in Indonesia.

Surf Breaks

Surfing is also a popular water activities in Indonesia and the sites are recognised as world class sites. The well-known spots are mostly located on the southern, Indian Ocean side of Indonesia, for example, large oceanic surf breaks on southern Java. However, the north coast does not receive the same surf from the Java Sea. Surf breaks can be found all the way along Sumatra, down to Nusa Tenggara, including Aceh, Bali, Banten, Java, Lombok, Mentawai Islands, and Sumbawa. On Bali, there are about 33 surf spots, from West Bali to East Bali. Sumatra is the second island with the most number of surf spots, with 18 spots. The common time for surfing is around May to September with the trade winds blowing from east to south-east. From October to April, winds tend to come from the west to north-west, so east coast breaks get the offshore winds.

Two well-known surf breaks in Indonesia are the G-Land in the Bay of Grajagan, East Java and Lagundri Bay at the southern end of Nias island. G-Land was first identified in 1972 when a surfer saw the break from the window of a plane. Since 6 to 8 foot (Hawaiian scale) waves were discovered by surfers at Lagundri Bay in 1975 the island has become famous for surfing worldwide.

National Parks

The biggest national park in Indonesia is the 9,500 square kilometre Gunung Leuser National Park in the north of Sumatra island. Together with Kerinci Seblat National Park and Bukit Barisan Selatan National Park, the total 25,000 square kilometres of national parks in Sumatra, named Tropical Rainforest Heritage of Sumatra, has been added to the UNESCO World Heritage list. Other national parks on the list are Lorentz National Park in Papua, Komodo National Park in the Lesser Sunda Islands and Ujung Kulon National Park in the west of Java.

To be noticed, different national parks offer different biodiversity, as natural habitat in Indonesia is divided into two areas by the Wallace line. The Wallacea biogeographical distinction means the western part of Indonesia (Sumatra, Java, Kalimantan) have the same flora and fauna characteristics as the Asian continent, whilst the remaining eastern part of Indonesia has similarity with the Australian continent.

Many native species such as Sumatran elephants, Sumatran tigers, Sumatran rhinoceros, Javan rhinoceros and Orangutans are listed as endangered or critically endangered, and the remaining populations are found in national parks and other conservation areas. Orangutans can be visited in the Bukit Lawang conservation area. The world's largest flower, rafflesia arnoldi, and the tallest flower, titan arum, can be found in Sumatra.

The east side of the Wallacea line offers the most unique and rarest and most exotic animals on earth. Birds of Paradise, locally known as cenderawasih, are plumed birds that can be found among other fauna in Papua New Guinea. The largest bird in Papua is the flightless cassowary. One species of lizard, the Komodo Dragon can easily be found on Komodo, located in the Nusa Tenggara lesser islands region. Besides Komodo island, this endangered species can also be found on the islands of Rintja, Padar and Flores.

Volcanoes

Hiking and camping in the mountains are popular adventure activities. Some mountains contain ridge rivers, offering rafting activity. Though volcanic mountains can be dangerous, they have become major tourist destinations. Popular active volcanoes are the 2,329 m high Mount Bromo in the East Java province with its little desert, the upturned boat shaped Tangkuban Perahu on the outskirts of Bandung, the most active volcano in Java, Mount Merapi and the legendary Krakatau with its new caldera known as anak krakatau (the child of Krakatau). Puncak Jaya in the Lorentz National Park, the highest mountain in Indonesia and the only mountain with ice caps, offers the opportunity of rock climbing. In Sumatra, there are the remains of a supervolcano eruption that have created the landscape of Lake Toba close to Medan in North Sumatra.

Cultural Tourism

Indonesia consists of at least 300 ethnic groups, spread over a 1.8 million km^2 area of 6,000 inhabited islands. This creates a cultural diversity, further compounded by Hindu, Buddhist, Islamic and European colonialist influences.

From the 3rd century until the 13th century, Hinduism and Buddhism shaped the culture of Indonesia. The best-preserved Buddhist shrine, which was built during the Sailendra dynasty in the 8th century, is Borobudur temple in Central Java. A few kilometers to the southeast is the Prambanan complex, a Hindu temple built during the second Mataram dynasty. Both the Borobudur and the Prambanan temple compounds have been listed in the UNESCO World Heritage list since 1991. In Bali, where most Hindus live, cultural festivals are major attractions to foreign tourists. Islam has also contributed greatly to the cultural society in Indonesia. As of 2006, about 88% of Indonesians are Moslem. Islamic culture is prominent in Sumatra, and a few of the remaining sultanate palaces can be seen in Medan and Pekanbaru.

Despite foreign influences, a diverse array of indigenous traditional cultures is still evident in Indonesia. The indigenous ethnic group of Toraja in South Sulawesi, which still has strong animistic beliefs, offers a unique cultural tradition, especially during funeral rituals. The Minangkabau ethic group retain a unique matrilineal culture, despite being devoted Muslims. Other indigenous ethnic groups include the Asmat and Dani in Papua, Dayak in Kalimantan and Mentawai in Sumatra, where traditional rituals are still observed. A discussion of cultural tourism is not complete without a mention of Yogyakarta, a special province in Indonesia known as a centre of classical Javanese fine art and culture. The rise and fall of Buddhist, Hindu, and Islamic kingdoms in Central Java has transformed Yogyakarta into a melting pot of Indonesian culture.

Metropolitan Tourism

Metropolitan tourism activities are shopping, sightseeing in big cities and enjoying modern amusement parks. The nation's capital, Jakarta, offers many places for shopping. Mal Kelapa Gading (the biggest one with 130,000 m^2), Plaza Senayan and Plaza Indonesia are some of the malls in the city. Another popular tourist activity is golfing, a favourite sport among the upper classes Indonesian and also foreigners. Some notable golf courses in Jakarta are Cengkareng Golf Club, located in the airport complex, and Pondok Indah Golf and Country Club. Bali has many shopping centers, for instance, the Kuta shopping center and the Galeria Nusa Dua. Nightlife of Indonesia is also popular among foreigners, especially in the big cities like Jakarta, Bandung, Surabaya and Denpasar.

Accommodation

The standards and types of accommodation available to the tourist varies from 5 star hotels to basic beach huts, with something to suit every taste and budget. Most large cities and tourist resorts have a selection of hotels, but the predominant form of accommodation is the family run hostel which can be found wherever there are budget travellers. These losmen provide not only accommodation, but often also will offer food and information for the traveller. In very remote villages, it might be necessary to discuss accommodation requirements with the village head. In Ubud, and elsewhere in Bali, many guest houses have been set up using the traditional family compound as their setting.

Food in Indonesia

The variety of cultures in Indonesia is reflected in the wide range of foods in the nation. Since the 15th century, many European traders have visited the archipelago to buy different kinds of spices, including pepper and mace. In modern times, many cultures and countries have influenced the cuisine of Indonesia, such as Western culture and Asian culture. Many claim that this diversity has resulted in one of the most unique cuisines in the world.

The main principle of almost all Indonesian food is halal. Rice is Indonesia's most important staple food. Most Indonesians eat rice twice a day, at lunch and dinner. The rice is usually served with a side dish, such as chicken, meats and vegetables. Although the meals are generally simple, the plentiful use of various roots, spices, grasses, and leaves adds flavour to most dishes. An Indonesian meal will often be accompanied by various condiments at the table, including sambal and kecap. Other main meals, such as potato, noodles, soybeans and wheat are common. The most common method for preparing food is frying, though grilling, simmering, steaming and stewing are also used.

Indonesian cuisine is also influenced by Western culture. The most obvious example is the presence of fast food companies in Indonesia, such as McDonald's, KFC and Pizza Hut.

To popularise the food of Indonesia, food related events were created, such as a food festival called "Enak-Enak", runs from August 15 to August 31, 2006.

INTERNATIONAL TOURIST ARRIVALS

International Airports

Each of the larger Indonesian islands, have at least one international airport. The biggest airport in Indonesia, Soekarno-Hatta International Airport, is located in Tangerang Regency, Banten. There are four more international airports on Java, Adisumarmo International Airport in Central Java, Juanda International Airport in East Java, Achmad Yani International Airport in Central Java and Adisucipto International Airport in Yogyakarta. On Kalimantan there is one international airport and there are two on Sumatra. Bali, which is part of the Nusa Tenggara Islands, has the Ngurah Rai International Airport.

Threats to the Tourism Industry

The 2002 Bali bombing was a major blow to the tourism industry in Indonesia. A series of travel warnings were issued by a number of countries. Subsequently, the rate of tourism in Bali decreased by 31%. Furthermore, a series of terrorist attacks-the 2003 Marriott Hotel bombing, the 2004 Australian Embassy bombing in Jakarta, and a second bombing in Bali-have worsened the situation for the tourism industry.

A recent outbreak of bird flu throughout the country has been affecting numbers of foreign travellers. It has resulted in at least 46 deaths since the spread of the disease last year, making Indonesia the country with the highest death-toll from the recent epidemic. However, since the disease has not yet been proven to mutate into a form that can transfer from human to human, the U.S. embassy, for example, has not yet issued a travel warning regarding the outbreak.

Another major threat to the tourism industry are sectarian and separatist conflicts in Indonesia. Papua is still affected by Papuan separatism, while Maluku and Central Sulawesi have suffered in recent years from serious sectarian conflicts. Conversely, decades of separatism-related violence in Aceh ended in 2005 with the signing of a peace agreement between the Indonesia Government and the Free Aceh Movement.

Transportation in Indonesia

Indonesia's transport system has been shaped over time by the economic resource base of an archipelago with thousands of islands, and the distribution of its more than 200 million people highly concentrated on a single island which is Java.

All transport modes play a role in the country's transport system and are generally complementary rather than competitive. Road transport is predominant, with a total system length of 370,500 km in 2003. The railway system has four unconnected networks in Java and Sumatra primarily dedicated to transport bulk commodities and long-distance passenger traffic. Sea transport is extremely important for economic integration and for domestic and foreign trade. It is well developed, with each of the major islands having at least one significant port city.

The role of inland waterways is relatively minor and is limited to certain areas of Eastern Sumatra and Kalimantan. The function of air transport is significant, particularly where land or water transport is deficient or non-existent. It is based on an extensive domestic airline network where all major cities can be reached by passenger plane.

Merchant Marine Vessels

Because Indonesia encompasses a sprawling archipelago, maritime shipping provides essential links between different parts of the country. Boats in common use include large container ships, a variety of ferries, passenger ships, sailing ships, and smaller motorized vessels.

Frequent ferry services cross the straits between nearby islands, especially in the chain of islands stretching from Sumatra through Java to the Lesser Sunda Islands. On the busy crossings between Sumatra, Java, and Bali, multiple car ferries run frequently twenty-four hours per day. There are also international ferry services between across the Straits of Malacca between Sumatra and Malaysia, and between Singapore and nearby Indonesian islands, such as Batam.

A network of passenger ships makes longer connections to more remote islands, especially in the eastern part of the archipelago. The national shipping line, Pelni, provides passenger service to ports throughout the country on a two to four week schedule. These ships generally provide the least expensive way to cover long distances between islands. Still smaller privately run boats provide service between islands.

On some islands, major rivers provide a key transportation link in the absence of good roads. On Kalimantan, longboats running on the rivers are the only way to reach many inland areas.

Waterways

Indonesia has 21,579 km of navigable waterways (2005), of which about one half are on Kalimantan, and a quarter each on Sumatra and Papua. Waterways are highly needed because the rivers on these islands are not wide enough to hold medium-sized ships. In addition to this, roads and railways are not good options since Kalimantan and Papua are not like Java, which is a highly developed island. With the current length of waterways, Indonesia ranked seven on the countries with longest waterways rant.

Ports and Harbours

Major ports and harbours include Cilacap, Cirebon, Jakarta, Kupang, Palembang, Semarang, Surabaya, and Makassar. Ports are managed by the various Indonesia Port Corporations, of which there are four, numbered I through IV. Each has jurisdiction over various regions of the country, with I in the west and IV in the east.

Roads and Highways

A wide variety of vehicles are used for transportation on Indonesia's roads.

Bus services are available in most areas connected to the road network. Between major cities, especially on Sumatra, Java, and Bali, services are frequent and direct; many services are available with no stops until the final destination. In more remote areas, and between smaller towns, most services are provided with minibuses or small vans. Buses and vans are also the primary form of transportation within cities.

Many cities and towns have some form of transportation for hire available as well, such as taxis, Busways and motorized autorickshaws (bajaj). Cycle rickshaws, called becak in Indonesia, are common in many cities, and provide an inexpensive form of in-town transportation. They have been blamed for causing traffic congestion and banned from most parts of central Jakarta. Horse-drawn carts are found in some cities and towns.

Private cars are far too expensive for the majority of the population, and are uncommon except in larger cities.

Indonesia has about 213,649 km of paved highways and about 154,711 km of unpaved highways (2002 estimate).

Indonesia has some toll roads. The most expensive is the Cipularang Toll road that connects Jakarta and Bandung.

Here are some Indonesian toll roads: Java:

- Jakarta Inner Ringroad
- Jakarta Outer Ringroad

- Jakarta-Merak Toll road
- Jakarta-Bogor-Ciawi (Jagorawi) Toll road
- Jakarta-Bandung Toll road,
  * Cikampek Toll road, connects Jakarta and Cikampek.
  * Cikampek-Purwakarta-Padalarang(Bandung) often called Cipularang
  * Padalarang-Cileunyi Toll road. Called Bandung Southern Ringroad
- Semarang-Ambarawa Toll road
- Surabaya-Gempol Toll road
- Surabaya-Mojokerto Toll road

Planned:

- Transjava Toll road
- Suramadu Bridge (In Progress)
- Merak-Bakauheuni (Sumatra) tunnel.

Sumatra:

- Medan-Tanjungmorawa Toll road
- Medan-Belawan Port Toll road

Planned:

- Medan-Kuala Namu International Airport

Railways

Most railways in Indonesia are on Java, which has two major rail lines that run the length of the island, as well as several minor lines. Passenger and freight service runs on all of the lines. There is also commuter rail service in the Jakarta metropolitan area, and Surabaya and the vicinities. A monorail mass transit system is under construction in Jakarta.

The only other areas in Indonesia having railroads are two separate regions of Sumatra, one in the north around Medan, and one near the southern tip.

Pipelines

Crude oil 2,505 km; petroleum products 456 km; natural gas 1,703 km (1989)

Airports

Total: 668 (2005)

Airports-with Paved Runways

Total: 161

over 3,047 m: 4

2,438 to 3,047 m: 15

1,524 to 2,437 m: 48

914 to 1,523 m: 51

under 914 m: 43 (2005)

Airports-with Unpaved Runways

Total: 507

1,524 to 2,437 m: 6

914 to 1,523 m: 26

under 914 m: 475 (2005)

Heliports

Total: 23 (2005)

Airlines

National airline:

- Garuda Indonesia

Other airlines

- Airlines of Indonesia

Culture

Indonesia has around 300 ethnic groups, each with cultural differences developed over centuries, and influenced by Arabic,

Chinese, Malay, and European sources. Traditional Javanese and Balinese dances, for example, contain aspects of Hindu culture and mythology, as do wayang kulit (shadow puppet) performances. Textiles such as batik, ikat and songket are created across Indonesia in styles that vary by region. The most dominant influences on Indonesian architecture have traditionally been Indian; however, Chinese, Arab, and European architectural influences have been significant. The most popular sports in Indonesia are badminton and football; Liga Indonesia is the country's premier football club league. Traditional sports include sepak takraw, and bull racing in Madura. In areas with a history of tribal warfare, mock fighting contests are held, such as, caci in Flores, and pasola in Sumba. Pencak Silat is an Indonesian martial art. Sports in Indonesia are generally male-orientated and spectator sports are often associated with illegal gambling.

Indonesian cuisine varies by region and is based on Chinese, European, Middle Eastern and Indian precedents. Rice is the main staple food and is served with side dishes of meat and vegetables. Spices (notably chili), coconut milk, fish and chicken are fundamental ingredients. Indonesian traditional music includes gamelan and keroncong. Dangdut is a popular contemporary genre of pop music that draws influence from Arabic, Indian, and Malay folk music. The Indonesian film industry's popularity peaked in the 1980s and dominated cinemas in Indonesia, although it declined significantly in the early 1990s. Between 2000 and 2005, the number of Indonesian films released each year has steadily increased.

The oldest evidence of writing in Indonesia is a series of Sanskrit inscriptions dated to the 5th century CE. Important figures in modern Indonesian literature include: Dutch author Multatuli, who criticized treatment of the Indonesians under Dutch colonial rule; Sumatrans Muhammad Yamin and Hamka, who were influential pre-independence nationalist writers and politicians; and proletarian writer Pramoedya Ananta Toer, Indonesia's most famous novelist. Many of Indonesia's peoples have strongly-rooted oral traditions, which help to define and preserve their cultural identities. Media freedom in Indonesia increased considerably after the end of President Suharto's rule, during which the now-defunct Ministry of Information monitored and controlled domestic media, and restricted foreign media. The TV market includes ten national commercial networks, and provincial networks that compete with public TVRI. Private radio stations carry their own news bulletins and foreign broadcasters supply programs. At a reported 18 million users in 2005, Internet usage is still limited to a minority of the population.

Heritage Sites in Indonesia

Borobudur

Coordinates: 7°36'29°S, 110°12'14°E

Borobudur is a ninth century Buddhist Mahayana monument in Central Java, Indonesia. The monument comprises six square platforms topped by three circular platforms, and is decorated with 2,672 relief panels and 504 Buddha statues. A main dome is located at the center of the top platform, surrounded by seventy-two Buddha statues seated inside perforated stupa.

The monument is both a shrine to the Lord Buddha and a place for Buddhist pilgrimage. The journey for pilgrims begins at the base of the monument and follows a path circumambulating the monument while ascending to the top through the three levels of Buddhist cosmology, namely, Kamadhatu (the world of desire); Rupadhatu (the world of forms); and Arupadhatu (the world of formless). During the journey, the monument guides the pilgrims through a system of stairways and corridors with 1,460 narrative relief panels on the wall and the balustrades.

Evidence suggests Borobudur was abandoned following the fourteenth century decline of Buddhist and Hindu kingdoms in Java, and the Javanese conversion to Islam. It was rediscovered in 1814 by Sir Thomas Raffles, the British ruler of Java. Since then, Borobudur has been preserved through several restorations. The largest restoration project was undertaken between 1975 and 1982 by the Indonesian government and UNESCO, after which the monument was listed as a UNESCO World Heritage Site. Borobudur is still used for pilgrimage, and once a year Buddhists in Indonesia celebrate Vesak at the monument. Borobudur is also Indonesia's single most visited tourist attraction.

Reliefs

Narrative Panels Distribution

section	location	story	#panels
hidden foot	wall	Karmavibhangga	160
first gallery	main wall	Lalitavistara	120
		Jataka/Avadana	120
	balustrade	Jataka/Avadana	372
		Jataka/Avadana	128
second gallery	main wall	Gandavyuha	128
	ballustrade	Jataka/Avadana	100
third gallery	main wall	Gandavyuha	88
	ballustrade	Gandavyuha	88
fourth gallery	main wall	Gandavyuha	84
	ballustrade	Gandavyuha	72
		Total	1,460

Borobudur contains approximately 2,670 individual bas reliefs (1,460 narrative and 1,212 decorative panels), which cover the façades and balustrades. The total relief surface is 2,500 m^2 and they are distributed at the hidden foot (Kamadhatu) and the five square platforms (Rupadhatu).

The narrative panels, which tell the story of Sudhana and Manohara, are grouped into 11 series encircled the monument with the total length of 3,000 metres (1.86 miles). The hidden foot contains the first series with 160 narrative panels and the remaining 10 series are distributed throughout walls and balustrades in four galleries starting from the eastern entrance stairway to the left. Narrative panels on the wall read from right to left, while on the balustrade read from left to right.

This conforms with pradaksina, the ritual of circumambulation performed by pilgrims who move in a clockwise direction while keeping the sanctuary to their right.

The hidden foot depicts the story of the karma law. The walls of the first gallery have two superimposed series of reliefs; each consists of 120 panels. The upper part depicts the biography of Buddha, while the lower part of the wall and also ballustrades in the first and the second galleries tell the story of Buddha's former lives. The remaining panels are devoted to Sudhana's further wandering about his search; terminated by his attainment of the Perfect Wisdom.

The Law of Karma (Karmavibhangga)

The 160 hidden panels do not form a continuous story, but each panel provides one complete illustration of cause and effect. There are depictions of blameworthy activities, from gossip to murder, with their corresponding punishments. There are also praiseworthy activities, that include charity and pilgrimage to sanctuaries, and their subsequent rewards. The pains of hell and the pleasure of heaven are also illustrated. There are scenes of daily life, complete with the full panorama of samsara (the endless cycle of birth and death).

Bukit Barisan Selatan National Park

Bukit Barisan Selatan National Park is a national park in Sumatra, Indonesia. The park has a total area of 3,568 km^2, and spans three provinces:

- Lampung,
- Bengkulu,
- South Sumatra

Starting as a Wildlife Sanctuary in 1935, the area became a National Park in 1982.

The park is home to many endangered species, including:

- Sumatran Elephant (about 500 animals, or 25% of the total remaining population of this sub-species live in the park)

- Sumatran Striped Rabbit
- Sumatran Rhino (an estimated 60-85 Sumatran rhinos live in the park, the largest population anywhere on Sumatra)
- Sumatran Tiger (approximately 40 adult tigers or 10% of the remaining Sumatran tigers live in the park).

The park has recently lost 20% of it's forests to illegal agriculture, according to the World Widę Fund for Nature. WWF found that more than 45,000 hectares of park land is being used for growing coffee, and the organisation is now working with multinational coffee companies (including Nestle) to help them avoid buying illegally grown coffee.

Gunung Leuser National Park

Gunung Leuser National Park is a national park covering 9,500 km² in northern Sumatra, Indonesia, straddling the border of North Sumatra and Aceh provinces. The national park, named after 3,381 m height of Mount Leuser, protects a wide range of ecosystems. An orangutan sanctuary of Bukit Lawang is located inside the park.

Kerinci Seblat National Park

Kerinci Seblat National Park is the largest national park in Sumatra; it park has a total area of 13,750 km², and spans four provinces:

- West Sumatra,
- Jambi,
- Bengkulu and
- South Sumatra.

It is located between 100°31'18"E-102°44'01"E and 1°07'13"S-3°26'14"S.

The park area includes a large part of the Barisan mountain range, including the highest peak in Sumatra, Mount Kerinci (3,805 m). The park includes hot springs, rivers with rapids, caves, scenic waterfalls and the highest caldera lake in Southeast

Asia-Lake Gunung Tujuh. The park is home to diversity of flora and fauna. Over 4,000 plant species grow in the park area, including the world's largest flower, Rafflesia arnoldi, and the tallest flower, Titan Arum. The fauna include Sumatran Tigers, Sumatran Rhinoceros, Sumatran elephants, Bornean Clouded Leopard, Malayan Tapir, Malay Sun Bear and 370 bird species.

Komodo National Park

The Komodo National Park is a national park in Indonesia located near the Lesser Sunda Islands in the border region between the provinces of East Nusa Tenggara and West Nusa Tenggara. The park includes the three larger islands Komodo, Rinca and Padar, as well as numerous smaller ones, and a total area of 1817 km² (603 km² of it land). The national park was founded in 1980 in order to protect the Komodo dragon. Later it was dedicated to protecting other species, including marine species. The islands of the national park are of volcanic origin. About 4000 people love within the park. In 1991 the national park was named aUNESCO World Heritage Site.

Scuba diving is popular Komodo National Park because of its high marine biodiversity, including whale sharks, ocean sunfish, manta rays, eagle rays, pygmy seahorse, false pipefish, clown frogfish, nudibranchs, blue-ringed octopus, sponges, tunicates, and coral.

Since 1995, the national park authority has been supported by The Nature Conservancy (TNC), an American environmental organization. A new management plan was co-authored with TNC and implemented in 2000 to address the problem of increasing resource exploitation, both marine and terrestrial. Most pressure on marine resources originates from fishing communities and commercial enterprises from outside the park. However, regulations and restrictions on resource use impact mostly on park residents, who have few options to make a living but rely on what the park has to offer. The provision of alternative livelihoods is part of the overall management strategy, but communities within the park are yet to benefit from appropriate measures addressing their needs (WALHI 2004).

The development of-largely marine-based-ecotourism is the main strategy to make the park self-financing and generate sufficient revenue through entrance fees and tourism licenses to cover operational and managerial costs. To this end, a joint venture between TNC and a tourism operator were granted a tourism concession, that also entails extensive park management rights (PKA & TNC 2000:78). This concession has generated an ongoing controversy. The joint venture has been accused of making decisions behind closed doors, and many people in and around Komodo claim that they haven't been consulted regarding decisions that ultimately affect their lives WALHI 2003, Dhume, 2000, Jurassic Showdown', Far Eastern Economic Review, March 16th, pp.50-52).

Most controversy, however, was caused by the death of several fishermen since the 1980s. The circumstances of the fishermen's deaths are contested. While park patrol (including, at the time, police and navy personnel) claim they acted in self-defense, fishing communities accuse park management of having deliberately killed the fishermen (Down to Earth 2003).

Komodo National Park remains an awe-inspiring experience for tourists and travelers, but the conflict between park management, TNC and local communities continues unabated.

Lorentz National Park

Lorentz National Park is located in the Indonesian province of Papua, formerly known as Irian Jaya (western New Guinea). With an area of 25,056 km² (9,674 mi²), it is the largest national park in South-East Asia. In 1999 Lorentz was declared a World Heritage Site by UNESCO.

An outstanding example of the biodiversity of New Guinea, Lorentz is one of the most ecologically diverse national parks in the world. It is the only nature reserve in the Asia-Pacific region to contain a full altitudial array of ecosystems spanning from marine areas, mangrove, tidal and freshwater swamp forest, lowland and montane rainforest, alpine areas, and equatorial glaciers. At 4884 meters, Puncak Jaya (formerly Carstensz Pyramid) is the tallest mountain between the

Himalayas and the Andes. Birdlife International has called Lorentz Park "probably the single most important reserve in New Guinea" (Birdlife International, 1999).

Lorentz Park contains many unmapped and unexplored areas, and is certain to contain many species of plants and animals as yet unknown to Western science. Local communities' ethnobotanical and ethnozoological knowledge of the Lorentz biota is also very poorly documented.

Cultural Aspects

The forests of Lorentz encompass the traditional lands of several ethnic groups, including the Asmat, Amungme, Dani, Sempan, and Nduga. It is widely acknowledged that conservation management strategies for the park will have to incorporate the needs and aspirations of these peoples if the park is to succeed in protecting biodiversity. Moreover, cultural diversity is another important measure of success for the park as well.

Threats

The main threats to the biodiversity of Lorentz are from commercial logging, forest conversion for plantation agriculture, smallholder agricultural conversion, mining/oil/gas development, and the illegal species trade. Climate change also poses a substantial threat.

As of 2005, there was no reported commercial logging or other large-scale threats present inside the park. There are no currently active forest conversion projects, and agricultural conversion is minimal. The illegal species trade is known to be a serious problem. A large gold/copper mining operation has been active for decades to the west and north of the park but is not active inside the park boundaries. Oil exploration inside and to the northeast of the park is ongoing.

The overall health of the biodiversity of Lorentz Park is currently excellent. While logging and other threats have yet to materialize, it is likely that this will become a threat in the future. Climate change poses a very real threat, but its specific implications for Lorentz are uncertain.

Conservation Status

As of 2005, there were no park staff or guards assigned to Lorentz. However, the park's success largely depends on local communities' understanding of and support for conservation, rather than external enforcement alone. Several conservation organizations are working in the Lorentz area.

Prambanan

Prambanan is the largest Hindu temple compound in Indonesia, located in central Java, approximately 18 km east of Yogyakarta (7°45'8?S, 110°29'30?ECoordinates: 7°45'8?S, 110°29'30?E). It was built around 850 CE by either Rakai Pikatan, king of the second Mataram dynasty or Balitung Maha Sambu, during the Sanjaya dynasty. Not long after its construction, the temple was abandoned and began to deteriorate. Reconstruction of the compound began in 1918. The main building was completed in around 1953, since it is next to impossible to find the original stonework, which has often been stolen and reused at remote construction sites. A temple will only be rebuilt if at least 75% of the original stones are available. Therefore only their foundation walls of most of the smaller shrines are visible and they will not be rebuilt.

Today, it is a UNESCO World Heritage Site and one of the largest Hindu temples in south-east Asia. It is characterised by its tall and pointed architecture, typical of Hindu temple architecture, and by the 47m high central building inside a large complex of individual temples.

The temple was damaged during the earthquake in Java in 2006. Early photos suggested that although the complex appears to be structurally intact, damage is significant, with large pieces of debris, including carvings, scattered over the ground. The temple has been closed to the public until damage can be fully assessed. The head of Yogyakarta Archaeological Conservation Agency stated that: "it will take months to identify the precise damage". However, some weeks later in 2006 the site re-opened for visitors. The immediate surroundings of the Hindu temples remain off-limits for safety reason.

The Complex

The compound is assembled of eight main shrines or candis, and more than 250 surrounding individual candis. The three main shrines, called Trisakti (Ind. "three sacred places"), are dedicated to the three gods Shiva the Destroyer, Vishnu the Keeper and Brahma the Creator.

The Shiva shrine at the center contains four chambers, one in every cardinal direction. While the first contains a three meter high statue of Shiva, the other three contain smaller statues of Durga, his wife, Agastya, a risi, and Ganesha, his son. The statue of Durga is also called temple of Loro Jonggrang (slender virgin), after a Javanese princess, daughter of King Boko. She was forced to marry a man she did not love, Bandung Bondowoso. After long negotiations she eventually agreed to the marriage, under the condition that her prince built her a temple ornamented with 1000 statues, between the setting and the rising of the sun. Helped by supernatural beings, the prince was about to succeed. So the princess ordered the women of the village to set a fire in the east of the temple, attempting to make the prince believe that the sun was about to rise. As the cocks began to crow, fooled by the light, the supernatural helpers fled. The prince, furious about the simple trick, changed Loro Jongrang to stone. She became the last and the most beautiful of the thousand statues.

The two other main shrines are that of Vishnu, to the north, and the one of Brahma, facing to the south. In front of each main temple is a smaller candis on the east side, dedicated to the mounts of the respective god-the bull Nandi for Shiva, the gander Angsa for Brahma, and Vishnus Eagle Garuda, which serves as the national symbol of Indonesia (cf. also to the airline Garuda Indonesia).

The bas-reliefs along the twenty sides of the temple depict the Ramayana legend. They illustrate how Sita, the wife of Rama, is abducted by an evil ogre. The monkey king Hanuman brings his army to help Rama and rescue Sita. This story is also shown by the Ramayana Ballet, regularly performed at full moon in front of the illuminated Prambanan complex.

The temple complex is surrounded by more than 250 individual temples of different sizes, called Pewara, believed to have been offered to the king as a sign of submission. The Pewara are arranged in four rows around the central temples, according to the rank of the people allowed to enter them. While the central row was accessible to the priests only, the other three were reserved for the nobles, the knights and the simple people respectively.

Not far to the west Candi Kalasan and Candi Sari, and to the south the Ratu Boko's Palace on higher ground-each provide further clues and details to the Prambanan complex and some of its mysteries.

Sangiran

Sangiran is an archaeological excavation site at the island of Java in Indonesia. The area comprises about 48 km^2 and is located in Central Java, about 15 kilometers north of Surakarta in the Bengawan Solo River valley. In 1996 it was accepted as World Heritage by the UNESCO.

In 1934 the anthropologist Gustav Heinrich Ralph von Koenigswald started to examine the area. During excavations in the next years fossils of some of the first known human ancestors, Pithecanthropus erectus ("Java Man"), were found here. About 60 more fossils, among them the enigmatic Meganthropus, have since been found here.

Tropical Rainforest Heritage of Sumatra

Tropical Rainforest Heritage of Sumatra site was listed in UNESCO World Heritage list in 2004. It comprises three Indonesian national parks on the island of Sumatra-Gunung Leuser National Park, Kerinci Seblat National Park and the Southern Hills National Park.

The site is listed under Criteria vii-outstanding scenic beauty; ix-an outstanding example representing significant on-going ecological and biological processes; and x-contains the most important and significant natural habitats for in-situ conservation.

Ujung Kulon National Park

Ujung Kulon National Park is located at the western-most tip of Java, Indonesia. It includes the volcanic island group of Krakatoa and other islands including Handeuleum and Peucang. The park encompasses an area of 1,206 km^2 (443 km^2 marine), most of which lies on a peninsula reaching into the Indian Ocean.

It is Indonesia's first national park and was declared a UNESCO World Heritage Site in 1992 for containing the largest remaining lowland rainforest in Java. It is also home to the last fifty to sixty members of the Javan Rhinoceros species. The mainland part of Ujung Kulon was formerly farmland until it was devastated and depopulated by the 1883 eruption of Krakatoa after which it returned to its original forested state.

Permits for the park are available at the town of Labuan, where there is a National Park office. There is also an office at Tamanjaya. Accommodation is available on Handeuleum and Peucang islands.

TOURISM IN SYDNEY

Sydney is a significant tourist destination, with 7.8 million domestic visitors and 2.5 million international visitors in 2004. The most well known attractions include the Sydney Opera House, and the Sydney Harbour Bridge. Other attractions include Royal Botanical Gardens, Luna Park, the beaches and Sydney Tower.

Sydney is also often referred to as Australia's showcase city, and tourists seem to think so as well with 70% of all tourists going to Australia, making a stop in Sydney.

Sydney Harbour

Port Jackson, containing Sydney Harbour, is the natural harbour of Sydney, Australia. It is known for its beauty, and in particular, as the location of the Sydney Opera House and Sydney Harbour Bridge. Bradley's Head within Sydney Harbour was used to shoot scenes for Mission: Impossible II. The house seen in the film was built on location, then removed after shooting was completed. Bradley's Head is now a unit of the Sydney Harbour National Park and managed by the New South Wales National Parks and Wildlife Service.

Sydney Opera House

The Sydney Opera House is located in Sydney. It is one of the most distinctive and famous 20th century buildings, and one of the most famous performing arts venues in the world. Sit uated on Bennelong Point in Sydney Harbour, with parkland to its south and close to the equally famous Sydney Harbour Bridge, the building and its surroundings form an iconic Australian image. It received attention during Sydney 2000 Olympics. It was included in the Olympic Torch route to the Olympic stadium, and involved Australian swimmer Samantha Riley standing on top of the Opera House waving the Olympic torch. It was the backdrop of some Olympic events, including the triathlon-which began at the Opera House-and the yachting events on Sydney Harbour.

Sydney Harbour Bridge

The Sydney Harbour Bridge is the main crossing of Sydney Harbour carrying rail, vehicular, and pedestrian traffic between the Sydney central business district (CBD) and the North Shore. The dramatic water vista of the bridge together with the nearby Sydney Opera House is an iconic image of both Sydney and Australia. The South-east pylon for many years operated as lookout and tourist attraction, containing a number of telescopes and antiquated arcade games which operated on pennies, long after that currency had gone out of operation. The couple that ran this tourist venue also kept a number of white cats which gave the interior of the pylon a memorable odour. The pylon has recently been renovated and returned to its tourist function.

Bridge Climb

Since 1998, BridgeClimb has made it possible for tourists to climb the southern half of the bridge. Tours run throughout the day, from dawn to dusk and are only cancelled for electrical storms or high wind. Night climbs are also available. Groups of climbers are provided with protective clothing appropriate to the prevailing weather conditions and are given an orientation before climbing. During the climb, attendees are secured to the bridge by a wire lifeline. Each climb begins on the eastern side of the bridge and ascends to the top. At the summit, the group crosses to the western side of the arch for the descent. Each climb is a three-and-a-half-hour experience.

The Rocks

The Rocks is an inner-city suburb, tourist precinct and historic area of Sydney, in the state of New South Wales, Australia. It is located on the southern shore of Sydney Harbour. The close proximity to Circular Quay and the views of the iconic Harbour Bridge, as well as the historic nature of many of the buildings, mean that the Rocks are very popular with tourists. It features a variety of souvenir and craft shops, and many themed and historic pubs. The Rocks Market operates each weekend, with around 100 stalls. There are numerous historic walks through the area, visiting historical buildings such as Cadman's Cottage and Sydney Observatory, and the Dawes Point Battery, which was the first fortified position in New South Wales.

Darling Harbour

The Darling Harbour precinct is home to a number of major public facilities and attractions, including:

- Sydney Entertainment Centre
- Paddy's Market
- Sydney's Chinese Gardens
- Tumbalong Park
- Sydney Convention and Exhibition Centre
- Australian National Maritime Museum (featuring museum ships including HMAS Vampire)
- Star City Casino
- Powerhouse Museum

- Sydney Aquarium
- the IMAX theatre
- Wildlife World
- Sega World Sydney (closed in 2000)

The Darling Harbour precinct is linked to the CBD by the Sydney Monorail.

Kings Cross

The Kings Cross area is infamous in Australia as being a red-light district, similar to Kings Cross in London with numerous strip clubs and "girlie" bars along Darlinghurst Road, although many now accuse the City Council of seeking to gentrify the area, and the demographics have changed in recent years. It is also known for its Neon signs and advertising posters, the most famous being the iconic Coca-Cola sign. It is often referred to by Sydneysiders by the affectionate colloquialism "the Cross".

The Kings Cross district was Sydney's bohemian heartland from the early decades of the 20th Century. From the 1960s onwards it also came to serve as both the city's main tourist accommodation and entertainment mecca, as well as its red-light district. It thereby achieved a high level of notoriety out of all proportion to its limited geographical extent.

Newtown

Newtown today is a vibrant Sydney suburb with over 600 stores, 70 restaurants, 40 cafes, pubs and entertainment venues along King Street and Enmore Road. Newtown and its surrounding areas have the highest concentration of independent theatres and live performance spaces in Sydney.

Newtown has traditionally been a hub for live entertainment. Throughout the 1990s it was particularly known as a centre for indie rock, with the suburb both home to many musicians and several live venues. However since the new millennium, the suburb has enjoyed a renaissance with the return of live music to the pubs and clubs in the area.

Sydney Tower

Sydney Tower (also known as the AMP Tower, AMP Centrepoint Tower, Centrepoint Tower or just Centrepoint) is Sydney's tallest free-standing structure, and the second tallest in Australia (with the Q1 building on the Gold Coast being the tallest). It is also the second tallest observation tower in the Southern Hemisphere (after Auckland, New Zealand's Sky Tower); though Sydney Tower's main observation deck is almost 50 metres higher than that of Auckland's Sky Tower. The Sydney Tower is a member of the World Federation of Great Towers.

Sydney Tower Skywalk

Sydney Tower Skywalk, or just Skywalk, is an open-air, glass-floored platform circling Sydney Tower at a height of 260m above ground level. The moving viewing platform extends out over the edge of the main structure of Sydney Tower. This attraction is more than twice as high as the popular BridgeClimb walk to the top of Sydney Harbour Bridge. From the platform the seaward horizon is 58 kilometres away, although inland features such as the Blue Mountains can be seen at further distances. See Sydney Attractions Group.

Sydney Wildlife World

Sydney Wildlife World is a zoo in the city of Sydney. It officially opened in September 2006. It is located on the shores of Darling Harbour and is attached to Sydney Aquarium. The Sydney Wildlife World is unusual for a zoo in that it is entirely enclosed and air-conditioned. The AUD$45 million development features a one-kilometre walkway which snakes through 7000 square metres of enclosures. The enclosure features around 6000 native animals.

Taronga Zoo

Taronga Zoo is the city zoo of Sydney, officially opened on October 7, 1916. It is located on the shores of Sydney Harbour in Mosman. Taronga is linked to Dubbo's Western Plains Zoo in terms of breeding programs. Taronga Zoo is home to over 2,600 animals on 28.7 hectares, making it one of the largest of its kind, and it divided into eight zoogeographic regions with numerous indoor pavilions and outdoor exhibits. Taronga Zoo has about 340 species and over 2600 individual animals. They are housed in a large variety of exhibits.

Museums

Sydney is home to a number of established museums. The Australian Museum is the oldest museum in Australia, and is particularly renowned in the fields of natural history and anthropology. The Powerhouse Museum specialises in science and technology, and its exhibits include the oldest steam engine in the world with a rotating action that is still in operation. The Australian National Maritime Museum focuses on Australia's maritime history.

Fox Studios

Fox Studios Australia is a major movie studio located in Sydney, Australia, occupying the site of the former Sydney Showground at Moore Park. Since opening in May 1998, the studio has been involved in the production of a number of blockbusters, including The Matrix, Moulin Rouge!, Mission Impossible II, Star Wars Episode II, Star Wars Episode III and Superman Returns.

Located ten minutes from the Sydney city centre, the 132,000 square metre (32 acre) site includes eight stages, production offices and heavy industrial workshops, and a community of over 60 independent businesses. These businesses provide services such as equipment hire, travel and freight, casting, postproduction, and explosives/pyrotechnic factory, adjoining residential properties.

An adjacent precinct provides restaurants and cafes, a retail complex, parklands, entertainment venues, and sporting facilities. The adjacent precinct was previously known as simply The Fox Studios Entertainment Precinct, however has since been renamed The Entertainment Quarter.

Beaches in Sydney

Sydney is renowned for its beaches and, with its warm climate, attracts people to the beaches almost all year round. Sydney's beaches are either ocean facing, such as the internationally renowned Bondi Beach, or harbour beaches, such as Balmoral Beach. The ocean beaches are usually divided into the Northern Beaches, north of the entrance to Sydney Harbour and those to the south, in the eastern suburbs and Cronulla. Most beach suburbs have one beach. A small few have two. Manly with eight beaches stands out. Those of Manly range from the massive 1.6 kilometre Ocean Beach to the tiny Fairy Bower Beach. Sydney also has beaches around Pittwater to the north and Botany Bay and Port Hacking to the south.

Bondi Beach

Large numbers of tourists visit Bondi Beach throughout the year with many Irish and British tourists spending Christmas Day there. Bondi Beach features many popular cafes, restaurants and hotels, with specatacular views of the beach. The beach itself is approximatly one kilometre long.

Manly Beach

Manly Beach is a well known beach situated in Sydney's Northern Beaches. Manly Beach is highly popular with tourists and locals alike; a popularity rivalled only by the famous Bondi Beach south of the harbour. Travelling to Manly from Sydney's main ferry terminal, Circular Quay, takes 30 minutes by ferry or 15 minutes by the faster 'Jet Cat' catamaran.

Cronulla Beach

Cronulla is a popular tourist attraction and attracts many beachgoers from all over Sydney. Cronulla Beach features a long stretch of sand that runs from Boat Harbour to North Cronulla, followed by rock pools and another sandy beach at South Cronulla. The beaches of Cronulla from north to south are: Boat Harbour, Wanda Beach, Elouera Beach, North Cronulla Beach, Cronulla Beach, Blackwoods Beach and Shelly Beach. The beaches are perfect recreational areas for swimming, surfing, bodyboarding, bodysurfing and other water sports. Port Hacking is also a popular location for such water sports as waterskiing and wakeboarding.

Places to see Outside the CBD

Blue Mountains

The Blue Mountains National Park is one of the most popular parks in Australia. The majority of tourists to the Blue Mountains see the National Park from one of the many lookouts between Wentworth Falls and Blackheath, and many of these never actually set foot in the park.

Despite this, there are many activities for the visitor. Short walks to impressive lookouts above cliff and waterfalls abound. Overnight and longer walks allow access to some of the more remote areas of the park. Other popular activities include canyoning and mountain biking.

Sydney Olympic Park

Sydney Olympic Park is a 640-hectare site located adjacent to the suburb of Homebush Bay, New South Wales, Australia. It was built for the 2000 Olympics and continues to be used for sporting and cultural events, including the Sydney Royal Easter Show, Sydney Festival, Big Day Out and a number of world class sporting fixtures. It is served by the Olympic Park railway line and station. There are also regular services to the nearby wharf which to and from run from various point around Sydney Harbour.

TOURISM IN THAILAND

Tourism in Thailand is a major economic factor of Thailand. The tourism industry received a boost when US soldiers went there in the 1970s pausing from the Vietnam war. In 2005, 13.38 million international guests visited Thailand, a 14.84% increase on 2004), staying 8.1 days in average.

According to the Tourist Authority of Thailand, 65% of tourists come from the Asia Pacific region, Japanese and Malaysians among the leaders. Western tourists come from

Britain, Germany, Scandanavia and the USA and increasing numbers arrive from the Middle East. Asian tourists prefer Bangkok and the historical sights nearby, western tourists prefer Bangkok and the southern beaches. The region having very little tourism is the Issan in the northeast. About 55% of tourists are return visitors.

In recent years Thailand has been losing out on tourists seeking cultural destinations, many of whom prefer Cambodia (Angkor Wat) and Laos (Luang Prabang). To counter this Thailand is seeking more niche markets such as golf holidays, or holidays combined with medical treatment. These are especially aimed at Japan and South Korea and in the future China.

Thailand offers a great variety of attractions which can be combined with hobbies or leisure.

This includes dive sites, sandy beaches, hundreds of islands, archaeological sites, museums, ethnic and religious sites and World Heritage Sites.

Sex tourism was an issue between the early 1970s until the late 1990s-however, this is no longer as common except in Pattaya.

TOURISM IN THE UNITED STATES

The United States of America has a large and lucrative tourism industry serving millions of international and domestic tourists. Tourism in the United States is mostly promoted at the state and local level, though the federal government does promote tourism itself, and sets visa entry requirements.

Tourists visit the U.S. to see natural wonders, cities, historic landmarks, and gambling venues. Americans seek similar attractions, but also gravitate to recreation and vacation areas.

Natural Wonders

- National Parks
    * Big Bend National Park
    * Denali National Park and Preserve

  * Death Valley
  * Devils Tower
  * Grand Canyon
  * Great Smoky Mountains National Park
  * Mammoth Cave
  * Yellowstone National Park
  * Yosemite National Park
  * Zion National Park
  * Arches National Park
  * Carlsbad Caverns National Park
- Other
  * Columbia River Gorge National Scenic Area
  * Great Lakes
  * Niagara Falls
  * Rocky Mountains

Vacation Areas

- Adirondack Mountains
- Brainerd Lakes Area, Minnesota
- Cape Cod
- Catskill Mountains
- Jersey Shore
- Key West
- Lake Tahoe/Reno
- Laurentian Mountains
- Martha's Vineyard
- Napa Valley
- Newport, Rhode Island
- Ocean City, Maryland
- The Ozarks

- Pennsylvania Dutch Country / Gettysburg National Military Park
- Pocono Mountains
- Savannah, Georgia
- South Padre Island
- Thousand Islands
- Virginia Beach
- New Hampshire White Mountains

Cities

- Boston, Massachusetts-important site for American history, several universities, beaches
- Charleston, South Carolina-important site for American history, several universities, beaches, golf courses, Arthur Ravenel, Jr. Bridge
- Chicago, Illinois-skyscrapers, blues music, museums, ethnic diversity, architectural phenomena
- Denver, Colorado-museums, rocky mountains, ski resorts
- Honolulu, Hawaii-beaches, exotic culture and cuisine
- Las Vegas, Nevada-casinos and entertainment
- Los Angeles, California-beaches, the movie industry, Disneyland
- Louisville, Kentucky-The Kentucky Derby, Louisville Slugger, Falls of the Ohio, Louisville Zoo, birthplace of Abraham Lincoln, Waterfront Park, University of Louisville, Frazier International History Museum, Actors Theatre of Louisville, Louisville Ballet, Bourbon Festival, fried chicken
- Memphis, Tennessee-Graceland, Beale Street, The National Civil Rights Museum, Sun Studio
- Miami, Florida-beaches, Cuban cultural center, the Everglades
- Myrtle Beach, South Carolina-beaches, resorts, tourist attractions, and shopping.

- Nashville, Tennessee-country music, Opryland
- New Orleans, Louisiana-French Quarter, birthplace of jazz, Louisiana Creole cuisine, Garden District, seafood, festivals (VooDoo, Jazz Fest, Mardi Gras, etc.), beignets, National World War II Museum
- New York City, New York-cultural attractions, skyscrapers, several American landmarks, Coney Island
- Orlando, Florida-beaches, Walt Disney World Resort, SeaWorld, Universal Orlando Resort
- Philadelphia, Pennsylvania-important site for American history, Independence National Historical Park
- Phoenix, Arizona-Sonoran Desert, arid climate, several renowned golf courses
- Salt Lake City, Utah-Mormon history, rocky mountains, ski resorts
- San Antonio, Texas-The Alamo, San Antonio Riverwalk, Tower of the Americas
- San Diego, California-Spanish colonial heritage, San Diego Zoo, Balboa Park, SeaWorld, beaches, historic Gaslamp Quarter
- San Francisco, California-Golden Gate Bridge, Chinatown, Alcatraz, beaches
- Santa Fe, New Mexico-Native American crafts and culture
- San Juan, Puerto Rico-El Morro Castle, Old San Juan historical district, El Yunque rain forest
- Seattle, Washington-Space Needle, proximity to Mount Rainier National Park and Olympic National Park
- Washington, D.C.-Smithsonian museums, federal monuments, capital city of U.S.

Historic Landmarks

- Fort Sumter
- Liberty Bell

- Independence Hall
- Washington Monument
- Statue of Liberty
- The Alamo
- San Juan National Historic Site
- St. Louis Cathedral
- Chalmette Battle Field (War of 1812)

Gambling Venues

- Atlantic City, New Jersey
- Biloxi, Gulfport, Tupelo, rest of Mississippi
- Las Vegas, Nevada
- Native American casinos, various reservations; varies throughout many states
- Mississippi riverboats
- Reno, Nevada
- San Diego, California hosts several Native American casinos and outlet centers

TOURISM IN SPAIN

After Francisco Franco's death Spain became the second most-visited tourism destination in the world after France. They welcome 52 million tourists per year, according to the World Tourism Organization. In fact, the headquarters of WTO are in Madrid.

Tourism in Spain includes the two largest cities of Madrid and Barcelona, and some other very interesting places include Vigo and Pontevedra in Galicia, Cordoba, Sevilla, Granada (cultural places) and Málaga, Huelva, Cádiz, Almería (beaches) in Andalusia, Salamanca, Toledo, Segovia are beautiful places in the rest of the country. Cáceres, Guadalupe and Merida are cultural places in Extremadura. Important tourist places (with incredible beaches) are Rías Baixas (in the province of Pontevedra), Salou, Benidorm, Mallorca, Ibiza (Balearic Islands),

Canary Islands, Valencia, Catalonia and Green Spain (north of Spain). The Basque Country, although it is an autonomous community inside Spain, is becoming a very important turistic point, with Bilbao Guggenheim Museum in Bilbao, Donostia, Vitoria, Iruñea, and Iparralde. The Basque Country coast is marvelous.

Spain's national airline is Iberia (or Iberia Airlines), but the country can also be flown into on many international passenger and charter airlines, both of which fly to many tourist spots in the region. There are good trains, for example AVE (Spanish high velocity) or Talgo. There are good freeways to the most important cities.

TOURISM IN TURKEY

Tourism in Turkey is focused largely on a variety of archaeological and historical sites, and on seaside resorts along its Aegean and Mediterranean coasts. In the recent years, Turkey is also becoming a popular destination for the SPA and health care tourism.

Turkey's largest city, Istanbul, has a number of major attractions derived from its huge historical status as capital of the Byzantine and Ottoman Empires. These include the Sultan Ahmed Mosque (the "Blue Mosque"), the Hagia Sophia, the Topkapi Palace, the Basilica Cistern, the Dolmabahce Palace, the Galata Tower, the Grand Bazaar, and the Pera Palas. Istanbul has also recently became one of the biggest shopping centers of European region by hosting malls and shopping centers like Metrocity, Akmerkez and Cevahir Mall (which is the biggest mall in Europe and second largest shopping center in the world).

Major cultural and historical attractions elsewhere in the country include the sites of Ephesus, Troy, Pergamon, House of Virgin Mary, Pamukkale, Hierapolis, Konya (where the poet Rumi had spent most of his life), Didyma, Church of Antioch, religious places in Mardin (such as Deyrülzafarân Monastery), and the ruined cities and landscapes of Cappadocia. (see List of Archaeological Sites Sorted by Country-Turkey)

Beach vacations, particularly for Turkish city-dwellers and visitors from Western Europe, are also central to the Turkish tourism industry. Most beach resorts are located along the southwestern and southern Aegean coast, especially along the Mediterranean coast near Antalya. Antalya is also accepted as the tourism capital of Turkey. Major resort towns include Bodrum, Fethiye, Marmaris, Kusadasi, Cesme, Didim and Alanya.

Foreign tourist arrivals increased substantially in Turkey between 2002 and 2005, from 12.8 million to 21.2 million, which made Turkey a top-10 destination in the world for foreign visitors. 2005 revenues are US$17.5 billion which also made Turkey the top-10 biggest revenue owners in the world.

Year-Arrivals (in millions)

1998	9,750,000
1999	7,460,000
2000	8,000,000
2001	10,400,000
2002	12,800,000
2003	13,300,000
2004	16,800,000
2005	21,200,000
2006	19,800,000
2007	

TOURISM IN SWEDEN

Sweden is visited most by tourists from its neighbouring countries Denmark, Norway and Finland. There after follow tourists from Germany and England.

A popular route for German tourists is to go by train from southern Sweden, through the European routes, up to Sweden's northern parts. Attractions along the way are historical, natural and cultural.

According to the CIA World Factbook, Sweden is the 21st most visited country in the world, with 7 627 000 arrivals in 2006.

Swedish Culture

The World Heritage Sites are reliable and popular goals to visit. Sites that can be visited are:

- The Agricultural Landscape on the island of Öland is popular for its geological and geographical features.
- Birka and Hovgården on the islands Björkö and Adelsö in Mälaren near Stockholm.
- The Church Village of Gammelstad, Luleå, northern Sweden.
- Drottningholm Palace, Theatre, and Royal Domain
- Engelsberg Ironworks
- The Hanseatic town of Visby
- The "High Coast" of Ångermanland
- Laponian area, Swedish Lapland, northern Sweden.
- The Mining Area of the Great Copper Mountain in Falun
- The Naval Port of Karlskrona
- Rock carvings in Tanumshede
- Skogskyrkogården in Stockholm

Swedish Nature

In the summer the sun hardly sets in Sweden, especially in the far north where it does not set at all. This allows activity until late in the evening, or even through the night.

Sweden has very many lakes and forests, and it is very good for fishing and canoeing. There are several large lakes, including lakes Vättern and Vänern. Walking is quite a popular activity in the summer. There are no very high mountains in Sweden, so climbing is somewhat limited. The highest mountain is Kebnekaise near Kiruna. Kebnekaise is 6926 ft, 2111 metres high. The Göta Canal from Stockholm to Gothenburg provides some good trips in the summer. Swedish horse racing is a little unusual, in that many races are actually trotting races. The horses are not allowed to gallop, and they pull a small trap with the racer on.

Northern Sweden and Winter Sports

In the winter, the Ice Hotel is built every year near the northern town of Kiruna. Kiruna is also a good place from which to see the Aurora Borealis or Northern lights. Tourists in the north of the country in winter often enjoy trips in reindeer sleighs with Sami drivers, or in dog sleighs.

It is also possible to ski, with downhill resorts at Åre and Vemdalen, and many cross country ski tracks throughout the northern part of the country. Vasaloppet in the beginning of March is the oldest, longest and largest cross-country ski race in the world. Ice hockey is a popular sport in winter. Many of the bays in the northern part of the country are frozen in winter, and it is possible to go ice yachting, or ice skating on the ice. Many lakes are also frozen, so ice fishing (pimpelfiske) is quite popular.

Cities

Most Swedish cities are small compared to other European cities such as those in England and Germany. The largest city is Stockholm, with approx. 750.000 inhabitants, followed by Gothenburg with 480.000 and Malmö with 250,000.

Stockholm has been Sweden's capital since at least the 14th century. It is Sweden's metropolis, the centre of the parliament, government, and media. Not only is its waterfront and adjacent Stockholm Archipelago one of a kind, but the old parts of Stockholm with its history and culture is spectacular in its own kind. For more information, see Tourism in Stockholm.

Gothenburg is a relatively young city dating from the 17th century, and is visited for its beauty, attractions, friendliness and shopping opportunities. Gothenburg is with over 60.000 students the largest university city in Scandinavia. According to a recent survey of Swedish media, Gothenburg was voted the most popular major city in Sweden. More than 60% of all Swedes would like to live in Gothenburg, which has a reputation of being even friendlier and more welcoming than the Swedish capital.

Malmö has recently emerged as the eastern part of the Oresund region, tied together with Copenhagen, Denmark, through the impressive Oresund Bridge. In the last 15 years, Malmö has been focusing more on culture, as it previously had a solid reputation as a working class city. The twisted skyscraper Turning Torso has become the new landmark, replacing the ship-crane at Kockums.

Other cities have solid places in Sweden's history:

- Uppsala became the seat of the Archbishop of Sweden in 1167, with Sweden's and Scandinavia's largest church building Uppsala Cathedral inaugurated in the 1440s. Uppsala also became the center of education in Sweden with the Uppsala University founded in 1477.
- Lund was among the cities belonging to Denmark until 1658. Previously, it had been the seat of Denmark's archbishop, in the city of Lund. In 1666, Lund was granted Sweden's second university, the Lund University.

Transportation

The Swedish rail system is called SJ and is quite excellent, offering slower-speed trains throughout the country and the faster X2000 trains connecting the major cities. Connection by rail is possible to Norway and Denmark, and to Finland by bus, due to rail gauge differences. It's possible to take the Silja and Viking Line boats from Stockholm to Helsinki, Finland, Rostock, Germany or Mariehamn island. Scandinavian Airlines System and other airlines provides access by air for longer trips.

Culture of Sweden

The Culture of Sweden is typically perceived as egalitarian, simple, and open to international influences. Sweden never had serfdom and peasant smallholders traditionally had a greater say in the nation's affairs than in virtually any other Western country. Protestant work ethic and trade unionism are other factors often said to have shaped Swedish mentality.

Foreign Influence

The greatest sources on influence on Swedish culture have been the Catholic church and Germany during the Middle Ages, France during the 18th century (mainly through king Gustav III), Germany again during the 19th century and the English-speaking world after World War II. Sweden is today very Americanized with a stongly adapted western culture.

Regions

The various historical provinces of Sweden, which earlier had poor communications, each have a distinct culture. Historically this was noted through the Swedish provinces that once (around 1,000 years ago) constituted separate countries. For brevity, one can make a crude distinction into seven areas. From north to south:

- Northern part: Norrland (Number 1 and 2).

This part was historically unexplored for centuries. For large parts wilderness dominates. The Scandinavian mountain range occupies its western part. The native Sami people have part of their habitat here, large parts of which have been declared a World Heritage Site under the name Laponian area.

- Lake and Folklore part: Dalarna, Värmland, Närke, Västmanland (Number 3 and 6).

The industry in these parts were dominated by mining, known as the Central Sweden mining district or Bergslagen. The Large Copper Mine of Falun, being active since 1347, has been declared a World Heritage Site. The falu red used on Swedish houses was created as a by-product from the copper mine. The traditional Swedish dish, the falukorv sausage, was also invented here and fed the miners for centuries.

- Stockholm and surroundings: lake Mälaren, the "east coast" (Number 4).

One of the three oldest parts of Sweden, together with Västergötland and Östergötland and home of the Suiones wherefrom the name Sweden is derived, the area has been the seat of the Swedish King since the captitol of Stockholm started to grow in the end of the 13th century. Uppsala near Stockholm has been the place of the archbishop for nearly a thousand years. Royal mansions are scattered around the lake Mälaren, and the royal palace Drottningholm has been declared a UNESCO World Heritage Site.

- Gothenburg and surroundings: Västra Götaland, Bohuslan, Dalsland (Number 8)

Historically the home of the Geats tribe, opposing the Suiones. People lived here at least since the Stone Age, for about 11.000 years ago (as shown by excavations along the Swedish west coast) and the rock carvings in Tanumshede, dating at least to the bronze age, have been declared a World Heritage Site.

- Forests and Glass: Småland (Number 7) and Östergötland, (Number 5).

The area is noted by glassworks such as Kosta Boda and Orrefors, for centuries providing both cheaper and costly glass products to the Swedish people. The land is generally unsuitable for agriculture, but has many dense forests leading to various wood-industries. Many industrious people stem from the area, including Carolus Linnaeus, Ingvar Kamprad (Ikea founder); and authors Astrid Lindgren and Vilhelm Moberg who characterized it in their worldwide appreciated works.

- Castles and plains: The Scanlan lands (Number 9).

Until the Treaty of Roskilde in 1658, this area belonged to Denmark, as did the counties of Bohuslän and Halland (Bohuslän originally Norwegian), who equipped it with around 200 castles and fortresses, along with many Romanesque countryside churches. Much of Sweden's crops are also grown in the plains of this area.

- Island of Öland (unnumbered-Off the coast of Smaland).

This region is known for its mesolithic settlements, Iron Age ringforts and Viking history. About one fourth of the island is a desgnated World Heritage Site, known as the Stora Alvaret, noted not only for its rich history but also as a limestone barren habitat, holding numerous rare and endangered species.

- Gotland (unnumbered-Island in the middle of the Baltics).

Regarded by some historians and linguists to be the original homeland of the Goths.

Generally the word goes that the farther north you come, the quieter people become. Experience as well as popular literature confirm the general truth in this.

It should be noted that these regions are made for cultural distinctions only. The two historical subdidivisions are the Provinces of Sweden (amounting to 26), and the Lands of Sweden (amounting to three).

Attitudes

Swedes have an egalitarian outlook. The concept of Jante Law is in many areas and fields still today strong in Sweden, and any form of elitism is likely to meet strong criticism. This attitude goes in hand with the Swedish lagomhet, the appraisal of modesty and humbleness. Swedes generally express themselves in very modest terms, especially when it comes to compliments and praises-when they say something is "totally okay" that means it is very good indeed. In the same way they are not likely to be harsh in criticizing others.

There is however also a strong drive for more individualist values, and these have during the 20th century taken over from the more collectivist tradition. Notably there is a very strong support for tolerance towards same-sex relationships compared to most European countries, and Sweden is often thought of (and most Swedes think of their country) as a country with little xenophobia, despite recent growth of racism.

The combination of embracing capitalist values and the Swedish agrarian modesty has produced an atmosphere that encourages hard work and honesty. Sweden generally has low corruption.

Environmentalism and animal protection are important values in Sweden.

January 1 is the New Years Day January 6 Twelfth Night March and April is Easter April 30 is the Feast of valborg

Food

Swedish food is traditionally simple, a typical meal consists of boiled potatoes, some kind of meat or fish, a simple sauce and some vegetables. Fish has historically been very important. Today Swedes eat roughly the same as other Westerners, spaghetti is rivalling the previously dominant potato in popularity.

Swedes are among the heaviest coffee drinkers in the world, second only to Finland. Brewed coffee is totally dominant. For meals beer, milk or water is standard.

Film

Swedish cinema is one of the most widely-known national film industries in the world. This is partly due to the innovation of its early days. The silent period saw the flourish of the gifted visionaries Mauritz Stiller and Victor Sjöström, who brought international attention to Swedish filmmaking and its particular vision of the world.

Ingmar Bergman, regarded as one of the most influential filmmakers of the 20th Century, emerged as a prominent figure in world cinema during the 1950s with his existential epic The Seventh Seal, which he followed with a host of critically revered psychological dramas. Two of his films in particular, Persona and Cries and Whispers, received unparalleled critical adoration and put Sweden in the map as a one of the most progressive cinematic entities. The revered naturalist Jan Troell as well as the socially conscious Bo Widerberg would quickly follow Bergman as the country's foremost visual artists.

Famous actresses and actors include Ingrid Bergman, Greta Garbo, Max von Sydow, Stellan Skarsgård, Ingrid Thulin, Lena Olin and Peter Stormare.

Music

In popular music, the group ABBA became the essence of Swedish music during the 70's and early 80's. Later emerged Roxette, where singing happy music into the 80's, and this band was unlike ABBA also successful in the U.S. Europe and Ace of Base are Swedish rock groups that have been popular in the world.

It can be noted that Britney Spears had at least one of her early albums produced in Sweden, and so have Bon Jovi and the Backstreet Boys.

In contrast to the beauty and vocal melody of many other types of music from Sweden, they also boast one of the most prolific death metal scenes in the world. Gothenburg is famed in the scene for the "Swedish Death" sound. Many of these bands such as In Flames, Dark Tranquillity, and Stockholm's Opeth have seen growing commercial success throughout Europe and the United States.

The Swedish hip hop scene is booming, but admittedly it has attracted no international fame. However, a sociolect / dialect has emerged in the foreigners-populated suburbs, which perhaps may spice up the language. (See the term Rinkeby Swedish, so named after the Rinkeby suburb).

There are several reputable Swedish singers. In the 1850s, Jenny Lind was touring the United States, and the admission to enter her performances was at a rate never seen before. Not for nothing was she referred to as the Swedish Nightingale. Later, in the 1950s, Jussi Björling was one of few non-Italian opera singers, and still today a household name in opera circles.

3

Historical Perspective of World Tourism

INTRODUCTION

The substantial growth of the tourism activity clearly marks tourism as one of the most remarkable economic and social phenomena of the past century. The number of international arrivals shows an evolution from a mere 25 million international arrivals in 1950 to an estimated 806 million in 2005, corresponding to an average annual growth rate of 6.5%

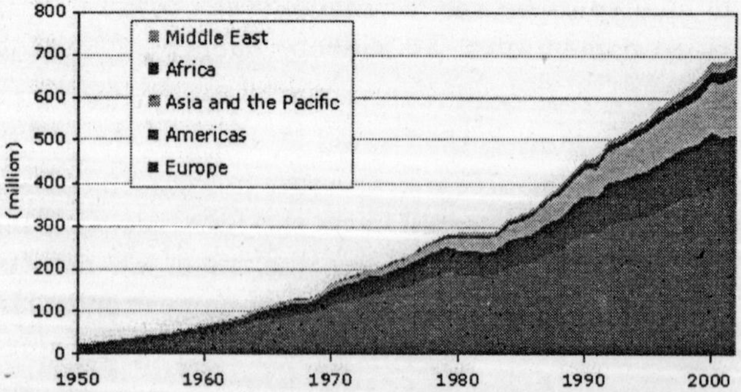

During this period, development was particularly strong in Asia and the Pacific (13% on average a year) and in the Middle East (10%) while the Americas (5%) and Europe (6%), grew at a slower pace and slightly below the world's average growth. New destinations are steadily increasing their market share while more mature regions such as Europe and the Americas tend to have less dynamic growth. Europe's world share declined by over 10 percentage points since 1950 whereas the Americas lost 13 percentage points. Though the Americas' performance has been most affected by the declines suffered in the past years, the fact is that its annual average growth rate for the period 1950-2000 was 5.8%, also bellow the average for the world (6.8%).

Europe and the Americas were the main tourist-receiving regions between 1950 and 2000. Both regions represented a joint market share of over 95 per cent in 1950, 82% forty years later and 76% in 2000.

CRITIQUE OF THIRD WORLD TOURISM

Tourism has become one of the most prominent and influential global industries. It directly or indirectly employs one in every 10 employed people on earth, and maintains 3.6 trillion dollars worth of goods and services which is 10.6 percent of the gross global product. (Brown, 24.)

Tourism has become the mainstay of countless countries worldwide and is one of the greatest sources of entrepreneurial activity. Yet, despite these impressive statistics, and contrary to what most tourists, myself included, have been taught, tourism, especially in the third world, is far from the benign panacea of benefits for 'host' countries it is regularly portrayed to be.

Tourism bears a nearly direct lineage to perhaps the first arbiter of the first/third world dynamic globalization: colonialism. This is most obvious in that nearly all tourists come from the first world, notably Europe and the United States, and are also the primary owners of the tourist infrastructure. Professor McCall's observation that whites are "living it up" in South Africa is true, to a large extent, throughout the world, with tourism among the central modes of their enjoyment. Tourism, like colonialism, involves an occupation and domination of space, in this instance by the tourist structure and tourists themselves. It is also an industry that, like colonialism, is enabled by expansions of power.

Tourists, especially those going to the third world, venture forth to survey the lands and peoples over which they reign: to catalogue it, exploit it, revel in its submission, and leave it, both in body and mind.

Tourism, contrary to popular belief, generally benefits the tourist far more than it does the residents of the country they visit. The often vast government subsidies poured into enabling tourism in many countries come at the expense of those funds being used to directly help the majority of the country's usually destitute residents. While such funds do help many residents to some extent, usually in the form of creating mostly low-paying, unskilled jobs, the resources are essentially being shared with, if not outright given to, tourists.

Additionally, the funds spent by tourists while on their sojourns rarely help the average resident. The spending, if it stays in the country, largely benefits the owners of the tourist structure in the country. In South Africa's case, this constitutes the often already wealthy, disproportionately white upper-class. However, much, and in some cases nearly all, of the money spent by tourists does not stay in the country at all. This is primarily due to a large portion of tourist infrastructure being foreign owned. Examples of this ownership include tour services, hotels, travel agencies, and many of the stores placed in tourist centers. Furthermore, these owners often employ expatriates or international workers instead of locals.

For instance, while on the return flight from South Africa I sat next to, and nearby, several groups who had spent the entirety of their stay in private game parks. Each group had a series of pictures of their loved ones proudly bestriding the various animals they had so bravely slain during the course of their so-called 'expeditions'.

Upon inquiry, I learned that by dealing exclusively with foreign-based outfitters, suppliers, agencies and owners, as apparently "all" of their friends did as well, these groups had managed to stay in South Africa for nearly a month without directly contributing a cent to the local economy. When I asked one group member, a portly man named Bill from Texas, why he had decided to only use foreign companies he, at first, seemed somewhat surprised by the question, giving me a quizzical look as if to say "surprised you'd need to ask". Then he answered "our outfitters are pros, they know what they're doin, the South Africans don't." In Kenya, Thailand, Fiji, and many other countries, this 'leakage', as it is commonly referred to, of tourist spending approaches, and often exceeds, 60%. (Brown 58), However, to lesser extents it is present in nearly every tourism integrated economy, including South Africa's.

As more tourists and wealthy first-world vacationers frequent a country, inflation and a rise in land prices begin to occur as a result of the strength of first-world currencies and by the disproportionate wealth of the foreigners. This hurts local residents by creating a barrier between their lives and the artificially created world of tourists. Tourist areas become far too expensive for locals to enjoy. Subsequently, the only use of the areas most local residents will have comes from working as the maids, cleaners, and other basic-service providing employees needed to run the sites.

In South Africa, we stayed in the "Waterfront" one area that demonstrates this point well. Of all the South African residents I spoke to not a single person frequented this area, the reason always being the, what one person at SABC called, "exorbitant" prices. This same effect has manifested itself in South African property, amusement parks, aquariums, museums, shopping centers, and even such national heritage sites as Table Mountain and Robben Island. In my story for SABC I interviewed over 25 South African residents on the streets of Cape Town and not a single person had visited either Table Mountain or Robben Island. They unanimously cited, what one school teacher called, "insane" prices, while also stating that they would love to go if the pricing was not so high. Aside from this essentially financial separation, there are many instances where local residents have been physically removed from an area to make way for tourism. Often, this consists of the destitute who are perceived as a blight and/or crime threat, as in Times Square, and are forcibly removed in these instances are moved out of the areas as they are perceived to make the area less desirable for tourists. For those remaining destitute residents in the Cape Town, Waterfront area, many of whom seem to subsist largely from soliciting money from tourists, life is made incredibly difficult by the harsh treatment doled out by nearly everyone they come into contact with. In one instance, while I was eating with our group in a café in the area, one ragged local man came to the door and, in plain view of all the patrons, the manager opened the door and yelled at the man "go away and don't ever come here again!". The man was most likely there to ask the patrons for money, and, as it could potentially disrupt business, I am not entirely surprised by the manager's reaction. It is the structural dynamic the example demonstrates that is most appalling: with most residents already priced out of the area, the most common remaining residents I encountered lived in various stages of destitution and had to resort to humiliating acts to get by.

(Another cause of local resident displacement is the growing trend of ecotourism. Ecotourists want to see so-called 'unspoiled' nature. This, of course, does not include people. However, communities reside in many areas that might make excellent ecotourist havens. This conflict of interest is increasingly leading to confrontations between the developers who envision their own Kruger Park (which itself, as Herman mentioned, displaced former inhabitants in its development) and the people, often indigenous, who reside on the land. Not surprisingly, with the all-powerful tourist lobby in their corner, the developers are not encountering much trouble.

Earlier this year, in an effort to clear the area for an ecotourism venture, 250 residents of the Ambulong shore village in the Philippines were evicted from their homes. As they had refused to leave earlier, the eviction was violent: police attacked the village, wounding many inhabitants and demolishing 24 houses. While the people have pledged to continue the fight for their homes, the outlook is clearly not good. In Bangladesh over 1000 families of the Khasi and Garoare indigenous groups face eviction from their tribal land for development of a park. In Brazil two villages near the resort town of Fortaleza have gone to court to show that a real estate agency that forced them off their lands to build an "ecological resort" broke the law. In Africa, more recent examples than Kruger include the Masai in East Africa and the Bushmen of Botswana. (Mail & Guardian June, 2002). Even when the indigenous peoples themselves propose to start ecotourism, as the Botswana Bushmen did, governments, as occurred in the Botswana case, often refuse to relinquish their potential earnings to the residents. (Mail & Guardian June, 2002)

Tourism also plays a significant role in the continuing economic subordination and dependency of the third world upon the core nations. The first world has a long tradition of forcing first world ideology and concepts upon drastically different third world countries, often their former colonies. One example if the first world (WTO/IMF)'s forcing of globalization and neo-liberal policies upon the third world instead of encouraging more third world appropriate concepts like localization. Another example is that by forcing third world economies to be based upon precarious and unpredictable exports (i.e. coffee and bananas) the first world effectively inhibits autonomous growth in the third world countries. Tourism is a similarly unpredictable and fluctuating business and is entirely dependent on, essentially, entertaining visitors from outside the country. Thus, tourist based third-world economies become both dependent on, and subordinate to, tourists. This comes at the expense of fostering more organic, autonomous and lasting growth. The result is the perpetuation of a structure in which strong, industrialized countries are able to impose terms of trade to their advantage upon weaker states. Within this broader perspective of relationships, the first world tourist visiting a third world tourist based economy is akin to a colonizer both visiting, and perpetuating the domination of, a colony.

This dependency in a tourist economy manifests itself in the subordination of the people, culture and structures of the society to tourist interests. If a third world country wants and IMF loan, it must demonstrate its compliance with the IMF's interests. The tourist/service relationship is, in some ways, a microcosm of this exchange. If a third world tourist economy wants tourist money, it must be sensitive to tourist interests.

In this sense, tourism is a form of domination and of the master/servant dynamic tracing its lineage to the colonial era. I could sense this dynamic in many instances on our trip. Nearly everyone staying at the Breakwater Inn were white tourists.

However, the staff, especially the cleaning and maintenance crew, was composed almost entirely of local blacks who had to serve us everyday, clean up after us, and ultimately treat us as if we were somehow above them. The people who would transport our luggage were like our servants, as well as the unseen maids at all the hotels we stayed at. The hundreds of vendors we encountered on the trip were entirely dependent on tourists, and many of them utilized, either by choice or desperation, that same master/servant dynamic. Often they would say things to me like "oh please sir, please buy something, I will never forget you, and my family will always remember you." I heard variations of that pitch throughout our trip from vendors of all kinds.

It seems that many tourists either consciously or unconsciously fulfill their 'master' role. I often encountered tourists treating vendors, staff and other employees with shocking rudeness and almost scornful disregard. Professor McCall drew my attention to one tourist becoming enraged at the black cooking staff for giving him what he called ¾ of an egg, as opposed to the whole egg he expected. On the return flight a member of the safari groups sitting near me verbally assaulted a stewardess when she said that she would need to take his suitcase to a storage compartment on the plane as the overhead bins were overflowing.

The tourist, after arguing with her about why she had no right to move his suitcase anywhere, on the plane or off, then yelled, as if to accuse the entire staff of being inept and corrupt, that "If anything and I mean anything is missing from that suitcase, there will be hell to pay!". These examples add to the countless instances I can recall throughout my experience of encountering stereotypically "angry tourists". They seem to consistently be appealing to a sense that they deserve better than everyone else, and are entitled to utter subservience. To this end, I have come to accept that I, like all tourists in a third world country, could, and probably often do, symbolize arrogance, oppression and the subservience of much of the country's people. In South Africa I often did feel people holding variations of this view of me, and I understand why they did. Several people said that they resented me, and people like me, who came to their country. Others mentioned my arrogance, which I am sure I do have to some extent, as well as the collective arrogance of the first world.

With the spread and intervention of capitalism into Third World societies, tourism has also had the effect of turning Third World places, landscapes and people into commodities. Essentially tourists consume elements of a vacation in the same way as we consume other objects or commodities. This is perhaps most obviously evident in the packaging of African culture, history and imagery into convenient souvenirs sold by vendors throughout the tourist enclaves. Another example is the play we saw, entitled "African Footsteps" which commoditized African history into a sanitized, tourist-pleasing, and overly simplistic package to be bought and consumed by tourists eager to move onto the next item. Trips to the country are sold as a package, but it is more importantly the country itself that is being transformed, along with its uniqueness, people, and cultural heritage, to be sold as a commodity to the golden hordes of tourists.

In the vein of commoditizing is the 'otherness' that is fostered by the separateness of tourism interactions with the local peoples and surroundings. Tourists, like the first world they come from, have come to view the core and periphery nations as a situation of 'us' and 'them', 'them' being the societies outside the first world which are variably defined by ideas of simplicity, disease, barbarism, instability, poverty and as generally problematic. Much tourism entrenches this sense of 'otherness.' For instance, the township tours (link to chapter on township tours) we went on consisted of driving through people's communities in buses, stopping occasionally to look around while guarded by police, perhaps asking a few questions (if the people are lucky) and then gathering to get back on the bus from whence we came, never to be seen again. We were, however, preceding, and will be followed by, a never-ending string of the same buses unloading the same people. Only the faces will really change, but even they won't change too drastically. Eventually it will just blend into a blur of otherness. Now I imagine if that was my community, if that backyard our bus pulled up in was my backyard.

If I had busses stopping in front of my house to momentarily let out peering faces and cameras who would peruse my driveway before getting back onto their bus. Then, a day later, another bus, and then another, and another. I would feel on display, like a commodity being captured in the visitors' cameras and taken away. Above all, I would feel like I was 'other'.

The yearning of first-world tourists to venture to third-world locales is a kind of postmodern reaction to a certain meaninglessness and dissatisfaction with modern life. One backlash against the post-industrial complex is the desire to return to the purity of pre-modern life and to experience the supposed authenticity of 'unspoiled' land, people and environments. As the continuing existence of any people or environment entirely unaffected by humans is nearly impossible, fabrications are necessary to satiate this yearning. Professor Wittenberg, in his introduction to Kruger Park, spoke at length about the desire of those who created the park to maintain a place where, in this case white men, could go to reconnect with pure nature and experience what their forefathers lived in, re-creating such lost rites of passage as "the first hunt". Kruger, however, is not a real, natural habitat. It is an artificially maintained semblance of a time long past. This also holds true for the Zulu cultural village many of us went to see. It utilizes the desire to see pure indigenous cultures, but is in fact, no more than a reenactment of a lifestyle long since altered by the very societies of many who now come to gaze at the sights. These things are not real, they remain in a romanticized vision of "untouched" land and peoples that exists today only as a fantasy in the mind of tourists. It is a mentality that encourages the "disneyizing" of culture and of environments, creating some romanticized fantasy rather than grappling with the modern day reality and conflicts of the places. The vision of "untouched" "virgin" land and peoples has a long history in the collective Western thought, tracing back to the mythologized colonial voyages and stories of explorers pushing to the frontier. For instance, as we drove through the Kruger terrain I wanted to imagine going to the area for the first time, I even remarked to Herman "imagine what it would have been like for the first voyagers coming to this area....how incredible and desperately hard it must have been". He then noted about the high death rate for them, but I was already drifting off into imaging how breathtaking it must have been to see these lands for the first time, yearning to have that experience as well. I had not realized it, but the efficacy of that idealized story had firmly enraptured my mind as well. This seems due, in large part, to the historical education I received. I was taught far more about the Indians of the 1700's in American high school than about the Indians of today. Additionally, I was bombarded with the supposedly heroic tales of explorers like Columbus and Magellan who first witnessed untouched people and lands. Few seem to care about, or have any desire to face, the complex, often difficult realities facing modern indigenous peoples or the crises facing many remaining tracts of actual wilderness. They would rather see a reenactment of a lifestyle long passed, or an artificially idyllic, maintained nature preserve, and leave with their preconceptions intact than have to deal with the often ugly and difficult reality. Tourists, after all, are not there to feel conflicted and are not paying to feel guilt; they want it to be simple, romantic, and easy to deal with.

In spite of all these problems, it must be noted that in many instances, utilization of third world tourism comes at a cost of less than many alternatives. For some areas, such as small islands, tourism is often the most viable means by which to develop the economy. Furthermore, given the desperate economic state of many third world countries, with unemployment often in double digits, it must be considered that there may be little choice other than tourism. While the jobs in the tourism market are mostly low-paying and unskilled, any job is better than none. Clearly, this does not excuse the multiplicity of problems endemic to third world tourism. Yet, it is often this lack of better economic alternative that leads countries to accept them. Thus, the goal must be to ensure that no country is in a position to need tourism to survive.

Tourism is, by many metrics, the world's largest industry. It has become a permanent part of the modern global economy and is only becoming more widespread. However, the third world tourism industry is obligated to address the multitude of aforesaid problems before it can become an equitable form of development. This will require the creation of alternate forms of tourism that truly benefit the majority of a country's residents as much, if not more, than the incoming tourists. Until then, third world tourism will continue to serve as a perpetuation of the colonial legacy, providing enjoyable exploration for tourists and festering exploitation for locals.

CHEAP SIGHTSEEING TOUR: YOUR NEIGHBOURHOOD

A cheap and easy sightseeing tour idea, explore your own neighbourhood like it were a new exotic location, introduction and tips.

Sightseeing in Your Own Neighbourhood

Whether we pay attention to it or not, we all belong to a neighbourhood of one sort or another. Some of us live in city neighbourhoods, some in suburban ones, others in rural neighbourhoods, such as the mountains or the high plains. What is your neighbourhood? Is it a place, a group of buildings, or a collection of people? Before you get into knowing your neighbourhood, look at the Almanac's neighbourhood map, drawn up by one who lived there. As he spotted items onto the map--which he got from the local town hall--he took notes on each item and keyed these notes to the map. You can do the same for your own neighbourhood.

Our sample neighbourhood is a suburb, about 1 1/2 hours from New York City. It contains 500 acres, about 200 houses, 275 apartments, and nearly 1,500 people. They are mostly young to middle-aged families with an average of slightly over 2 children per household. It can be described as a solidly middle-class neighbourhood. Listed below are its parts and a description of each:

1. *Shopping Center*. People from all over this town and surrounding towns come here to shop. The land was developed and owned by a national company and the stores are leased to large chains which are not oriented to the neighbourhood. Some smaller shops like the stationery and gift shops, however, are owned by neighbourhood people. They like the heavy traffic which the chains bring in. The neighbourhood on the whole, however, doesn't like it. Three years ago the shopping center was an orchard.
2. *Highway, U.S. Route* 1. Follows the old Boston Post Road. Four lanes of heavy traffic carry outsiders through this edge of the neighbourhood as well as neighbourhood residents to and from work and the many stores that line the highway strip. Two private companies have buses connecting the neighbourhood to the town and the nearest city. But the service is poor and is nonexistent on Sundays or in the evenings. The very young and the old who don't drive can't get out of the neighbourhood to do things. Take, for example, Mrs. Robin McKenna. You can meet her easily enough because, although she's 75 years old, you'll often find her hitchhiking along Shore Drive (4). Pick her up and she'll tell you that since the old trolley was abandoned 25 years ago, it's been harder and harder for oldsters like her to get into town. She doesn't drive, but all the large stores, doctors' offices, and meeting places are in the town or nearby city. She tells her friends to hitchhike but they're afraid. Mrs. McKenna admits that some strangers are weird, but most are friendly and all are interesting. Her regular rides get cookies from her at Christmas.
3. *Alps Road*. A feeder street for the neighbourhood it bounds. It is so narrow and winding over the small hills in the neighbourhood that the old farmers called it

"Alps Road." Some of them live in older farmhouses along the road, but most have been squeezed out by single-family homes built over the last 10 years costing $30,000 to $40,000.

4. *Shore Drive.* Another feeder street and neighbourhood divider. It is also State Highway 142 and carries outsiders through the neighbourhood to the nearby shore and beaches which gave the road its name. Summer traffic is heavy and generally keeps people from crossing it to go to stores and schools in the next neighbourhood. The road has mostly older, single-family houses, lived in by older couples whose children have grown up.

5. *Echlin Company.* This factory makes automobile parts. It is owned by outsiders, employs a few people from the surrounding neighbourhood, and uses many inner-city blacks who commute by car from the nearby city because owning a house in the neighbourhood is expensive and nearby apartments are small and lived in only by whites. But according to realtors of the area, no discrimination takes place here. Bob Gillings thinks differently. He's black, lives in the nearby city, and hasn't found a place to live in this neighbourhood. "When the company moved from the city to this town, they promised the town fathers they'd bring good taxes but none of the workers. Too expensive for us to buy a house here. We can afford the rents here but we always get the 'no vacancy' sign when we ask. Heck, me and my wife are more comfortable in the city anyway."

6. *Old Colonial Farmhouse.* "For Sale." Although some of the town's famous families lived here, this home's place on the highway (2) makes its land more valuable for stores.

7. *Vacant Lot.* Owned by the owners of the shopping center next door (1), who want to build 152 apartments here. The neighbourhood opposes them because apartments would bring in more traffic, especially to Shore Drive (4), alter streams through the land (8), and possibly

bring in low-income residents, such as the blacks who work nearby.

8. *Streams.* These collect water from the sloping land and carry it to the nearby river. These streams are relatively unpolluted since this part of the neighbourhood has been provided with sewer pipes beneath the streets to carry waste water to a plant which treats it before letting it flow out to the river. During rains, the streams here often flood the lot (7), which temporarily holds the water before it goes downstream. Buildings around these streams would make the water overflow faster and flood downstream houses. This kind of flooding already happens at the nearby apartments, where one building has been situated in the path of a stream.

9. *Apartments.* Seven buildings have 55 apartments. Developed and sold as condominiums, only about half are owner-occupied. Nonresidents own the rest as rental investments. They provide little in the way of maintenance or play facilities for those who rent from them. The renters tend to have lower incomes than the owners, are younger, and have young children. Because the owners tend not to have children living at home, they don't want to spend money on building a play lot. So the children play in the parking lots.

10. *More Apartments.* All 150 are rented to older couples or young families. The neighbourhood used to be all single-family or lots. But a major developer bought the land, made a large contribution to the local political party in power, and got permission to build apartments here. Because the earth is too rocky to absorb so much sewage, the developer 1st had to put in a sewer line. The chairman of the Sewer Authority, who doesn't live in the neighbourhood, is a land developer himself as well as the boss of the political party which received the contribution. So Mr. Chairman was happy to extend the sewer lines. This made the entire neighbourhood suitable for apartments, and developers are madly rushing to buy up the open space.

11. *Open Space*. The play area for the apartments (10) was supposed to be here. But the developer forgot to build it. Instead he quickly sold the land and buildings to outside investors such as Dr. Robert Kelley. Dr. Kelley is a dentist who has his offices in the local town center and lives in a wealthier part of town. Many of his patients live in our sample neighbourhood but they don't know that their dentist owns these apartments. Dr. Kelley doesn't want them to know.
12. *Vacant Lot*. But not for long! Another developer wants to fill in the pond with rock and dirt from the nearby hill, which he'll tear away to build 150 apartments. Mark Robbins, who lives in the apartments (9) with his mother and 2 sisters, has spotted a muskrat family living in the pond. But the developer would rather have wealthier, childless families in condominium apartments living here instead of muskrats or little boys like Mark who befriend the local wildlife.
13. *Ballou Road*. A small, single-family housing tract owned and lived in by older, working-class families. Joe Ballou lives here. He built most of the houses and named the street that he put in for them. His youngest daughter, Lisa, is still in high school, but his other children are married and live in other suburbs. Joe doesn't build houses anymore. "The market isn't so good," he says. "And besides, my wife and I are getting old enough where we'd like to enjoy life." So he and his wife have spent the last 4 winters in Florida. During the rest of the year Joe occasionally remodels bathrooms and kitchens.
14. *Footpath*. Apartment dwellers shortcut to the shopping center or bus, rather than walk along the streets, which have no sidewalks in this part of the neighbourhood.
15. *Homes*. New, one-family houses worth $40,000 to $65,000. A typical owner is Bud Anderson. He is an accountant with a large firm in the city but he's planning to start his own firm soon. He and his wife Vicki send

their 2 children to a private school on the other side of town rather than to the public one nearby (26) because "the quality of public schools here is poor." Streets in this section or tract have been named by the developer.

16. *Condominium Townhouses.* These townhouses have just been built on a lowland and marsh. The builder has installed a pond to collect the water that used to flow to the marsh, but this doesn't work and flooding now occurs. People who are buying the townhouses, according to the realtor, are very successful older couples. No one under the age of 18 is allowed to live here. "No burden on the schools," says the realtor. So far, families who have moved here all have 2 cars, which has added significantly to the traffic on Alps Road. The designer of these townhouses, an architect by the name of George Boswell, has won an award for his scheme. He admits, however, that they should never have been built on this land: "It was really too wet for townhouses, but if it's going to be built it may as well be designed well." Whether the well-designed buildings survive on this soggy ground, only the future will tell.
17. *Streams.* Water on this side of the neighbourhood flows into a nearby tidal marsh and then into the bay.
18. *Farm.* This farmer presently raises corn for sale, vegetables for his family and friends. He also keeps some old horses and cows which graze on the fertile hillside. He has good, well-drained, upland soil which developers of nearby condominium townhouses covet. They've asked the farmer to sell, but he's holding out.
19. *Marsh.* Gradually being filled in by yet another developer, who plans 75 apartments here. His action has destroyed the marsh, forcing out ducks and other birdlife that once used the area. But, the developer argues, now that the area is filled in, how can the town deny me permission to build here? The neighbourhood wouldn't grant permission if it had its way, but it's the town's planning and zoning commission that will give permission. Its members don't live around here.

20. *Homes.* Large, newer homes on large lots. Mostly wealthy families live here with 2 to 4 children. Of course, they oppose the nearby apartments because they will reduce property values.

21. *Drain.* In this part of the neighbourhood, water flows directly into the bay either through a natural stream bed or storm drains beneath the built-up areas.

22. *Old Section.* Homes in this section of the neighbourhood were built on small lots and narrow streets over 50 years ago, as summer cottages for city people who wanted to be near the beach during the humid months. The houses are mostly wooden. Many have screen porches running around 3 sides. Since the soil here is quite rocky and there are no sewers, waste often flows untreated and unabsorbed by the land, directly into the bay with its beaches. The area is no longer a desirable resort spot and over the years has become a year-round neighbourhood. Owners have winterized their cottages, closed in the porches, and either live here themselves or rent their places out to students during the winter.

23. *Baseball Diamond.* The only playground in the neighbourhood. Because the neighbourhood does not support the political party which has run the town for many years, the town doesn't build recreational facilities here. So Geno Pantani decided to take matters into his own hands. Geno moved here shortly after he married his wife Deborah. Ever since that time he's been a policeman for the local town. Now he's a sergeant. Having a lot of respect from his neighbours, he was able to get them to form a neighbourhood association. He was elected their 1st president and he took as his 1st task the building of a play lot. The association put up money for the land by taxing themselves. With their own hands they filled in the marsh, then bought benches and swings 2nd-hand from the city. Now they have a small play lot and baseball diamond, a facility that is well-used by kids and their parents alike.

24. *Vacant Land.* Held by a private local foundation that administers it for the benefit of town residents. Old evergreens line the pond on one side, steep cliffs line it on the other. Many hiking trails wind their way through the area, often alongside stone walls which mark the boundaries of old farms which were here in the last century. The pond is used by neighbours for swimming in summer and for ice skating in winter. It is called Altmansburger's Pond after the family who once owned and farmed the land. Their descendants live in houses at the end of the pond.

25. *Store.* At this corner is a local "mom-and-pop" grocery store owned by an older man and his wife who have lived next door for over 50 years. They know the neighbourhood--its residents and its history. Their son was not interested in continuing the business, however, so mom and pop may close the store soon and the supermarket chain (1) will probably get their business.

26. *Public School.* Because it's on the edge of this neighbourhood, the school receives 1st through 4th graders from this neighbourhood and outside neighbourhoods. Older children attend the town-wide middle and high schools.

27. *Footpaths.* A narrow sidewalk along the road, trodden-down dirt paths through the woods. The town built the sidewalks so nearby children could walk safely to the school. The paths were made by children wearing down the shortest route home from school.

28. *Old Stone Wall.* An old property divider dating from the 18th century. Colonial farmers here cut the trees, and then dragged stones out of the fields and piled them along the edges. Crops no longer grow here and a 2nd generation of trees has sprung up--birch, pin oak, hickory, some maple and pine trees. According to the old-timers the elms were wiped out by the Dutch elm disease.

Now that you've examined the sample neighbourhood, you can start asking questions about your own neighbourhood: What makes it different? What makes it a neighbourhood? Is it part of a larger unit? You'll have to do a bit of legwork to answer some of these questions. But walking is the best way to get to know your neighbourhood. First, get an overview, maybe by car or bus. Whether you're new or old to your neighbourhood, you'll enjoy a special tour given by someone else. Many large cities offer such guided tours on foot or by bus. But if your area doesn't have one, be your own tour guide. Pretend you're a stranger and look around your neighbourhood through his eyes.

Determine the shape and boundaries of the neighbourhood by looking for physical obstacles. Our sample neighbourhood is shaped by the major streets that cut off foot traffic. Would you ever think of walking across a 4-lane highway to borrow a cup of sugar? There are natural boundaries, too, such as rivers and hills. These characteristics often give names to the neighbourhoods, such as "Riverside," "Valley Acres," or "Hollywood Hills."

Next, notice the street and road system. Generally they are the 1st things built. Houses and shops come after the roads or trolley lines have been built to link the neighbourhood to the city and other neighbourhoods. What are the links in your neighbourhood? Some streets are laid in regular, straight lines while others, like those in the older section of our sample, follow the crooked foot and cow paths of another century. Go to the town clerk and ask how the streets were named. Some street names follow an alphabetical pattern such as Ash, Bay, Church streets. Or they may be named for States, such as Michigan Avenue in Chicago. Or they may be named for historical events or personalities. Most cities have a Madison Avenue or Washington Street. The avenues may run in one direction, the streets in another.

Traffic arteries, heavily traveled streets, are often called boulevards or highways. What happens along such arteries is different from what happens along smaller residential streets. Arteries often form commercial strips. Because they draw more traffic, stores, apartments, and factories are often located along arteries and major intersections.

Not only the homes, stores, and factories of your neighbourhood feed traffic to local roads. So do outside neighbourhoods. Ask yourself where your neighbourhood's roads and streets begin and end. Are they carrying your neighbours' cars or outsiders'? What about buses and heavy trucks? They may be carrying goods or people to and from or through your area. Since streets, roads, and parking lots can consume as much as 50% of your neighbourhood's land area, it's good to question who uses so much of your area's resources. By comparison, look to see how much of your area's land is given over to sidewalks, bicycle trails, parks, or pure open space. In our sample neighbourhood, one apartment area (9, 10) provides parking for cars but no play area for children. You might also note the noise level of major streets and compare it with that of smaller ones.

Walking or bicycling not only gives you more time to look closely at your neighbourhood, but also the occasional opportunity to talk to your neighbours. In addition, walking or bicycling will put your legs directly in touch with the land. In a car we tend to pay attention only to man-made features. On foot we know immediately if we're walking up the slightest hill.

The lay of the land is often hidden from us. Most neighbourhoods do not have mountains or rivers in or around them. But they may have been there at one time. Unknown to most residents are the natural and artificial streams flowing under the neighbourhoods. Fresh water is often obtained from these sources. Dirty water is put back. Do you know where water drains from your neighbourhood? Does it settle into the ground? What if the ground is too rocky? Perhaps the waste water is carried off to a nearby river or sewage plant. These natural and man-made watercourses follow the land downhill and sometimes carve it out. Find the low points and gulleys of your neighbourhood and you will find the spots where water is collecting either below or above the ground. Follow the streams. Find their sources and outflow.

If you need help, get a topographic map of the area from a local library or the U.S. Geological Survey. The map will show elevations, streams, roads, buildings, and other prominent physical features. Agricultural maps go further and tell the types of soil and vegetation. But even without the maps you can examine the earth directly: Is it sandy or rocky? Light or dark? Wet or dry? The soils of your area will often tell you its history. What was your neighbourhood before it was built up? An Indian burial ground? A farm? The Back Bay neighbourhood of Boston and the Marina neighbourhood of San Francisco were built upon dirt hauled in to fill what was once part of a bay. Perhaps your neighbourhood stands upon a sliced-off hill or a filled-in valley. If you can't find any old-timers to tell you, go to the nearest library and ask for some old maps.

A good place to go to find out about your neighbourhood's soils and vegetation is the nearby park. Look at the trees and shrubs that can be grown locally and talk with other strollers. The park caretaker can certainly tell you a lot about the trees and plantings. Ask him which trees were planted and which were standing before the park was built. Ask why certain kinds of trees are popular in the area. Perhaps the evergreens were planted in your neighbourhood to give privacy around the houses. Perhaps some trees have been planted to help retain sandy soil. Or still others, such as eucalyptus, might have been planted to shield crops from the wind when the neighbourhood was a farm.

You may find that the land in your neighbourhood once bore a forest. Was it cut for timber to build the neighbourhood's buildings? Or was the forest cut to clear the land for farming? Find out which crops grew successfully in your soil and test your answer by growing them in your own backyard.

Look also at the features of the park. Statues, monuments, markers, bandshells. They may reveal some local history. Find out what cultural events take place there. There are often important neighbourhood events such as parades or picnics. What was used to build the walkways or walls or fences in the park? These building materials will tell you a lot about the architecture and history of your neighbourhood. The same brick that was used to pave the walkway may have been used to build your house.

BUILDING STRUCTURE

What are most of the buildings in your neighbourhood built of? Wood? Stucco? Concrete blocks? Very often whole neighbourhoods or streets have been built at the same time and in the same style, sometimes by the same builder. Pay close attention to the shapes and styles of the buildings. Are the roofs flat or peaked? Do all houses have porches? Why?

What happens behind the building faces? How many families are in each building? Do the families who live in the buildings rent or own the property? If your neighbourhood has many apartments, most likely it is a rental neighbourhood, although apartments can also be owned as cooperatives or condominiums. Rental neighbourhoods differ from owner-occupied neighbourhoods. Renters stay for shorter periods of time than owners would. Who owns the apartments that are rented? Landlords may live in the building or they may live in a different neighbourhood altogether. If outsiders, they may or may not be concerned about the neighbourhood. Find out. Go to city hall, the tax office in particular, and compare the residential addresses of the property owners and the addresses of the properties they own.

How many of your neighbours work within the neighbourhood? How many outsiders come to your neighbourhood to work and make money? It may take some time before you're comfortable enough to ask such questions of your neighbours. If you prefer not to ask them directly, go to the main library and look up the census information for your area. The census will tell you the age of buildings, their condition, whether owned or rented. It will also tell you about the people: how many people live in the neighbourhood, where they work, and how long they've lived there.

But the best way to get to know the people of your neighbourhood is to get into friendly conversations with them.

To do this, go to the local gathering spots and involve yourself in the activities which draw the people of the neighbourhood together. Such spots include the corner market, newsstands, the local bar or the drugstore. Store proprietors are a mine of information, especially if they're native to the neighbourhood. Supermarkets and chain stores, while their prices may be lower (you should find this out), are generally not as friendly. Moreover, find out if the larger stores draw shoppers from more than one neighbourhood. When you find the nearest small store, get to know the owner and ask him about his shoppers. He will probably tell you that they all come from the local neighbourhood and that he is devoted to them and the neighbourhood.

Activities which draw people together and tighten their sense of neighbourliness are such things as day-care centers, churches, schools, block parties, sports events, and politics. Canvassing for a political party or a legitimate charity provides a ready-made excuse to knock on doors and talk to your neighbours. You can find out what they think about their neighbourhood and where it's going, its needs, and their goals for it. Such activities not only will tell you about a neighbourhood, but they will make you a part of it.

4

TOURISM DEVELOPMENT IN INDIA

INTRODUCTION

Tourism development in India has passed through many phases. At Government level the development of tourist facilities was taken up in a planned manner in 1956 coinciding with the Second Five Year Plan. The approach has evolved from isolated planning of single unit facilities in the Second and Third Five Year Plans. The Sixth Plan marked the beginning of a new era when tourism began to be considered a major instrument for social integration and economic development.

But it was only after the 80's that tourism activity gained momentum. The Government took several significant steps. A National Policy on tourism was announced in 1982. Later in 1988, the National Committee on Tourism formulated a comprehensive plan for achieving a sustainable growth in tourism. In 1992, a National Action Plan was prepared and in 1996 the National Strategy for Promotion of Tourism was drafted. In 1997, a draft new tourism policy in tune with the economic policies of the Government and the trends in tourism development was published for public debate. The draft policy is now under revision.

The proposed policy recognises the roles of Central and State governments, public sector undertakings and the private sector in the development of tourism. The need for involvement of Panchayati Raj institutions, local bodies, non-governmental organisations and the local youth in the creation of tourism facilities has also been recognised.

The other major development that took place were the setting up of the India Tourism Development Corporation in 1966 to promote India as a tourist destination and the Tourism Finance Corporation in 1989 to finance tourism projects. Altogether, 21 Government-run Hotel Management and Catering Technology Institutes and 14 Food Craft Institutes were also established for imparting specialised training in hoteliering and catering.

TOURIST ATTRACTIONS

India is a country known for its lavish treatment to all visitors, no matter where they come from. Its visitor-friendly traditions, varied life styles and cultural heritage and colourful fairs and festivals held abiding attractions for the tourists. The other attractions include beautiful beaches, forests and wild life and landscapes for eco-tourism, snow, river and mountain peaks for adventure tourism, technological parks and science museums for science tourism; centres of pilgrimage for spiritual tourism; heritage trains and hotels for heritage tourism. Yoga, ayurveda and natural health resorts also attract tourists.

The Indian handicrafts particularly, jewellery, carpets, leather goods, ivory and brass work are the main shopping items of foreign tourists. The estimates available through surveys indicate that nearly forty per cent of the tourist expenditure on shopping is spent on such items.

GROWTH

Domestic tourism is as old as the Indian society. According to available statistics, domestic tourism has grown substantially during the last one decade. It increased to 167 million in 1998 from just 64 million in 1990, thus registering a compound annual growth of 12.8 per cent.

The growth of inbound tourism since Independence has been quite impressive. It was just around 17 thousand in 1951. From this level it rose to 2.36 million in 1998. Tourism receipts on the other hand have grown at a phenomenal rate of 17 per cent to Rs.11,540 crore in 1998 from Rs.7.7 crore in 1951.

ECONOMIC IMPACT

Tourism has emerged as an instrument of employment generation, poverty alleviation and sustainable human development. During 1998-99, employment generation through tourism was estimated at 14.79 million.

Foreign exchange earnings from the tourism sector during 1998-99 were estimated at Rs.12,011 crore. Tourism has thus become the second largest net foreign exchange earner for the country.

Tourism also contributed Rs.24,241 crore during 1998-99 towards the country's Gross Domestic Product (GDP).

THRUST AREAS

In order to speed up the development of tourism in the country several thrust areas have been identified for accomplishment during the Ninth Five Year Plan (1997-2002). The important ones are development of infrastructure, products, trekking, winter sports, wildlife and beach resorts and streamlining of facilitation procedures at airports, human resource development and facilitating private sector participation in the growth of infrastructure.

ORGANISATION

The organisations involved in the development of tourism in India are the Ministry of Tourism with its 21 field offices within the country and 18 abroad, Indian Institute of Tourism and Travel Management, National Council for Hotel Management and Catering Technology, India Tourism Development Corporation, Indian Institute of Skiing and Mountaineering and the National Institute of Water Sports.

BOOSTING TOURISM

Some of the recent initiatives taken by the Government to boost tourism include grant of export house status to the tourism sector and incentives for promoting private investment in the form of Income Tax exemptions, interest subsidy and reduced import duty. The hotel and tourism-related industry has been declared a high priority industry for foreign investment which entails automatic approval of direct investment up to 51 per cent of foreign equity and allowing 100 per cent non-resident Indian investment and simplifying rules regarding the grant of approval to travel agents, tour operators and tourist transport operators.

CELEBRATIONS

During the Golden Jubilee celebrations of India as a Republic, the Ministry of Tourism made special efforts to publicise the tourism potential of India. The first-ever Indian Tourism Day was celebrated on January 25, 1998. Bauddha Mahotsav was organised from 24th October to 8th November 1998. The Year 1999 was celebrated as Explore India Millennium Year by presenting a spectacular tableau on the cultural heritage of India at the Republic Day Parade and organising India Tourism Expo in New Delhi and Khajuraho. The Wong La Millennium was held from April 1999 to January 2001. A special calendar of events has been formulated for highlighting contributions to Millennium events by various places in all the States. An official website of the Ministry of Tourism has also been created for facilitating dissemination of information on tourism.

CONSTRAINTS

The major constraint in the expansion of international tourist traffic to India is non-availability of adequate infrastructure including adequate air seat capacity, accessibility to tourist destinations, accommodation and trained manpower in sufficient number.

Poor visitor experience, particularly, due to inadequate infrastructural facilities, poor hygienic conditions and incidents of touting and harassment of tourists in some places are factors that contribute to poor visitor experience.

To sum up, Indian tourism has vast potential for generating employment and earning large sums of foreign exchange besides giving a fillip to the country's overall economic and social development. Much has been achieved by way of increasing air seat capacity, increasing trains and railway connectivity to important tourist destinations, four-laning of roads connecting important tourist centres and increasing availability of accommodation by adding heritage hotels to the hotel industry and encouraging paying guest accommodation. But much more remains to be done. Since tourism is a multi-dimensional activity, and basically a service industry, it would be necessary that all wings of the Central and State governments, private sector and voluntary organisations become active partners in the endeavour to attain sustainable growth in tourism if India is to become a world player in the tourist industry.

ECO TOURISM AND SUSTAINABLE DEVELOPMENT

The Draft Tourism Policy 1997 states that "in the context of economic liberalisation and globalisation being pursued by the country, the development policies of no sector can remain static." The policy further states that "the emergence of tourism as an important instrument for sustainable human development including poverty alleviation, employment generation, environmental regeneration and advancement of women and other disadvantaged groups in the country" requires support to realise these goals. India's tourism resources have always been considered immense, in a tourism audit. The geographical features are diverse, colourful and varied. The coastline offers opportunities for developing the best beaches in the world. There are a wealth of eco-systems including bio-sphere reserves, mangroves, coral reefs, deserts, mountains and forests as well as an equally wide range of flora and fauna.

The Policy further states that "international tourists visiting interiors of the country for reasons of purity of the environment and nature contributes to the development of these areas particularly backward regions". Thus Tourism "should also become a reason for better preservation and protection of our natural resources, environment and ecology". The policy recognises that sustained growth of tourism can give rise to conflicts. To ensure that the growth of tourism takes place along desired lines, certain guidelines have been framed: 1.to remove the constraint of the information gap.

1. To create a tourist product that is desirable and supported by an integrated infrastructure.
2. To involve all agencies, public, private and government, in tourism development.
3. To create synergy betweèn departments and agencies that have to deliver the composite tourist product.
4. To use both the circuit and scheme approach so that peoples participation through panchayats, local bodies, NGO's, and youth organisations will create a greater awareness of tourism. The Central Government can thus concentrate on larger investment oriented projects.
5. To create direct access for destinations off the beaten track.
6. To diversify the product with new options like beach tourism, forests, wild life, landscapes and adventure tourism, farm and health tourism.
7. To ensure that the development does not exceed sustainable levels.
8. To develop the seven north-eastern states, the Himalayan region and Islands for tourism.
9. To maintain a balance between the negative and positive impacts of tourism through planning restrictions and through education of the people for conservation and development.

The strategy for development should take into consideration the carrying capacity, local aspirations and benefits likely to accrue to the community. In particular specific policies and guidelines for eco-tourism development and adventure tourism are to be formulated, primarily through a regulatory framework.

The Draft Guidelines have been approved at a State Ministers Conference and have been circulated to various trade and industry bodies. The guidelines draw a distinction between mass or resort tourism and nature or eco tourism, as the kind of tourism that has a lower impact on the environment and requires less infrastructural development. The Ministry hopes that the environment conscious international tourist will be made aware that India is taking steps to protect its ecology and environment.

Apart from the do's and don'ts, the guidelines are governed by a tourism management plan, the key elements of which are the protection of natural resources and a positive involvement of local communities, along with an optimum number of environmentally conscious visitors.

The principles of management are scientific planning, effective control and continuous monitoring, development of physical infrastructure, zoning and a Management plan for public use of natural sites. The management plan should establish standards for resort development, style and location of structures, waste disposal, treatment of sewage, control of litter, use of public spaces and fragile areas. The operational guidelines rely on sensitisation of all the role players and this programme is based on a self-regulated environmental code.

Area specific rather than universal development plans keeping in mind the unique character of the location and its economic and social environment are important. This would help the State Government to coordinate with the industry in managing visitors and their activities. NGO's working on socio-economic programmes in forest and remote areas could have a closer coordination with tourism service operators to transfer economic benefits, particularly the handicraft production and marketing sector.

The guidelines are only a beginning, and it is hoped that with increasing awareness of the visitor the industry will regulate its practices. There is an emphasis on the needs and perceptions of the international tourist running through the discussion on the guide lines although the data from the National Parks makes it evident that the domestic tourists outnumber international visitors, although they do not pay the same amount as the foreign visitor either in entry fees or for board and lodging and transport facilities.

They do however demand a much higher per capita use of resources like water, fuel for heating and cooking and transport. They also make the same intensive use of time and try to maximize their stay by the number of animals and birds they can view in the 24-hour period.

It is interesting to note that no democratic participation has been called for in the policy formulation process, and all the amendments to the policy have come from trade associations and government think tanks. The tourism Advisory Committee also consists of eminent persons and community representation has been ignored. The elite nature of the policy makers is well represented in the quotations given above from the policy document.

The policy clearly recognises the debate on the tourism issue which has surfaced wherever tourism development, particularly in the case of tourism projects relating to the "gifts of nature" like beaches, rivers, mountains and forests, have already been developed. However, mere recognition of the hostility of people to tourism development is not enough to change the nature of tourism development or the resistance to tourism or what many have termed a poor tourism culture. Perhaps to understand this in a better perspective, we should look at the issue of sustainable development in a critical way. Perhaps we can question the impact of sustainable development on the environment and sift through the jargon of development planners, international agencies, and environmental activists to see how sustainable development can be achieved without all the contradictions that are apparent as in the case of the tourism sector.

Phrase SUSTAINABLE DEVELOPMENT Concepts Sustainability Development Connotations Literal, ecological, Social Process Objectives Meaning sustains sustains sustains growth/ anything, ecological social basis change basic needs basis of of human human life life conditions ecological social conditions conditions interpretations SD sustaining growth SD achieving traditional objectives + ecological and social sustainability (contradictory, trivial) (mainstream, meaningful) Semantic Map Sustainable development has become the developmental paradigm of the nineties but it remains a fashionable phrase that everyone pays homage to but no one cares to define. (Tolba, 1984).

To some extent the value of the phrase lies in its ambiguity. It allows people with irreconcilable positions in the environmental debate to appear to have found common ground without having to compromise their positions. The absence of semantic and conceptual clarity hampers a real debate. S. M. Lele (1991) has attempted a semantic map of Sustainable Development, which will help us to understand some of the positions in the debate. Is sustainable development ecologically sustainable and environmentally sound or is it a process of change that has sustainability added to it? Is it to be understood as sustained growth or successful development? Literally sustainable development is change that can be sustained or continued for the time period concerned. Development we can say with some confidence is a process of directed change, but any process embodies both the objectives and the means of achieving the stated objectives.

Objectives

Can we set sustainable objectives (as growth in sustained consumption of) for resources that now are recognised to have ultimate limits or what we may call non-renewable resources or what we may call the balance between the use and conservation of such resources? Even where we are concerned with socio-economic change, the discussion is not meaningful unless we state the objectives of change and why we should be concerned with continuing the process of change indefinitely. Is the change so envisaged to be broadly understood as social welfare? Can the increase in welfare continue indefinitely, and what will be its cost? Even where welfare is based on beneficiary oriented design (grass roots participation) as a procedural imperative, it tells us nothing about the overall goal of the developmental process since the beneficiaries need not conserve resources to achieve their welfare. The concept of sustainability originated in the context of renewable resources like forests and fisheries and was subsequently adopted by the environmental movement. In most cases it is understood to mean "the existence of the ecological conditions necessary to support human life at a specific level of well being through future generations." However, in addition to ecological conditions there are social conditions that influence ecological sustainability in a nature-people interaction. The social connotations have been described by Barbier (1987) who has defined social sustainability as "the ability to maintain desired social values, traditions, institutions, cultures or other social characteristics."

The term sustainability came into usage in 1980 when the IUCN presented the World Conservation Strategy where sustainable development was linked to conservation of living resources. However, the fundamental goals have often been lost sight of because of operational goals (e.g. food, water, shelter, health are fundamental goals to be realised through self reliance, cost effectiveness, appropriate technology, people centred-ness etc.) Consequently, the WCED made its definition brief: Social Development is development that meets the needs of the present without compromising the ability of future generations to meet their own needs. They did not make any assumptions on the direction in which changes in demand would take place. (E.g. equity, social justice, self-determination, or cultural diversity). India's tourism policy follows the mainstream SD thinking by adopting all the critical objectives: revive growth change the quality of growth meet essential needs for jobs, food, energy, water and sanitation ensure sustainable levels of population conserve and enhance the resource base reorient technology and management risk merge environment and economics in decision making reorient international economic relations make development more participatory.

These objectives are responsible for building a very broad consensus on the issue of sustainable development, yet the debate at the operational level continues. Most participants in the debate now accept that many human activities are reducing the long-term ability of the natural environment to provide goods and services, which will eventually affect human health and well being. Many also accept that poverty is devastating the lives of millions in the Third World since there is no consensus between what is environmentally necessary and what is economically and developmentally feasible. The level of interdependence between the two insights is yet to be incorporated in the concept of Social Development. Some problem areas are: Environmental degradation, already affecting millions in the Third World, is likely to reduce human well being across the globe. Who is responsible for this rapid degeneration? Is it the poor or the rich?

The poor have no option but to exploit resources for short-term survival. If we take the example of forests and their resources, which have been traditionally outside the market system and in the sphere of tribal or indigenous peoples rights, they are today seen as exploiters of the forests as against tourists, with all their demand for infrastructure and superstructure, who are seen to be conservationists. The inter-linked nature of the problem of sustainability is such that the impact of degradation will be quicker on the poor than on the rich. Can Sustainable Development be the metafix it claims to be in reconciling increasing industrial, agricultural and resource use productivity with environmental needs. The weakness of the Social Development argument lies in the techno-economic approach to solutions with regard to common property resource management, through know how transfers, resource pricing, subsidy policies and building management capabilities. (World Bank, 1987) Deeper processes such as land reforms, industrial demands on raw materials, over consumption, changing legal and political structures are either ignored or looked at in a cursory manner.

For instance how can we claim a consensus between those who are concerned for the survival of future generations with those who are concerned with the survival of wild life, or human health and subsistence? Unless we can identify the trade-offs necessary for each specific objective of sustainability, we will not have clarity in the discussion. We will also fail to understand why, even when there is a broad consensus, projects on the ground result in conflicts. Suggested refinements could be: a distinction between ecological and social sustainability and in the process an identification of the inter-linkages a distinction between renewable and non-renewable resources, between environmental processes crucial to human life and crucial to other forms of life dependent on the resources, a distinction between the techno-economic aspects of social sustainability (infrastructure, services, government) with political and cultural sustainability, a distinction between equitable development and local participation, and decentralisation, what many have called NGOisation of sustainable development.

This is because no rigorous testing of local participation leading to social equity or to sustainable resource use have been reported. Case studies reflect personal, organisational or political preferences. Tourism is one of the activities which has caused concern because of the effects of increasing human traffic on fragile environments. Countries which are looking towards Tourism as a means of economic growth, like India, have limited resources and cultural restraints and they have the greatest need to pay heed to the possible negative impacts of tourism.

Environmental Impact

The environmental impact of tourism is a basic issue, whether we are looking at a developed or an underdeveloped area, region or country. The costs of tourism for a country like India include extensive investment in fixed assets with a low rate of return for infrastructure, transportation, accommodation, cultural institutions, exhibition centres, and park facilities. To this maybe added the social and cultural costs like additional demands on infrastructure like land, water, health services; the creation of new jobs for displaced people; the cost of positive community relationships; the disparity between the lifestyle of visitors and those who serve them; the possible friction between local residents and new users of valued local resources; the perception of local residents of the spending of scarce capital resources on what they consider low priority areas like tourism; cultural cost of alterations in local ceremonial or traditional values; loss of privacy for local communities as tourists come to gape at their living conditions and rituals. Tourism also causes increasing congestion and pollution as thousands of visitors flock to parks and sanctuaries in motorised vehicles; there are changes in accessibility, landscape and the ecological balance between man and nature; there is the cost, both monetary and human, of creating conservation zones (core/ buffer) with unforeseen or undesirable side effects; which have been observed in the ecotourism movement.

The benefit of revenue from tourism does not always redress these problems but goes towards the cost of administering the project. The tourism industry is generally self-centred and not given to educational, cultural or exchange programmes on a philanthropic basis. The natural environment, with the best will in the world, cannot escape damage with the volume of visitors. As more and more tourists, both domestic and international seek the exotic and remote destinations around the world, the likelihood of the environment suffering as a result become greater. Forests can suffer from trampling, fires, tree felling for facilities and waste. Wildlife, despite the protection in national parks, has suffered a loss of habitat, hunting and poaching, viewing and photographing, leading to an interruption of feeding and breeding patterns or hunting for food undisturbed. These are the prized moments for the viewer. The trade in wild life trophies or tourist souvenirs is the more deliberately destructive aspect of such tourism. The building of tourist lodges in materials that are not integrated with the environment and the pressure they put on the land and water bodies is also wilfully destructive. Management techniques that include being less user friendly or control of numbers by closing access or by multiplying the number of attractions and areas or charging higher admission fees are generally not popular with the tourist or the tour operator and are also difficult to implement because of high administrative costs.

CONCLUSION

EQUATIONS, through its involvement in the field have had a variety of experiences relating to the debate on eco tourism and sustainable development. The major issues that have emerged after the policy of notification of wild life sanctuaries and their management by the Forest Departments are quite disturbing. Wherever notification has led to displacement of people the experience of rehabilitation has not been successful and the conservation aims have not been met. Several sanctuaries have witnessed militant action by displaced communities against the developers of tourism. In many cases the tourism aims have also not been met in making the sanctuary accessible to viewers, naturalists, wild life photographers. Tourism has not been able to counteract poaching and the most extensive and the oldest conservation project, Project Tiger has not been able to save the tiger population. The commercialisation of the experience, like the privileging of one species, for example the tiger, has led to congestion and noise pollution and this has put a pressure on the management of the sanctuary to organise tiger shows which are putting a pressure on the feeding and mating habits of the tiger. These are very invasive techniques of experiencing the wild.

On the plus side, the concept of beneficiary led development has helped indigenous people to organise against their displacement and exploitation as well as to fight for the retention of their traditional rights and life styles. Environmentalists have not only been involved in such organisations and movements but have done valuable documentation. This has influenced many urban visitors to be more sensitive to the wild and to follow the rules when participating in eco-tourism. This has also led to the development of a code of conduct for the tourist, the industry and the administrator. These attempts are in a very nascent stage. The kind of co-ordination that is required between the environmentalist and economist is just beginning to emerge and have still to counter the myths of neo-classical economists in the field of tourism. But a beginning has been made.

5

Tourism Policy of India: An Exploratory Study

INTRODUCTION

The objective of this report is to assess the impact of Tourism Policy on the tourism sector and make a preliminary study of the possible impact such policy imperatives might have on the socio-economic fabric of the country. The study, commissioned by EQUATIONS, Bangalore, utilised a methodology involving a historical preview of the evolution of Tourism Policy since 1982, and an exploratory assessment of the impact. The study material included documentation available at EQUATIONS and relevant publications of the Union Government.

The impact assessment of the sectoral policies on the specified sector suffers from a serious methodological problem. Briefly, it may be argued that the development of a sector is not solely dependent on the factors within the sector: it is influenced by the general socio-economic environment, the political system and the overall policy framework.

Thus the study integrates within itself the dynamic aspects of historical changes that are taking place at the macro-economic level. Similarly, Tourism Policy would not have evolved on its own without being influenced by the general tenor of macro-economic policy. Tourism policy thus has a socio-political grounding as much as it has a macro-economic colouring.

The 1980s witnessed the era of liberalisation initiated by the Congress Government at the Centre. The process of liberating the Indian economy from the shibboleths of 'license-permit Raj' culminated in the initiation of the structural adjustment programme in 1992.

"Objectives, Thrusts and Macro-economic Dimensions of the Eighth Plan" endorsed by the National Development Council, clearly outlines the context within which the structural reforms were initiated: "The need to restructure our systems of economic management has become an imperative if India is to emerge as a vibrant and internationally competitive economy in the 90's. Systems of control and regulation, developed for good reasons in the past have outlived their utility and some positively (sic) stand in the way of further progress. Such dysfunctional systems have to be overhauled in the light of emerging realities.

" The process of structural adjustments has brought about far reaching changes in the Indian economy at a breath-taking pace. The impact of these changes over the tourism sector need to be studied in a dynamic context. Nevertheless, the above should not be taken as ignoring the fact that sectoral policy does have a direct and unambiguous impact over the concerned sector.

Tourism Policy, as a statement of intent by the Government, would form the reference point for action and criticism. Any initiative by Government in Tourism by way of legislation or direct investment is envisaged within the framework of Tourism Policy. The debates in Parliament had taken recourse to the received policy of the Union Government while making references to particular cases. The backdrop of a policy always serves as a guideline for further executive and legislative initiatives. It would be cynical to regard these policy statements as mere exercises in eloquence and additions to the already existing volumes of wishful thinking.

Furthermore, Policy statements by Government should be viewed in their evolutionary stance. It would be a negation of the democratic content of our political system to view a Policy statement as a static and rigid formulation, at a point in time, applicable for years to come. Thus, since 1982, various initiatives undertaken by the Government need to be perceived as additions or modifications to the received Policy. While it may be argued that these changes in the policy are only marginal and superficial from the viewpoint of equity and social justice, it would be an oversimplification to view the latest policy statement as nothing but the "nth" version of the Policy formulated in 1982. Recognising the all-pervading inertia that looms large in matters governmental, one is often tempted to deny the scope for lobbying which makes possible the desired modifications in the policy corpus. In short, policy, as a body incorporating proactive intentions, is amenable to periodic reviews and possible modifications.

The issues stressed in the preceding paragraphs provide the framework within which Tourism Policy needs to be considered. In brief, there is more to policy in tourism than is found in the Tourism Policy. Perhaps, the links within a macro-economic framework need no special mention.

MAJOR POLICY INITIATIVES

The first ever Tourism Policy was announced by the Government of India in November 1982. It took ten long years for the Government to feel the need to come up with a possible improvement over this. Thus the National Action Plan for Tourism was announced in May 1992. Between these two policy statements, various legislative and executive measures were brought about. In particular, the report of the National Committee on Tourism, submitted in 1988 needs special mention. In addition, two five-year plans-the Seventh and the Eighth-provided the basic perspective framework for operational initiatives.

The Seventh Plan advocated a two-pronged thrust in the area of development of tourism, viz., to vigorously promote domestic tourism and to diversify overseas tourism in India. While laying stress on creation of beach resorts, conducting of conventions, conferences, winter sports and trekking, the overall intention was to diversify options available for foreign tourists.

The Tourism Policy, 1982 was more an aggressive statement in marketing than a perspective plan for development. Its main thrust was aimed at presenting India to the foreigners as the ultimate holiday resort. With a view to reach this destination, the following measures were suggested by the Policy:

1. To take full advantage of the national heritage in arriving at a popular campaign for attracting tourists;
2. To promote tourist resorts and make India a destination of holiday resorts;
3. To grant the status of an export industry to tourism;
4. To adopt a selective approach to develop few tourist circuits; and,
5. To invite private sector participation into the sector.

The Planning Commission recognised tourism as an industry by June 1982. However, it took ten years to make most of the States to fall in line and accord the same status within their legislative framework. At the beginning of the Eighth Plan (1992-97), 15 States and 3 Union Territories had declared tourism as an industry. Four States had declared hotels as an industry.

The National Committee on Tourism was set up in July 1986 by the Planning Commission to prepare a perspective plan for the sector. Within the broad framework of the Seventh Plan, the Committee had to evolve a perspective plan for the coming years.

The Committee, headed by Mr. Mohammed Yunus, submitted its recommendations in November 1987. The list of Members was as impressive Mr. S.K. Mishra (Secretary, Department of Tourism), Mrs. Kapila Vatsayan, Mr. K.L. Thapar, Mr. Rajan Jaitley, Mr. A.B. Kerker, Mr. R.K. Puri and Mr Pran Seth. The Committee in its Report recommended that the existing Department of Tourism be replaced by a National Tourism Board. It suggested that there be a separate cadre of Indian Tourism Service to look after the functioning of the Board. It also submitted proposals for partial privatisation of the two airlines owned by the Union Government.

By September, 1987, the Central Government declared more concessions for the sector: these included tax exemption on foreign exchange earnings from tourism (a 50% reduction on rupee earnings and a 100% reduction on earnings in dollars), a drastic reduction in tariff on import of capital goods, and concessional finance at the rate of 1 to 5% per annum.

The Tourism Development Finance Corporation was set up in 1987 with a corpus fund of Rs. 100 crores. Until then, the sector was financed on commercial lines by the Industrial Development Bank of India, Industrial Credit and Investment Corporation of India and other commercial banks.

The National Action Plan for Tourism, published in May 1992, and tabled in the Lok Sabha on 5 May 1992, charts 7 objectives as central concerns of the Ministry:

- socio-economic development of areas;
- increasing employment opportunities;
- developing domestic tourism for the budget category;
- preserving national heritage and environment;
- development of international tourism;
- diversification of the tourism product.,
- and, increase in India's share in world tourism (from the present 0.4% to 1% during next 5 years)

As per the Action Plan, foreign exchange earnings are estimated to increase from Rs.10,000 crores in 1992 to Rs.24,000 crores by 2000 AD. Simultaneously, the Plan aims at increasing employment in tourism to 28 million from the present 14 million. Hotel accommodation is to be increased from 44,400 rooms to 1,20,000 by 3 years. Other provisions in the Action Plan include a discontinuance of subsidies to star hotels, encouraging foreign investment in tourism and the setting up of a convention city for developing convention tourism.

The Action Plan envisages the development of Special Tourism Areas on lines of export processing zones. Special Central assistance is to be provided for the States to improve the infrastructural facilities at pilgrimage places. It proposes to set up a National Culinary Institute, and projects a liberalised framework for recognition of travel agents and tour operators.

The Eighth Plan document makes a special mention that the future expansion of tourism should be achieved mainly by private sector participation. The thrust areas as enumerated in the Plan include development of selected tourist places, diversification from cultural related tourism to holiday and leisure tourism, development of trekking, winter sports, wildlife and beach resort tourism, exploring new source markets, restoration of national heritage projects, launching of national image building, providing inexpensive accommodation in different tourist centres, improving service efficiency in public sector corporations and streamlining of facilitation procedures at airports.

The Eighth Plan aims at luring the high spending tourists from Europe and USA. It also envisages a 'master plan' to integrate area plans with development of tourism. This is envisaged to ensure employment opportunities for the local population.

In April 1993, the Government announced further measures aimed at export promotion. The existing Export Promotion of Capital Goods Scheme (EPCG) was extended to tourism and related services. Against the existing 35%, the tourism sector would now pay an excise duty of 15% only on capital goods import, subject to an export obligation of 4 times the cargo, insurance and freight (CIF) value of imports. With an obligation period of five years, this came as a boon to the hotel industry. The cost of construction had also come down by 20%.

In addition to the above policy pronouncements by the Union Government, our planners had envisaged the possibilities of developing specific regions on a zonal plank. Special area programmes like the Hill Area Development Programme and the Western Ghats Development Programme form part of the overall national plan.

The Eighth Plan document stipulates that the strategy in such designated special areas is to devise suitable location-specific solutions, so as to reverse the process of degradation of natural resources and ensure sustainable development. This approach perhaps needs to be integrated into the project of special tourism areas, now being made popular by the Government. Administrative Control and Developmental Compromises

The federal principles enshrined in the Indian Constitution require that the tourism sector be treated as a State subject. As such, the Department of Tourism (under the Ministry of Civil Aviation and Tourism at the Centre) undertakes certain promotional and developmental activities with a view to enhance the sectoral potential. The Department has certain regulatory functions to perform involving the hotel industry, travel agencies and tourist operators.

Over the years, there has been considerable erosion of powers so far as State Governments are concerned. The sustained campaign for privatisation in all the policy documents has left limited space of operation for the States. The public sector is increasingly being perceived as an agent of inertia than of change and hence the pressure for a hands-off policy. On the other hand, the Union Government has been usurping the powers of the State with some pretext or the other. Promotion schemes, designed at the Centre, are transferred for implementation at the State level.

The special Central Assistance, for example, granted for the development of infrastructure at the pilgrim centres, carries with it a pre-defined scheme and mode of execution. Furthermore, there are occasions when the Centre forces the State Governments to extend certain subsidies and concessions to the sector. The terms of such concessions would have been fixed by the Centre and the States would have no choice but to fall in line.

For example, during the State tourism minister's conference in December 1991, the States were urged to freeze water and electricity rates for 10 years. They were also asked to exempt certain hotels from local and state taxes for 10 years. Seventeen circuits and destinations were identified under the National Action Plan for development through Central assistance and investment by the States and the private sector. The centres were identified by the Centre and the States were asked to do the needful. There were also times when the federal division of power resulted in operational contradictions.

For instance, by 1989, many foreign hotel chains like Hilton, Hyatt, Penta and Kempinski had applied for licenses for investing in India. However, the revenue departments of the respective States failed to locate and allocate land for the construction of hotels.

The scheme, thus, fell flat. Curiously, the Union Government was not hesitant to make use of Constitutional provisions when it suited its interests. As has been stated earlier, the Yunus Committee had suggested the creation of the Tourism Board on lines of the existing Railway Board. (Perhaps, it was the brainchild of Mr. K.L. Thapar, then adviser to the Planning Commission, in charge of Transport and Tourism Sector. Being from the Railway Service, it is not surprising that Thapar thought about a 'Tourism Board'). To begin with, the empowered committee of secretaries challenged the idea of creation of a Board.

It was said that the Railway Board as an independent entity was created for historical reasons. It would be difficult for tourism to be looked after by a Board, because legally the sector would come under the Industrial (Development) Act. It was also found that such a Board would not be viable financially. In 1991, the think-tank on tourism created by Minister Madhavarao Scindia rejected the idea of a Board in toto. It was emphasised that the Board cannot be in charge of a sector that is basically under the jurisdiction of the States! Scope for Federal Interventions The previous section highlights the dubious ways by which the Centre attempts to hijack initiatives at the State-level. This is achieved essentially by threatening to curtail Central assistance or by cajoling through promises of more financial aid.

It is common knowledge that the resource-base of the States is very narrow, making them vulnerable at the negotiating table. However, States have the freedom to resist the Centre's strong-arm tactics, provided State assemblies stand-by the interests of the States. For instance, State legislatures may refuse to freeze water and electricity rates on grounds of revenue generation.

In that event, the concerned Chief Minister or the Minister of Tourism may convey the intensity of resistance that he is confronted with, and thus refuse to comply with the Centre's diktats. It is heartening to realise that the States have often exercised their power of self-determination and consequently refused to toe the line drawn by the Centre. This offers enough scope for possible interventions at the federal strata of our political system in matters of policy formulation. Privatisation and its Implications According to the Approach Paper to the Seventh Plan, " there is a vast potential for development of tourism in the country.

Tourism should be accorded the status of an industry. Private sector investment will have to be encouraged in developing tourism and public sector investments should be focused only on development of support infrastructure". Thus the seeds of private initiatives were sown during the Seventh Plan. The Government took the matter of privatising the tourism sector seriously by 1988. It was during the tenure of Mr. S.K. Mishra as Tourism Secretary that the talk of inviting private investment into the sector began.

The Government permitted foreign equity participation up to 5 1 %in tourism projects. Foreign charters were allowed to operate in the country for the first time. Foreign companies were allowed to repatriate their profits to the extent of 3%. The structural adjustment programme, initiated in June, 1992, paved the way for privatisation in almost all sectors of the economy. The Annual Plan (1992-93) document emphatically enunciated the Government's position vis-a-vis tourism: "(T)he future growth of tourism will have to be achieved mainly through private initiative.

The State will contribute to tourism by planning broad strategy of development, provision of monetary and fiscal incentives to catalyse private sector investment." The process of privatisation brought in its wake big investments and private involvement at various levels. As an offshoot, environmental considerations were thrown to the winds and there were instances of large scale human rights violation. The self-correcting nature of policy made provisions for stricter controls in this regard. More seriously, privatisation meant alienation of the majority of our population and their deprivation. Employment generated in tourism is generally seasonal and ill paid. The private sector-induced pockets of tourism had the potential of turning into centres of pollution, drug trafficking and prostitution. Industry Status Granted to Tourism The Seventh Plan proposed that tourism be declared an industry. However, it took time for the States to implement this, even though they agreed in principle.

The smokeless industry had the advantage of generating maximum value-added, because of low-cost inputs. The Tourism Policy Statement carried certain provisions in favour of the hotel industry. It stated that there should be provision for depreciation in the balance sheets of hotels. Being an export industry, hotels were to be given excise concessions. The provisions of the Monopolies and Restrictive Trade Practices (MRTP) Act were relaxed for hotels, because any hotel with 300 or more rooms would have incurred an investment of Rs. 25 crores. The document also hinted at lower tariffs for power and water and regulations for easy import of equipment. As a follow-up, hotel and shipping were added to the list of 27 industries exempted from Section 22 A of the MRTP Act. The consequences of declaring tourism as an industry need to be studied in detail. It is not possible to capture its implications in an exploratory work like this. However, it is obvious that the private sector has primarily benefited to a great extent by this measure. Importing Modifications to Policies We have earlier stated that the arena of policy formulation should be self-evaluating and self-correcting. In the case of Tourism Policy, this has proved to be the plus point.

As an illustration, the Policy statement of 1982 made no mention of infrastructure development. The successive governments at the Centre failed to create proper tourism infrastructure, thus resulting in loss of traffic. This lacuna was corrected in the National Action Plan. However, much of this change was due to intensive lobbying by such agencies like the Indian Association of Tour Operators (IATO), the Travel agents Association of India (TAAI) and the Indian Hotels and Restaurants Association (IHRA). It is for the voluntary agencies and pro-people forces to exploit the avenue of lobbying at various levels. The environmental implications of tourism development did not form part of the 1982 Policy.

The consequences are too obvious to be written about. However, the NAP, 1992 did carry specific provisions for environmental protection and harnessing. From Policy to Cartooning Policy statements may also lead to justifiable flights of fantasy. Two examples would illustrate how policies were used to justify stands taken by the politicians: a. Shri Devi Lal, the then Deputy Prime Minister wanted a 50% discount for farmers at Five Star Hotels run by India Tourism Development Corporation. The scheme had teething problems since it was not easy to distinguish a farmer from amongst the clients who visit such hotels. However, on his insistence, the so-called CHAUPALs recreated a village ambience to the amazement of foreign tourists, who took a liking for them. b. Pursuing the objective of the Seventh Plan to diversify overseas tourism to its logical conclusion was what prompted A&. Jagdish Tytler to float the idea of casinos. It was an attempt to provide some entertainment for foreigners during the evenings. It was said that Indian classical music would not provide much needed entertainment for foreign guests because the artistes spend a lot of time tuning their instruments! Folk dances get over in an hour. So much for our much touted cultural diversity.

It is embarrassing to believe that the consultative committee attached to the Ministry of Civil Aviation and Tourism had endorsed the idea. Conclusion Broadly, our successive policy pronouncements in the realm of tourism falls within the "liberalising" framework of the macro-economic policy environment. The Finance Bill, 1988, had assured 50% tax exemption on foreign exchange earnings in the sector, and a further 50% exemption if re-invested. In effect, it amounts to 100% tax concession. Luxury hotels enjoy exemptions of all kinds with a view to encourage tourism earnings. These tax exemptions coupled with provision of soft loans to the sector led to a boom in the tourism related private investment. The Economic Survey 1991-92 aptly summarises the ultimate aim of such incentives for private sector participation: " The Government has tried to expand the economic space in which the people can exercise their initiative and ingenuity.

It hopes to do more to expand their opportunities, to enhance their potential. But what shape the economy takes ultimately depends on what the people make of it. In that sense, the future is in their hands." We should not forget that tourism is an industry which emerges in the context of unresolved socio-economic structural issues, such as land distribution patterns or the take over of traditional occupations by modem mechanised capital. Tourism happens to be a source of livelihood for millions in India and aggressive privatisation does not ensure social and economic safety nets. In the face of the unhindered entry of international capital and successive alienation, perhaps, it is difficult to agree that "the future is in our hands"

RURAL AREAS BENEFIT FROM RECREATION AND TOURISM DEVELOPMENT

Beautiful scenery-lakes, mountains, forests-attracts people to rural resort areas in the United States. Rural recreation areas have grown rapidly in recent years, and recreation and tourism development has become a popular vehicle for rural economic development.

Recreation development involves more than just tourist-related businesses, such as hotels and restaurants; it encompasses all economic growth that results from people moving into the community to take advantage of its recreational amenities. This kind of development has the potential to dramatically transform a stagnant rural community into a thriving community by attracting retirees, entrepreneurs, and young workers, diversifying the economy, and improving the quality of life with a broader array of goods and services.

But recreation development comes with potential problems. Some problems are growth-related-such as congested roads, crowded schools, environmental strains, housing shortages, despoiled scenic views, and conflicts over land use and public policies. Other problems are specific to the tourism industry's workers (unskilled or foreign), many of whom earn relatively little and have few fringe benefits. And another downside: Criminals may be particularly attracted to some recreation areas. Is recreation and tourism development a viable economic option for rural areas? ERS examined some key questions about the socioeconomic effects of rural recreation development. The answers are generally favourable, with improved employment conditions, earnings, and incomes; lower poverty rates; and healthier and better educated populations. However, conditions vary by type of recreation area, and higher housing costs and crime rates can accompany the more favourable outcomes.

DEFINITIONS AND METHODOLOGY

The word "recreation" is used in this article to refer to the leisure activities of tourists as well as seasonal and permanent residents. However, when discussing recreation's estimated impact on various socioeconomic indicators, the term 'recreation development' usually refers to the extent to which a county depends on recreation development for employment, income, and housing.

ERS used the 2002 version of its recreation county typology developed by Ken Johnson and Calvin Beale to analyze rural recreation areas nationwide. The number of recreation counties studied was 311, including 11 types varying by geographic location, natural amenities, and form of recreation.

ERS examined selected indicators of socioeconomic well-being in rural recreation areas nationwide, using county-level data from the 2000 Census and other Federal data sources. First, socioeconomic conditions and trends in rural recreation counties were compared with those in other nonmetro counties (excluding metro areas). Socioeconomic conditions and trends were also compared across various types of rural recreation counties. Next, multiple regression analysis was conducted to estimate the impact of recreation-dependency on socioeconomic conditions and trends in the 311 rural recreation counties. Because of rapid employment growth in rural recreation areas and a potentially broader array of jobs, including more seasonal and part-time positions that appeal to residents unable to work full-time, year-round jobs, employment options would likely be enhanced by recreation development. However, it may not be easier for residents to find jobs due to competition with other workers who have recently moved to the area.

ERS researchers found that recreation development, measured by the extent to which a county's employment, income, and housing depend on recreation and tourism, is linked to a higher percentage of the working-age population having jobs. This percentage-employed measure encompasses discouraged workers who had dropped out of the labor force, making it a more comprehensive and meaningful measure of employment conditions. Moreover, recreation development led to an increase in this employment measure during the 1990s for all age groups, except the population ages 65 and older.

Jobs that are usually associated with recreation development, such as those in hotels and restaurants, are assumed to be low paying with few fringe benefits. Some related service jobs, such as those in retail businesses, may also pay low wages. However, low-wage workers in recreation areas may have access to more opportunities to work part-time and seasonal jobs to supplement their incomes, and some service and construction jobs associated with recreation development pay quite well. Recreation development appears to have increased the growth in earnings per job during the 1990s. But average earnings per job in 2000 were not significantly higher in rural recreation areas.

To better measure what residents earn from employment, ERS looked at total earnings per resident worker, which includes earnings from second jobs (part-time and seasonal). Second jobs are expected to be more readily available in recreation counties than elsewhere. Total earnings per resident were substantially higher ($2,000 more per worker) in recreation counties than in other rural counties. Contrary to conventional wisdom, recreation development seems to have increased residents' earnings.

COST OF LIVING HIGHER, BETTER EDUCATION AND HEALTH

Anecdotal evidence suggests that housing costs have risen rapidly in some of the most well-known recreation areas, becoming so high that many workers can no longer afford to live in the area, sometimes requiring long commutes. In addition, higher housing costs may prevent the children and grandchildren of some long-term residents from finding housing in their home towns. While this may be true in some recreation areas, it is not known how widespread this higher cost of living is. However, median rent for housing (an important component in cost of living) in recreation counties is 23 percent higher than in other nonmetropolitan (nonmetro) counties, reducing some of the economic advantages for recreation county residents, but only partially. Median household incomes are $3,185 higher in recreation counties than in other counties, while median annual rent is only $1,080 higher in recreation counties. This implies that the higher rent offsets about a third of the recreation county income advantage.

Recreational development might attract migrants who tend to have higher levels of education than nonmigrants. As expected, ERS research found that recreational development leads to a more educated population, particularly when education is measured by the share of adults with college degrees. Recreation development is also associated with good health (measured by age-adjusted death rates), as might be expected from the higher number of physicians (per 100,000 residents) in recreation counties than in other rural counties. The availability of physicians, however, was not responsible for the good health of residents. Other factors, such as greater opportunities for physical exercise, may explain the health advantages associated with recreation development. In addition, the pristine environments of many recreation counties, with clean air and water, might lead to better overall health.

MORE CRIME, OTHER SOCIAL PROBLEMS

When recreation development is unplanned or occurs too rapidly, it can lead to congested roads and can strain the capacity of public services. Recreation areas have significantly higher rates of population growth than other rural areas, suggesting that some growth-related social problems, such as school crowding, housing shortages, pollution, and loss of identification with the community, may be present. ERS researchers examined road congestion by looking at commute times and found that recreation development was not linked to the commute time to work in 2000. If anything, recreation development appears to have helped keep down commute times in recent years because recreation counties had smaller increases in average commute times during the 1990s than other rural counties. Recreation development can also result in higher poverty rates if significant numbers of low-wage, low-skilled workers arrive to work in tourist-related service establishments. However, ERS research indicates that recreation development results in significantly lower levels of poverty in rural recreation areas. In addition, recreation and tourism development appears to have contributed to declines in local poverty rates during the 1990s.

Another possible disadvantage is higher crime rates: Criminals may be drawn to recreation communities to prey on tourists, or certain types of recreation, such as casino gambling, could attract illicit activity. Crime rates (for serious crimes) are higher in recreation counties than in other rural counties. However, the way crime rates are calculated may be biased inherently against recreation areas. Crimes against tourists and seasonal residents are counted in the crime statistics, but tourists and seasonal residents are not counted as part of the population base upon which the crime rates are calculated.

Thus, even if people in recreation areas do not have a higher chance of becoming victims of crimes, the crime rates for these areas will appear higher than elsewhere because of this bias. Nevertheless, one could still argue that recreation-related crime adds to the local cost of policing and incarcerating criminals, just like recreation-related traffic adds to the cost of maintaining roads.

CONDITIONS VARY FROM PLACE TO PLACE

The benefits of recreation development for rural areas appear to be generally positive. This finding, along with the finding that socioeconomic effects vary significantly from one place to another, will inform policymakers seeking to achieve meaningful development through this strategy. The rural recreation counties in this analysis exhibit a considerable degree of diversity in socioeconomic conditions. For example, counties with ski resorts have among the wealthiest, best educated, and healthiest populations among all recreation county types. These counties also have relatively high crime rates.

In contrast, counties with reservoir-based recreation facilities (mainly located in parts of the Great Plains and the Midwest) and recreation counties in the southern Appalachian region have among the poorest, least educated residents among all recreation county types and relatively high age-adjusted death rates, but they have relatively low crime rates.

Counties with casino facilities had among the highest rates of job growth and large increases in earnings per job during the 1990s. Casino counties also had among the highest rates of growth in the share of employed people ages 65 and older, perhaps reflecting the greater need for jobs among older people in these high-poverty communities. Because recreation county types are not evenly distributed across the country, some of the differences may reflect interregional diversity.

This analysis focused on counties that have already succeeded in developing recreation as a significant industry. Most of these places have amenities that attract people. In contrast, some places that employ recreation as a development strategy may encounter difficulties because they lack natural amenities or other attributes that can attract large numbers of people. In these less attractive places, the socioeconomic benefits of recreation development are likely to be smaller.

6

Tourism Geography

INTRODUCTION

Tourism Geography or Geotourism is the study of travel and tourism as an industry, as a human activity, and especially as a place-based experience. From a geographical point of view, tourism consists of the places of tourist origin (or tourist generating areas), tourist destinations (or places of tourism supply), and the relationship (connections) between origin and destination places, which includes transportation routes, business relationships, and traveler motivations.

Geography is fundamental to the study of tourism because tourism is geographical in nature. Tourism occurs in places, it involves movement and activities across geographic space (between places), and it is an activity in which both place characteristics and personal self-identities are formed through the relationships that are created among places, landscapes and people. Physical geography provides the essential background against which tourism places are created, and environmental impacts and concerns are major issues that must be considered in managing the development of tourism places.

Human geography provides an understanding of the social and economic relationships that exist in providing tourism and U.S. National Park Service nature-based outdoor recreation opportunities and activities, as well as the special meaning that these places have to individuals. A destination's sense of place is often a key element behind tourism development--after all, without the uniqueness and diversity of places, tourism would be mundane and uninteresting.

TOURISM TECHNOLOGY

Tourism Technology is a term coined by the Korea tourism organization that refers to the recent trend of incorporating technology with the tourism industry.

DEFINITION OF TOURISM TECHNOLOGY

The convergence of industries has forced people to create terminology such as information technology, biotechnology, ubiquitous technology and even cultural technology to explain frequently talked about topics. Tourism Technology is a term that encompasses all social, cultural, managerial, and value-adding activities of the tourism industry. Tourism Technology also incorporates and encourages technological advancements and economic development in the tourism industry.

ORIGIN

"Tourism Technology", initially based on the concept of cultural technology, is a more comprehensive term covering knowledge used to add to the value of tourism products on a micro level and the management of the travel and tourism industry on a macro level. New tourism products are also the end result of tourism technology combining with other industries. These include medical tourism, educational tourism, agricultural tourism, marine tourism, and the application of information technology to the travel and tourism industry.

APPLICATION

The term "technology" can easily call to mind scientific achievements, computer graphic skills, special effects and other engineering-related images. However, "Tourism Technology" encompasses the integrated fields mentioned in the previous paragraph, statistics, managerial and socio-cultural know-how, and skills that the tourism industry can adopt to design, produce, and market various tourism products. In addition to coordinating various aspects of human resources in the travel and tourism industry, "Tourism Technology" describes a comprehensive field containing but not limited to such widely referred to subjects as entertainment technology, contents technology and creative technology. Examples of how tourism technology can be applied are as follows.

- Development of tourism products that tell a story
- Convergence with other industries such as medical and film industries
- Application of advanced information technology to provide tourist information via navigation systems or PDAs.

BIBLIOGRAPHY

Andrew Holden: *Tourism: A New Perspective*, London, Prentice Hall, 1995.

Andronicou, Antonios: *Tourism in Cyprus*, New York, Oxford University Press, 1979.

Ashworth, Gregory J.: *Marketing Tourism Places*, London, Routledge, 1990.

Bennett, O.: *Financing for Tourism Projects in Developing Countries*, England, Wiley, 1994.

Bevan, D. L., and D. W. Soskice: *Appraising Tourist Development in a Small Economy*, London, Heinemann, 1976.

Boissevain, Jeremy: *Coping with Tourists: European Reactions to Mass Tourism*, England, Berghahn, 1996.

Bruce, David : *Tourism Strategies for Rural Development*, Sackville, New Brunswick, 1993.

Cooper, C.: *Tourism: Principles and Practice*, London, Pitman, 1993.

Daniel, R.: *Recent Advances in Tourism Marketing Research*, New York, Hawthorne Press, 1996.

David W.: *Tourism Planning*, Chicago, Council of Planning Librarians, 1995.

David, L.: *International Tourism Policy*, New York, Van Nostrand Reinhold, 1990.

Davidson, R.: *European Business Travel and Tourism*, England, Wiley, 1994.

Douglas C.: *Heritage Tourism is in the Future of Many Alabama Communities*, Auburn Univ., Auburn, 1991.

Douglas, Pearce: *Change in Tourism: People, Places, Processes*, New York, Routledge, 1995.

Edward, M.: *In International Tourism: Identity and Change*, London, Sage, 1995.

Forbes, A. H.: *Tourism and Transport Policy in the European Union*, England, Wiley, 1994.

Fowler, Peter: *Heritage and Tourism*, New York, Routledge, 1993.

Frew, E.: *International Charter Travel—a New Opportunity for Australian Tourism*, England, Wiley, 1994.

Gorman, Michael: *Design for Tourism: An ICSID Interdesign Report*, New York, Oxford University Press, 1972.

Harrison, David: *Tourism and the Less Developed Countries*, London, Belhaven, 1992.

Heise, Dorothy: *Promoting Tourism in Rural American*, Maryland, National Agriculture Library, 1991.

Hitchcock, Michael: *Tourism in South-East Asia*, London, Routledge, 1993.

Hudman, Lloyd E.: *Tourism: A Shrinking World*, Columbus, Grid, 1980.

Inskeep, E.: *Training for Tourism in Developing Countries*, Chichester, England, 1994.

Jenkins, C. L.: *Tourism in Developing Countries: The Privatisation Issue*, Chichester, England, 1994.

Knox, J.: *Tourism Research Priorities in Hawaii and the Pacific*, Honolulu, University of Hawaii, 1979.

Martinus J.: *Tourism by Train: Its Role in Alternative Tourism*, Philadelphia, University of Pennsylvania Press, 1992.

Richard, W.: *Tourism and Recreation in Rural Areas*, Chichester, U.K., 1998.

Stabler, Michael J.: *Tourism and Sustainability: Principles to Practice*, New York, CAB International, 1997.

Stephen F.: *Linking Tourism, the Environment, and Sustainability*, Ogden, Utah, 1995.

Valentine, Udoh: *Tourism Development: A Research Note on Africa*, Connecticut, Praeger, 1996.

Victor T. C.: *Sustainable Tourism: A Marketing Perspective*, Woburn, Massachusetts: Butterworth-Heinemann, 1998.

William W. Swart: *Planning for Tourism Development: Quantitative Approaches*, New York, Praeger, 1976.

INDEX

R

S

T

U

W

□□□